Titles in this series

Obstacles to disarmament and ways of overcoming them

Edited by Swadesh Rana

Joseph Owona
Sergiu Verona
Swadesh Rana
Marek Thee
Michael Randle
Jaime Diaz
Betty Reardon
Serge Wourgaft
O. V. Bogdanov
Uma Chopra

The Unesco Press

Published in 1981 by the United Nations
Educational, Scientific and Cultural Organization
7 place de Fontenoy, 75700 Paris
Printed by Imprimerie des Presses Universitaires
de France, Vendôme.

ISBN 92-3-101879-5

Preface

At its historic special session devoted to disarmament in 1978, the General Assembly of the United Nations urged Unesco 'to step up its programme aimed at the development of disarmament education as a distinct field of study through the preparation, *inter alia*, of teachers' guides, textbooks, readers and audio-visual materials'. Indeed, for Unesco, it is essential that a greater awareness be developed at all levels of formal, non-formal and informal education of the dangers to peace and security and the harmful impact on development prospects of the arms race and its social, political, economic and cultural repercussions. As part of its campaign to launch disarmament education during the Second Disarmament Decade proclaimed for the 1980s, Unesco is endeavouring to provide educators and the general public with teaching materials which may be used in the classroom or in more informal educational environments.

The essays contained in this publication were prepared for an expert meeting which Unesco convened in April 1978 on 'obstacles to disarmament and ways of overcoming them'. An introduction was written by Dr Swadesh Rana, who was elected president of that meeting and subsequently accepted the editorial responsibility for this volume. Unesco wishes to express its sincerest thanks to Dr Rana, not only for carrying out the arduous task of editing this work, but also for animating the expert meeting and contributing her expertise and personal involvement to numerous Unesco activities concerning peace and disarmament. Unesco also expresses its gratitude to each of the authors for participating in this project. The authors are responsible for the choice and the presentation of the facts contained in this book and for the opinions expressed therein, which are not necessarily those of Unesco and do not commit the Organization. Indeed, it is only through the expression of a plurality of views that one can develop an understanding of the complexities and ramifications of the subject with which this book deals. There can be no unanimity on precisely what steps should be taken, and under what conditions, to bring a stop to the arms race and embark upon genuine disarmament; we are convinced, however, that unanimity can be reached on the imperative of the ultimate goal of general and complete disarmament under effective international control.

This book in no way claims to outline all the obstacles which have so far kept this goal out of our reach, nor does it define in any systematic manner the ways of overcoming them. What it offers is an *approach* to the analysis of disarmament issues. This approach consists essentially in using the results of research from all relevant disciplines to elucidate the intricacies of these obstacles according to various perspectives (political, diplomatic, technological, economic, sociological, cultural, psychological, etc.) and then applying imagination and creativity to devising means of countering the processes thus elucidated according to all appropriate levels of action.

As regards the perspectives for the analysis of the obstacles, the essays in this book offer some reflections on political, diplomatic, technological and psychological dimensions of the problem, with certain economic and cultural factors being taken into account.

Perhaps the perspectives that are the most fundamental for a deeper understanding of the obstacles to disarmament are the economic and cultural ones however, these are only briefly dealt with in several chapters. Indeed, the economic factors operate to a large extent independently of the more controllable political and diplomatic ones and determine the orientations of the latter. The economic interests involved in military research and development, the arms trade, the determination of military budgets and a myriad of other social and economic phenomena are enormous and often have their own dynamic, which may not be a function of a perceived threat. The study of the economic and social consequences of the arms race and of military expenditures, carried out by a Group of Consultant Experts appointed by the Secretary General of the United Nations and recently up-dated,* has become a standard reference. In order to assist researchers, students and officials, particularly in

* United Nations publication, Sales No. E.78.IX.1

countries where libraries may not contain adequate collections of the vast literature on this aspect of the obstacles to disarmament, Unesco has published a review of research trends and an annotated bibliography, which is available on request.* Given the complexities of the subject and the wealth of material available, it was felt that the economic dimensions could not be adequately dealt with in one or two chapters of this work; it is therefore suggested in several places and remains a priority area for further research. In this regard the United Nations study on the relationship between disarmament and development, now being completed, will be a major contribution.

Similarly, the cultural obstacles to disarmament require much more thorough study than the few references made to them in this work. Whether it be the role of patriarchal society and the attitudes it engenders towards conflict resolution, the content of masterworks of literature, the attitudes transmitted through children's literature and games and mythology or any of the multifarious manifestations of culture, one of the richest fields for future investigation is that of the interrelations between culture and militarism.

The approach suggested by this book would involve the application of relevant research in political science, economics, sociology, psychology, strategic studies, peace research, history and law, to name only the most obvious disciplines, to all of these dimensions of the problem.

Similarly, the reflections on the ways of overcoming the obstacles identified attempt no more than to illustrate the approach proposed. Emphasis is placed on education, international agreements and mobilizing public opinion. Much more could be said about each of these means and many others, be they local, national, or world-wide, nongovernmental or governmental. The possibilities are as varied as human endeavour. The aim of proposing this selection of attempts to identify the ways of overcoming the obstacles to disarmament is to stimulate further thought and action by the reader.

Over two years have elapsed since the meeting on which this book is based. In the meantime a special session of the General Assembly has been held and several activities of Unesco have been undertaken on the basis of the work of the 1978 expert meeting. The remainder of this preface will highlight some of these activities.

* Unesco publication, Reports and Papers in the Social Sciences, No. 39.

Several of the recommendations of the meeting, which appear in the final report (Appendix 1 of this book) were addressed to the special session, which took place less than two months later. The Final Document of that session reflects most of the ideas of the meeting, which were brought to the attention of the General Assembly in particular on the occasion of the address by the Director-General of Unesco on 26 May 1978. The role of research, co-operation with specialized institutes and non-governmental organizations, and the promotion of disarmament education as a distinct field of study are all mentioned in the Final Document in terms reflecting the preoccupations of the expert meeting. The special mission of Unesco as defined by the special session was quoted in the opening paragraph of this preface.

The expert meeting made three major recommendations, the first of which concerned the World Congress on Disarmament Education. As recommended, the Congress was held at Unesco Headquarters from 9 to 13 June 1980, and 132 specialists from 48 countries and 122 observers from 97 non-governmental organizations and 55 Member States took part. The Final Report and Document are reproduced in Appendix 2 of this publication. A selection of the proceedings has been published in the *Bulletin of Peace Proposals* (Vol. II, No. 3, 1980).

The second major recommendation of the 1978 meeting concerned the preparation of a book on the international law of disarmament. A volume in Unesco's series 'New Challenges to International Law' is being devoted to this subject and will be published in the near future.

The third major recommendation concerned the organization of a 'disarmament day' or a 'disarmament week'. In paragraph 102 of the Final Document of the Special Session of the General Assembly devoted to Disarmament, the General Assembly proclaimed the week starting 24 October as Disarmament Week, and of course Unesco participates actively every year in celebrating this week.

The specific recommendations of the meeting concerned each of Unesco's fields of competence. In the field of education, efforts have been made to reinforce the implementation of the recommendation concerning education for international understanding, co-operation and peace, and education relating to human rights and fundamental freedoms, including textbook revision. Regional training seminars have been planned in order to prepare university-level teachers to include disarmament-related subjects in their curricula. Numerous other activities are foreseen further to the World Congress on Disarmament Education.

In the field of science, a new project has been launched on the role of scientists in the arms race and disarmament, which will include an expert meeting and a publication. The concept of the responsibility of scientists and the recommendation on the status of scientific researchers occupy a central place in these activities. Most of the research projects suggested by the 1978 meeting have been either implemented or are part of the approved programme for the next few years. In particular, a special issue of the journal *Impact of Science on Society* was devoted to military R&D under the title 'Weapons from science. Civilization's pitfall' (Vol. 31, No. 1, January–March 1981), and a book on the same subject has been prepared for publication in 1982. The subject of contemporary strategic doctrines and their alternatives is also the subject of a book to be published soon.

Pursuant to the recommendations of the meeting as regards culture a new project has been launched on 'images of war and peace as conveyed through various modes of cultural expression'. This activity will involve an expert meeting and lead to a publication.

As proposed by the 1978 meeting, the recommendations concerning information were brought to the attention of the International Commission for the Study of Communication Problems, which took them into account in its final report, *Many Voices, One World. Communication and Society, Today and Tomorrow* (1980). New activities, based on the recommendations of the 1978 meeting, are planned to examine the role of the media in disarmament matters and the possibilities of using the radio to expand information in this area. The Declaration on Fundamental Principles concerning the Contribution of the Mass Media to Strengthening Peace and International Understanding, to the Promotion of Human Rights and to Countering Racialism, Apartheid and Incitement to War, adopted by the General Conference at its twentieth session (1978) has been translated into over fifteen languages and is being widely disseminated.

Another specific recommendation of the meeting was that Unesco publish its reader on disarmament. This work, entitled *Armaments, Arms Control and Disarmament* (edited by Marek Thee) is being published in 1981. Other publications, such as the *World Directory of Peace Research Institutions* (Reports and Papers in the Social Sciences, No. 49) and the *Unesco Yearbook on Peace and Conflict Studies*, contribute to establishing and reinforcing relations between researchers dealing with disarmament matters in different parts of the world.

The General Conference of Unesco at its twenty-first session (Belgrade, 1980) adopted several resolutions concerning Unesco's contribution to peace and disarmament. The one most directly related to the subject of this book is resolution 21 C/11.1 on creation of a climate of public opinion conducive to the halting of the arms race and transition to disarmament. The text of this resolution is reproduced in Appendix 3 of this book.

Though a very brief summary of some of the activities undertaken following the 1978 meeting, this preface is aimed at illustrating how the materials contained in this publication marked a starting point for a new direction in Unesco's programme relating to disarmament. The understanding of the obstacles to disarmament is an ongoing process. This publication offers some limited observations on the subject. The reader, *Armaments, Arms Control and Disarmament*, being published almost simultaneously, provides many more.

The challenge Unesco is trying to meet is that of applying international co-operation in the fields of education, science, culture and information to the search for solutions to these obstacles. Its success will depend on the active contribution of all who can help. In the words of the final document of the World Congress on Disarmament Education: 'Disarmament education should be the concern of all sectors of society and public opinion. Indeed, schools, non-formal and informal education circles such as the family, community organizations and the world of work, universities and other research centres and information media, all have a part to play in this task.'

Unesco intends to pursue its own efforts to find the ways and means in each of its fields of competence—education, science, culture and communication—of contributing to overcoming the obstacles to disarmament. The urgency of such efforts has been stressed for over a generation. Twenty-five years ago Bertrand Russell and Albert Einstein, along with nine other outstanding men of science, issued a manifesto in which they said: 'We have to learn to think in a new way. We have to learn to ask ourselves not what steps can be taken to give military victory to whatever group we prefer, for there no longer are such steps; the question we have to ask ourselves is: what steps can be taken to prevent a military contest of which the issue must be disastrous to all parties?'

The approach proposed in this volume aims at encouraging all men and women to ask that question. If this book can stimulate such reflection, it will have accomplished its purpose.

Contents

Introduction

Senior Researcher at the
Institute for Defence Studies
and Analysis, New Delhi
(India) and consultant to
the United Nations on
disarmament and
development

Swadesh Rana

No other field of international endeavour has yielded more unsatisfying results than those attained in the attempt to restrain and discourage the global military effort. Beginning with major initiatives at the Hague Peace Conference in 1899, several proposals for arms control and disarmament have been forthcoming from numerous quarters. By and large, these proposals fall into three different categories: first, budgetary constraints through percentage cuts in national military expenditures; second, physical constraints on national force levels and arsenals; and, third, measures discouraging a resort to the arms option as a means of resolving national security concerns.

No formal agreements on budgetary constraints have been concluded since the Second World War; the current global military expenditure of 500 billion dollars a year is likely to increase at the rate of at least 40 billion dollars per year. A number of bilateral and multilateral agreements on limiting force levels and weapons systems have either been concluded or are being considered, but there is a side effect: the limitation on particular forces or weapons has resulted in compensatory increases in outlays on other military elements or even in qualitative improvements of elements put under constraint. Renunciation of the use of force has been a frequent subject of declaratory agreements as well as of national constitutional charters. The past three decades, however, have witnessed not only a more frequent reliance on the arms option—as compared with the first post-Second World War decade—but they have seen that option used for a wider range of objectives, from protection of national frontiers to the waging of soccer wars.

Are these trends irreversible? Is it possible to identify the obstacles that make disarmament a highly elusive goal?

The experts assembled at Unesco Headquarters in Paris, from 3 to 7 April 1978, pooled the findings of their research and insight to answer these questions. A comprehensive report of their discussion, prepared by Sergiu Verona, Malvern Lumsden and the staff of Unesco's Division of Human Rights and Peace, is appended as the conclusion to this volume. The purpose of this brief introduction is merely to capture the intellectual essence of the essays which were presented as working papers at the meeting referred to above.

The grouping together of essays identifying obstacles, in contradistinction to those suggesting ways to overcome them, is more thematic than functional, since most of the essays discuss both. Betty Reardon's suggestion for 'demilitarization of education' also identifies the relation between competitive values taught in schools and the attitudes of nations towards arms acquisition. 'The highest degree of competitive social-ization exists in those societies which are the most active in the arms race', says Betty Reardon. Marek Thee's suggestion for a sort of Hippocratic Oath against the socially irres-ponsible use of scientific knowledge also analyzes the asym-metry between the 'energizing' and 'restraining' forces in armament dynamics and concludes that to date the stimulants are overwhelmingly stronger than the elements of restraint.

In identifying obstacles, all the essays juxtapose myths and realities to emphasize the need for rational imperatives. Discussing militarism, Michael Randle says: 'Historically, militarism has been associated with stridently aggressive regimes such as Prussia under Bismarck, Germany under Hitler, Italy under Mussolini. But there is a good case for interpreting militarism in a broader sense. Regimes which differ very much from these and from one another have also come to be dominated by the dynamics of military expansion.' Perpetuation of economic disparities to sustain the political stratification of the international power structure provides strong incentives for reliance upon explicit and tacit use of military force. The essay on strategic factors discusses the compulsions of the most heavily armed nations to match insufficient resources with expanding political interests, demonstrating the limits of the political readiness to accept meaningful arms control and disarmament measures of both the industrialized and the developing countries.

The choice of correctives to redress the present situation reveals little enthusiasm for the institutionalized international machinery for disarmament negotiations. O. V. Bogdanov's comprehensive treatment of the subject, while listing the formal agreements promoted by the United Nations, details a long list of the unaccomplished tasks on subjects related to disarmament. Sergiu Verona expresses serious reservations about the composition of the negotiating machinery as well as its scope of activity. Understandably, those excluded from the process of decision-making view with suspicion the decisions taken in restrictive forums which appear to them as ignoring their interests or affecting them adversely. Sergiu Verona describes the 'irrelevance' of formal agreements signifying activity without movement. 'Pressing topics of general and immediate concern for international peace and security, like thermonuclear weapons, for example, have gradually receded into the background, while a systematic attempt is made to focus attention on problems which may arise in future', says Verona, adding that 'the danger of war is being sought at the poles, on the moon, in other planets and at the ocean floor, while one loses sight of the fact that explosive materials have been heaped and piled on our own planet and are ready to cause a world disaster.' Michael Randle questions the concept of negotiation itself and suggests that the unattainability of disarmament is related to a particular approach which sees disarmament coming about as a result, and virtually only as a result, of bilateral or multilateral agreements.

Is disarmament merely a subject for formal negotiations among sovereign nations? Should it not be made a subject for education too?

Believing that 'school is both a child and mother of warfare ideology', to quote Jaime Díaz, both Díaz and Reardon plead for an educational curriculum which would replace the present compartmentalization of history within territorially confined national frontiers and the current socialization in educational systems based upon the notion of competitiveness among different cultures. Serge Wourgaft, drawing upon his long experience in a non-governmental organizations' concern for subjects vital to human survival, suggests a mass movement for a better allocation of global resources instead of the current outlay patterns, which sustain 70 per cent of the world's population on merely 30 per cent of its resources.

The essays in this volume are a collective endeavour to

pull disarmament-related problems out of the marginality of human consciousness and to place them in the forefront of international concern. The contributors are extremely grateful to Unesco and its Division of Human Rights and Peace for providing them with both a forum and a milieu which encourage transnational discussion of disarmament as a subject for education instead of the widely accepted tendency to treat it as a problem for negotiation alone.

Obstacles
to disarmament

International political structures as obstacles to disarmament

Director of the International
Relations Institute of
Cameroon (IRIC), Yaoundé
(United Republic of
Cameroon)

Joseph Owona

Introduction

Disarmament is and has been a fundamental problem of international relations on more than one score. Applied universally and comprehensively, it would constitute a miracle cure for the problem of world security and reliance on the use of force.[1] Effective universal disarmament would make it possible to release astronomical sums for the financing of development by the reallocation of thousands of millions of dollars now dedicated to the arms race.[2]

Nevertheless, disarmament has remained a problem, with obvious persistence over the centuries: 'the most telling failure of the law of nations'.[3] The first Hague Peace Conference (1899), which brought together twenty-six powers —mainly European—on the initiative of Tsar Nicholas, reached the conclusion that any joint limitation of arms was impossible; it simply adopted rules to make land warfare more humane and established the text of a convention for the Pacific Settlement of International Disputes. The second Hague Conference (1907) did not even examine the question of arms reductions in depth. Disarmament became a major preoccupation of the League of Nations following the First World War, and the Covenant of the League recognized that the maintenance of peace required 'the reduction of national armaments to the lowest point consistent with national safety and the enforcement by common action of international obligations'.[4] The Treaty of Versailles undertook to impose disarmament upon Germany. But the Geneva organization was no more successful in resolving the issue.

Apart from the Saint-Germain-en-Laye convention, the first international instrument for the control of the international arms trade,[5] no noteworthy results were achieved.

The conclusion of the 1932 World Disarmament Conference, although in favour of armament reductions, was merely the Benes resolution.* Efforts to bring about the limitation of naval armaments produced imperfect results of limited duration:†

The Treaty for the Limitation and Reduction of Naval Armaments (Washington, 1922) merely regulated the naval arms race by establishing parities.

The London naval treaty (24 June 1930) set a quantitive limit on cruiser, destroyer and submarine forces.

The second London naval treaty did no more than limit the maximum tonnage of warships and the calibre of their guns.

In the spirit of the Atlantic Charter, which stated the necessity of 'complete and general disarmament', various agencies of the United Nations were later to set back in motion the difficult process of disarmament, urged on by the appearance of nuclear arms.[6]

The scope of the goal to be attained by disarmament had widened to the point of becoming ambiguous.[7] The aim was now not only the elimination by one or more states of their military resources and the retention of only the most necessary of these, but also the reduction and limitation of armaments,[8] implying even total or partial demilitarization, neutralization or denuclearization.

At the conclusion of these 'confused negotiations'[9] the major powers merely arrived at a definition of the general principles that were to serve as guidelines for negotiations,[10] namely: a step by step movement towards disarmament; and the maintenance of the existing balance of power.

So far, there has been no question of complete and general disarmament. Achievements remain partial. Obstacles are commensurate with the dimensions of the problem, especially where the political structure of international society is concerned. On the one hand, the international community, because of the heterogeneity of its component parts, has a built-in tendency to every kind of belligerence of the 'hot' or 'cold' type. On the other hand, because of its decentralization, it displays a considerable aversion to any type of international administration of worldwide arms control.

* The Benes resolution prohibited aerial bombardment of the civilian population and the use of bacteriological and incendiary weapons, set limits on the unit-weight of tanks and on the calibre of land artillery, and envisaged the possibility of on-site inspection.
† The Washington Treaty of 1922 and London Treaty of 1930 expired on 25 March 1936.

International society and its inherent tendency to conflict

The international structure can be seen to have a built-in tendency to belligerence of all types, for several reasons:

The militarized state constitutes a virtually irreducible international phenomenon. The poles of state power are multiplying. The charismatic appeal of belligerence remains a constant factor in international activity and international relations are marked by considerable 'ideologization'.[11]

The irreducibility of 'the armed state'

At the present time, international public law recognizes the sovereign right of states to organize their national armed forces. It is a privilege of sovereignty and a distinctive mark of independence.[12] It is also one of the normal tasks of the public services, and a means of enabling the state to exercise its freedom of recourse to force. The major powers equip themselves at great cost with considerable armies in the form of land, sea and air forces. The small and medium-sized powers do not escape the phenomenon. Indeed it is very marked among them, for the national army appears to be the symbol and the guardian of a new-found sovereignty acquired and defended with ostentation.[13]

Exceptions to the sovereign right of raising national armies and stockpiling weapons are rare. The various situations of neutrality do not necessarily imply a ban on national armies or the reduction of the neutral state to a disarmed state. Ordinary neutrality is defined as the legal and political status of a state which, in the event of a war between two or more other states, takes no part in hostilities, abstaining from assisting one or other of the belligerents.[14] Perpetually neutral states are bound by international treaty to abstain from participation in any eventual conflict[15] and may not be members of an international military organization (Switzerland, Austria). There is nothing here to prevent exercise of the sovereign right to raise autonomous military forces. International law even finds a place for 'armed neutrality'[16]—that is, the taking of military measures by a state to protect its neutrality. In such cases the state must raise the forces required for the defence of its frontiers.

The irreducible nature of the armed state in fact has few exceptions in international law:[17]

Certain micro-states or other small states agree to have their defence ensured by the neighbouring power.

Demilitarization—a security measure consisting in a more or less complete ban on military forces and installations within a specified territory, and sometimes even stipulating the destruction of the existing military apparatus—is still strictly a measure imposed by the victors upon the defeated (Rhineland, 1919).

Finally, the Japanese constitution of 3 May 1947 lays down, under article 9, a perpetual ban on armed forces (land, sea and air) and on all other military potential.

The irreducibility of the 'armed state' is unquestionable. States, whether small or large, are military powers, unlike the international organizations which do not have permanent armed forces at their disposal; the constitution of the United Nations emergency forces (Cyprus, Sinai, Congo) results mainly from short-term political crises.

The multiplication of the poles of armed power

The present international structure is characterized by nuclear polycentrism and the multiplication of the conventionally-armed powers.

Command of atomic weapons is shared among a few major powers; the two giants (the Soviet Union and the United States), China, France and the United Kingdom, followed by India. This spreading of the poles of nuclear power is a major obstacle to disarmament.

It should be noted that the development of this poly-centric nuclear structure has been accompanied by the multiplication of conventionally armed regional powers: the Socialist Republic of Viet Nam and Indonesia in South-East Asia; Argentina, Brazil and Cuba in Latin America; Egypt, Israel and the Syrian Arab Republic in the Middle East; Iran and Saudi Arabia in the Gulf region; the Republic of South Africa, Ethiopia and Nigeria in Africa. Overlapping strategic interests and the spread of territorial irredentism jeopardize the prospects for even limited disarmament.

The ideological responsiveness of the other transnational forces

The other actors on the international scene appear to be highly receptive to ideological extremism.

Groups operate according to ideological affinities. Political solidarity has become institutionalized among parties: the Communist International, now replaced by a congress of Communist parties; the Socialist International; the Christian Democratic World Union; the World Liberal Union.[18] International labour groups (World Federation of Trade Unions, World Confederation of Labour, the Christian-inspired International Confederation of Free Trade Unions) still exist. The various forums for the expression of world public opinion should also be noted.

These ideological divisions are reflected in the debates on disarmament, making it difficult to reach a consensus on the very concept and methods of disarmament,[18] or on the choice of the forums for the discussion of disarmament issues.[19]

The appeal of belligerence

A number of territorial conflicts and ideological clashes set states against one another the world over. Certain political leaders with charismatic appeal embody, or try to embody, the spirit of these conflicts, diminishing the chances for universal or regional disarmament by exacerbating distrust among states. In the recent past, international society has witnessed an increase in such pernicious forms of leadership—Hitler, Mussolini and several others provide the most prominent examples. Such situations can further retard the disarmament process, particularly when the heads of state or of government increase their personal participation in the conduct of international politics against the background of a society which is hostile to any type of control.

An international society with no institution for the monitoring of disarmament

International society today appears to reject all permanent institutions for the control of disarmament, refuses all forms of global monitoring, and tolerates only partial or regional control systems.

The absence of a world authority
for disarmament control

There is no worldwide authority for the control of disarmament, nor has there ever been one. The Hague Conferences
did not contemplate any such mechanism. According to the
provisions of the Covenant of the League of Nations, the
Council of the League was to prepare plans for the reduction
of armaments, taking into account the geographical situation
and special conditions of each state. The members entrusted
the League with the general supervision of the trade in arms
and ammunition with the countries in which the control of
this traffic was necessary in the common interest.[20] The
Preparatory Disarmament Commission, after five years of
deliberation, succeeded in bringing the question of control
within the scope of negotiations.[21] The World Disarmament
Conference, which began its meetings in 1932, failed to
establish a specific supervisory authority and broke down
in the face of German rearmament.

In turn, the Charter of the United Nations renewed the
effort to reduce to a minimum the volume of world economic
and human resources channelled into armaments. As far
back as 1945, the United Nations General Assembly established an Atomic Energy Commission and the Security
Council set up a Commission for Conventional Armaments composed of its eleven members and Canada.
Both bodies suffered setbacks. The creation of an authority on atomic development ran into Soviet opposition
with regard to the international inspection of nuclear
installations.

The Joint Statement of Agreed Principles for Disarmament Negotiations by the Soviet Union and the United States
(20 September 1961) proposed more extensive supervision,
to be ensured in conjunction with an *international disarmament organization*, which has never come into being. Negotiations were pursued in the context of the Eighteen-Nation
Committee on Disarmament, which replaced the Ten-Nation
Committee, and the principle of a limited number of international inspections was envisaged. France, which has not
occupied its seat on the Committee since 1963, suggested
in 1977 the creation of a world agency for satellite surveillance of armaments.[22] The insurmountable problem of
supervision and the evolution of military technology have

resulted in the notion of disarmament being superseded by the concept of arms control and inspection and have led to the implementation of certain controls by sector.

Sectoral controls of a contractual nature

A number of international treaties have provided for partial and purely contractual control of regional or global scope.

Demilitarization

The Antarctic Treaty signed in Washington on 1 December 1959 prohibits the establishment of military bases and fortifications, the carrying out of military manoeuvres and the testing of any type of weapons, including nuclear explosions, in the region. Antarctica is to be used for peaceful purposes only.[23] The states party to the treaty ensure the efficacy of these demilitarization provisions through national inspections and through the exercise at any time of their right of supervision, including missions by inspection teams to any location, with the right to visit any station, permanent installation, ship or aircraft.

The Agency for the Control of Armaments, within the framework of the Western European Union, is responsible for a two-fold control task: verification that undertakings by the Federal Republic of Germany not to manufacture certain types of armaments are observed; and the controlling of levels of stocks of armaments held by any of the European states party to the treaty.

Denuclearization

A large number of controls have been laboriously worked out in the nuclear field, covering both regional and international aspects:

The regional control system under a treaty (1967). The Tlatelolco Treaty (Mexico City, 1967), which seeks the banning of nuclear weapons in Latin America, provides for a control system designed more especially to ensure that installations intended for the peaceful uses of atomic energy are not employed for military purposes and that no activity prohibited by the treaty is exercised on the territory of the states which are party to the treaty. The Agency for the Prohibition of Nuclear Weapons in Latin America (OPANAL), with headquarters in Mexico City, is responsible for ensuring compliance with the treaty's provisions. It has a general conference, a council and a secretariat.

Unilateral control systems for nuclear-free zones. The ocean floor and seabeds as well as outer space have been the subject of denuclearization provisions under international treaties.

A system of access, on a reciprocal basis, to all stations, installations, equipment and space vehicles on the moon and other celestial bodies, for the purpose of their inspection and verification, is provided for by Article XII of the treaty on the Principles Governing the Activities of States in the Exploration and Use of Outer Space, including the Moon and other Celestial Bodies, of 27 January 1967.

The treaty on the Prohibition of the Emplacement of Nuclear Weapons and other Weapons of Mass Destruction on the Sea-bed and Ocean Floor and in the Subsoil Thereof, of 11 February 1971, seeks to prevent the extension of the nuclear arms race to the sea-bed and ocean floor beyond a limit of twelve nautical miles from shore. Article III gives states party to the treaty the right of verification and observation, and of notifying the other states, in order to ensure compliance with the treaty's provisions. Indeed, the treaty provides for the referral of matters to the Security Council in the case of any unsuccessful consultations.

It should be noted that the systems of control prevailing in both cases favour national procedures by the states which are party to each treaty rather than a supranational authority.

Control under arms-ban treaties

Another series of international agreements seeks to bar either specific types of weapons or the testing of these weapons:

The de facto supervision of the nuclear test ban. The Moscow Treaty of 5 August 1963, which binds the three major powers and a large number of other states, bans nuclear weapon tests in the atmosphere, in outer space and under water. It is significant that no control mechanism—even of a unilateral kind—is provided for. A '*de facto modus vivendi*' may exist however,[24] permitting the three main 'Original Parties' to exercise some measure of supervision.

The priority of bilateral control over the non-proliferation of nuclear weapons. The Treaty on the Non-Proliferation of Nuclear Weapons (July 1968) had the effect of restricting the number of nuclear powers. It contains obligations of two types: the obligation of the nuclear-weapon states to refrain from assisting other states in the manufacture of such devices and that of the other states to abandon their development while retaining the benefits of the peaceful applications of the atom.

The treaty (Article V) refers to 'appropriate international observation' and the obtaining of the benefits of peaceful applications by non-nuclear-weapon states through 'an appropriate international body' with adequate representation of these states on it. This allows of action by the International Atomic Energy Commission. But according to the terms of bilateral agreements, the nuclear supplier state is to inspect the activities of the recipient state. Such 'competitive' supervision by the supplier state is likely to have an adverse effect on the working of impartial international control.

The control system of the Convention on the Prohibition of the Development, Production and Stockpiling of Bacteriological (Biological) and Toxic Weapons. This convention, prepared in 1971, is designed to supplement the Geneva Protocol of 1925 by prohibiting the production and stockpiling of micro-biological, biological or toxin agents.

The initial control system, by the state itself, involves a set of domestic measures aimed at ensuring compliance with the undertakings given. The second set of control measures is of an international character, and includes consultations between the parties and comparative scrutiny of the measures taken, examination by an international body of experts covering both qualitative and quantitative factors, and a complaints procedure consisting of an inspection after the complaint has been lodged and an impartial investigation. Thirdly, the Security Council may take action if one of the parties complains of violation of the Convention.[25] No specific or specialized body is required for purposes of control, which is left to the discretion of states as far as domestic measures are concerned.

Monitoring of the SALT agreements
by national technical facilities

The bilateral SALT agreements signed in Moscow in 1972 are principally concerned with strategic arms limitation. The method of verification provided for in these agreements consists of national technical facilities such as electronic detection and other devices mounted on satellites, aircraft and ships. It is mandatory for the parties not to impede verification.

In short, there is clearly no international control body as such. Provision is made in three international instruments for the possibility of inspection: these are the Antarctic Treaty of 1959 (Article VII), the Treaty on Outer Space of 1967 (Article XII) and the Nuclear Non-proliferation Treaty. Only the Mexico City Treaty provides for the creation of a monitoring body, whereas all the others rely on national facilities.

Conclusion

International political structures are such that they are too receptive to conflicts. It is therefore difficult to set up organizations to monitor disarmament measures, and these have remained in an embryonic state.

Is there reason to despair in the face of these impediments to general and complete disarmament? The slow progress made leads us to believe that the most appropriate method in this area would be to take our inspiration from the 'old Yukong' of the mountains of Chinese legend and to embark on a long-term process spreading over several generations.

Notes

1. Charter of the United Nations, Article 2.
2. In the words of an official report of the United Nations of 1962.
3. L. Delbez, *Les principes généraux du droit international public* (3rd ed.), Paris, Librairie générale de droit et de jurisprudence, 1964.
4. Covenant of the League of Nations, Articles 8(1) and 9(1).
5. Naoum Scoutzky, 'La Société des Nations et le contrôle du commerce international des armes de guerre (1919–38)', *50 ans de la Société des Nations*, Geneva, Centre Européen de la Dotation Carnegie pour la Paix Internationale, 1969.
6. Cf. paragraph 8 of the Atlantic Charter.

7. P. Gonidec, *Relations internationales*, 2nd ed., p. 3, Paris, Précis Domat. Montchrestien, 1977.
8. Basdevant, *Dictionnaire de terminologie du droit international*, Paris, Sirey, 1960.
9. P. Reuter, *Droit international public*, p. 366, Paris, Presses Universitaires de France, 1966.
10. H. Thierry, *Droit international public*, p. 616, Paris, Précis Domat, Montchrestien, 1975.
11. G. Arbatov, *Lutte idéologique et relations internationales*, p. 27, Moscow, Éditions du Progrès.
12. C. Rousseau, *Droit international public*, p. 97, Paris, Précis Dalloz.
13. SIPRI, *The Arms Trade With the Third World*, Harmondsworth, Penguin.
14. Basdevant, *op. cit.*
15. J. Charpentier, *Institutions internationales*, 4th ed., p. 21, Paris, Mémentos Dalloz.
16. Basdevant, op. cit.
17. Charpentier, op. cit
18. 'Conceptions du désarmement' as treated in the work by Daniel Colard, *Le désarmement*, Paris, Armand Colin, Collection U2, 1972.
19. Clashes between delegates from the Soviet Union and the United States at the World Conference of the International Woman's Year, Mexico City (June–July 1975).
20. Covenant of the League of Nations, Article 23.
21. Charles Zorgbibe, *Les relations internationales*, 1st ed., p. 330, Paris, Presses Universitaires de France, Collection 'Thémis', 1975.
22. *Le Monde*, 26 January 1978.
23. R. J. Dupuy, 'Le Traité sur l'Antarctique', *Annuaire français du droit international* (AFDI), 1960, pp. 111–32.
24. G. Delcoigne, G. Rubinstein, *Non-prolifération des armes nucléaires et systèmes de contrôle*. Études de science politique, Éditions de l'Institut de Sociologie, Université Libre de Bruxelles, p. 65–7.
25. G. Fischer, 'Chronique du désarmement', *AFDI*, 1971, pp. 85–130.

International, legal
and diplomatic aspects

Specialist on disarmament
questions at the Institute of
Political Science, Bucharest
(Romania)

Sergiu Verona

A survey of today's world economic and political issues spotlights, among other phenomena, the immense waste of that human wealth and intellect which is devoted to destructive purposes. Even statistics become helpless when faced with the ongoing limitless accumulation of weapons. We are witnessing an unprecedented competition aimed at destroying the very assets of human civilization. Military budgets have increased severalfold in the postwar period. Nuclear weapons are stockpiled in immense quantities, and their destructive capacity is several times bigger than the Hiroshima bomb. The nuclear arsenals today, even if partially used, would destroy not only this planet but also a good part of the entire solar system. Missiles of intercontinental range, carrying one or several nuclear loads, have grown by fifty times in less than twenty years.[1] New types of conventional weapons, more sophisticated and more destructive as compared to those used during the Second World War, have been developed. Above all, the difference between the nuclear and conventional weapons is becoming increasingly meaningless.[2] More than fifteen years ago, a well researched study on disarmament stressed that 'unless there is nuclear disarmament of all countries, we shall be living in a world threatened with the mass extermination of many millions of us, fifteen minutes (or perhaps very much less) after a decision (rational or irrational) for war has been taken in any one of several capitals'.[3] This warning is even more pertinent today.

Although historically rooted in the search for naval supremacy among the maritime powers of Europe, the contemporary dimensions of the arms race both nuclear and conventional can be traced to the situation existing immediately after the Second World War. There was an overriding concern for the military capability of the victorious powers, including the demands of occupying forces in different countries, an industrial infrastructure which was still war-oriented, and nuclear weapons which were emerging together with the economic and political interests they created. The arms race benefited from these factors and from an incapacity, or more accurately an unwillingness, to halt it, despite pressures by peoples throughout the world.[4]

While debates in international forums like the United Nations, even in the immediate aftermath of the Second World War, were indicative of the general desire to restrain the arms race, the dominant trend outside the United Nations was to institutionalize it as a major instrument of policy in the balance of power. Growing in intensity, breadth and depth, the arms race increasingly acquired a dual position in relation to the existing international order, eventually becoming both cause and consequence. The arms race was stimulated and perpetuated by the structure and machinery of an international order based upon the hierarchy of power. Since states were graded according to their military capacity, the possession of military power—either singly or through military blocs—became a primary concern for any actor interested in participating in the international system. If possession of overwhelming military strength was essential for entry into the hierarchy of power, acquisition of greater strength became a guarantee against any threats to that order. The arms race thus became a constant objective of those who found their hierarchical position threatened by the revolutionary changes—whether social, economic or political—which have occurred in the past and are likely to occur in the future.

It is our conviction that a credible disarmament strategy is determined by, and indissolubly linked to, the causes and compulsions which underlie the arms race. In our view, disarmament never was—nor is it at the moment—a goal in itself. It is a political strategy meant to put an end to the arms race and to its effects. That is why an attempt to identify the obstacles created by the international economic and political order to a real process of disarmament must take into account the causes of the exacerbation of the arms race. It is in this context that we propose to examine the available legal and diplomatic framework for negotiating disarmament. In our view, the most pertinent problems are those related to (a) the limitation of the negotiation framework to a restricted number of states, (b) the inadequate structure, both bilateral and multilateral, for negotiation, and (c) the role and capacity of the states in contributing to disarmament.

Problems of the limitation of the negotiation framework to a restricted number of states

More often than not, experts have underlined that an effective strategy for disarmament should view the problems in general and comprehensive terms. Discussing these issues, Hedley Bull wrote in 1966:

The doctrine that disarmament, to be effective, must be general and comprehensive, takes as its starting point the proposition that the arms race is general and comprehensive. The present international society is a worldwide one, and is a single military theatre. No power, group of powers or region can be isolated from military contact with the rest of this society. Consequently, a disarmament agreement to which only some powers are party, e.g. a regional agreement, will not stop the arms race, and will be difficult to negotiate. . . . [5]

This, however, was not the approach adopted in practice. A survey of the United Nations documents, dating back to the first years of the Organization, show that some powers were always unwilling to accept any conclusive decisions on the various aspects of the disarmament debate.

This situation can be partly attributed to the fact that the Charter of the United Nations does not include any clear-cut and definite provisions on disarmament. A number of noted United Nations analysts have pointed out that, although formulated less than three months after the atomic bomb was dropped on Hiroshima, the United Nations Charter makes no reference to either the atomic bomb or to atomic power. William Epstein, for example, noted that it was strange that Articles 1 and 2 of the chapter devoted to the Purposes and Principles of the Organization, did not refer to disarmament.[6] Article 11 points out that 'the principles governing disarmament and the regulation of armaments' were included among the general principles of co-operation in the maintenance of international peace and security, with regard to which the General Assembly might make recommendations to the Members or to the Security Council or to both. Article 26 is more specific and stipulates that the Security Council 'shall be responsible for the formulation of plans to be submitted to the Members of the United Nations for the establishment of a system for the regulation of armaments'. Article 47 defines the responsibilities of the Military Staff Committee, entrusting it with the responsibility 'to advise and assist the Security Council on all questions relating to . . . the regulation of armaments, and possible disarmament'.

Based upon these United Nations Charter provisions, the United Nations, acting through the United Nations General Assembly and the Security Council, had established two commissions by 1951: the Commission for Atomic Energy; and the Commission for Conventional Armaments. The membership of both commissions was the same, namely all the members of the Security Council plus Canada—in all, twelve states.

The year 1952 saw the establishment of the Disarmament Commission, which also consisted of twelve members. Negotiations on disarmament were carried on within that framework for two years. In 1954, Resolution 715 (VIII) of the United Nations General Assembly suggested that the Disarmament Commission should study the establishment of a Sub-Committee mainly comprising 'the representatives of the powers concerned'. It was a formula meant to institutionalize the hierarchy of power recognized earlier. The Disarmament Sub-Committee, comprising five members—the major powers and Canada—was to examine the possibility of reconciling divergent proposals. These arrangements echoed a regrettable trend of the disarmament debates in the inter-war period, when the major powers considered themselves authorized to take decisions on behalf of all the countries concerned, particularly on problems of such crucial importance as disarmament. In more than three years, the Disarmament Sub-Committee held 157 meetings, and their negotiations turned both the Disarmament Commission and the United Nations General Assembly into bodies endorsing decisions taken elsewhere.

In 1959, a new negotiating body was created. The Ten-Nation Committee included, apart from the four major powers, six members representing the North Atlantic Treaty Organization (NATO) and the Warsaw Pact. Although numerically larger than the earlier bodies, the Ten-Nation Committee proved neither more useful nor more representative. It marked, in fact, a crucial watershed in the negotiating framework by openly shifting from general to bloc-to-bloc negotiations.

It was only in 1962 that this closed framework of major powers and military blocs was replaced by a multilateral one with the creation of the Eighteen Nation Disarmament Committee (ENDC), subsequently named the Conference on Committee for Disarmament (CCD). This body, too, has been faced with several obstacles.

The fourteen-year period from 1946 to 1960, when disarmament negotiations were restricted to a few, also witnessed an expansion of the arms race, almost entirely among those who were in fact entrusted with the duty to stop it. By the end of the 1950s, the existing arsenals had been supplemented with continental ballistic missiles which further complicated possible agreements in the field of disarmament.

Practically speaking, the framework of disarmament negotiations was becoming steadily narrower. The heterogeneous Security Council membership, reflecting different grades of power and alignment, was expanded but only to include representatives of the military blocs in the negotiating machinery for disarmament. Others concerned were shut out from an exercise which had serious political, economic and security consequences. Justifiably, those excluded from the process of decision-making viewed with suspicion the decisions taken. The solutions, suggested in restrictive forums, appeared to them as either ignoring their interests or affecting them adversely.

Problems related to inadequate negotiation structures—bilateral and multilateral

The establishment of the CCD was generally welcomed as a step forward in comparison with the previous disarmament negotiation structures. The CCD was governed by the well-known Zorin-McCloy statement. In guidelines for the negotiations to follow, the Zorin-McCloy statement stipulated wider participation, particularly in working towards a general disarmament treaty for universal acceptance. While that ultimate goal remains unattained, many fundamental changes have occurred in the world. The number of sovereign and independent states has grown by one third at least, and international relations are no longer confined to a rigid East-West framework. Serious international problems, disarmament included, cannot be viewed pragmatically as the domain of a restricted number of states and their military alignments. Every state, regardless of its size, social system, degree of development and economic potential, has acquired a stake in its independent survival. The unprecedented risks of a nuclear holocaust make it imperative that disarmament and related problems should be approached globally. Any legal or diplomatic norms evolved for that purpose must consider that the security of every state, large or small, is equally important.

A detailed analysis of the activities of the CCD falls outside the scope of this paper. The main concern is to determine the extent to which the CCD negotiations were affected by the power hierarchy of the international order and to examine why they turned into what Alva Myrdal called the 'game of disarmament'.

In the sixteen years since its establishment, the CCD has recorded a spectacular output: close to 800 sessions, roughly 600 working papers by various participants and over 25,000 pages of verbatim proceedings. The regularity and volume of their proceedings notwithstanding, the states participating have often expressed dissatisfaction with the nature and contents of their negotiations. Some of them regret that the necessary decisions have not been taken, despite the fact that CCD discussions do not conform to the rigid disciplines of bloc-to-bloc negotiations. The coercive influence of hierarchical gradations has not always been enforced in the CCD. Experts refer to this phenomenon as a horizontalization of positions, which enables participants to seek agreements outside the constraints imposed by the major powers. The negotiations for the conclusion of the Nuclear Non-Proliferation Treaty (NPT), for example, demonstrated this phenomenon.

Nevertheless, the CCD is gradually witnessing a drift towards (a) the removal from within its competence of key problems relating to nuclear disarmament in particular and the emphasis on complete disarmament in general, and (b) the evolution of special privileges for the major powers. The best way to describe the CCD membership would be to call it a presence that does not ensure participation so far as powers other than the major ones are concerned.

The removal of key problems from the CCD is the result of a tendency to feel that, since the great military powers have the capacity of negotiating and, therefore, analysing priority concerns, the other participating states should play the role of some *chœur à l'antique*. To quote Arthur H. Dean, the United States representative in the Geneva negotiations in the first years of existence of CCD:

Saying that disarmament problems are peculiarly a great power problem leads straight into another bramble patch. In any negotiations or detailed brass tacks discussion of disarmament or arms control, what is most important is what the nations possessing the arms say and what in fact they do. The attainment of concrete results will depend on their decisions. This is a plain fact. What the great powers do or do not do, however, will affect millions of people all over the world who do not have significant arms but who do feel a lively concern over, and would be vitally affected by, the consequences of war, especially a nuclear war.[7]

Writing a book after the completion of his terms at the CCD, Dean also stated:

It is a fact that very few nations in the world are in a position to carry out the necessary research and analytical thinking on disarmament matters . . . This is not to ignore the stimulating ideas that emerge from other countries. But too many statesmen, with an eye on the Nobel Peace Prize, come forward with proposals that hit the front page but are both unrealistic and dangerous.[8]

Arthur Dean explains the role of the other states present at the negotiations, especially the non-aligned states:

By being there, they (the eight non-aligned countries) serve as a constant and poignant reminder of the interest of the smaller states in disarmament and of their yearning to avoid major war. They also serve to reassure the other Member States that their voice is being heard by the great powers. Furthermore, their presence and their vocal interest make it more difficult to break off the discussion.[9]

Unfortunately, this political and philosophical perception of disarmament has also prevailed in actual negotiations. In the 1962 debates of the ENDC, two draft treaties on general and complete disarmament were submitted by the Soviet Union and the United States in quick succession.* Almost all the problems relating to general disarmament were covered. The two draft treaties referred to reduction

* From 14 March to 7 September and from 26 November to 20 December 1962, 95 working sessions were held; a double record for number of sessions and their duration.

and prohibition of delivery systems for nuclear warheads, prohibition of nuclear weapons and nuclear weapon tests, measures for the reduction of conventional armaments and number of troops, etc. Compromise proposals to reconcile different positions were forwarded for the purpose of adopting a general disarmament treaty including definite provisions for nuclear disarmament. Comparative studies were even produced to identify the common ground for discussion on the two draft treaties.[10] The representatives of the major powers submitted a number of proposals to freeze and limit the delivery systems for nuclear weapons with a view to their ultimate prohibition. As emphasized by Arthur Lall, former representative of India to the 1962–64 debates of the ENDC, 'This issue, in all its aspects, took more of the time of the Geneva Conference than any other single issue'.[11] Soon after, the examination of the problems identified was abandoned, and substantial discussions became a prerogative of the Strategic Arms Limitation Talks, conducted between the Soviet Union and the United States. Thus the issues initially discussed in multilateral debates were eventually restricted to a bilateral framework. It is significant to note that neither of the participants in the SALT has ever submitted any of its position papers to the CCD. These were brought to the attention of the CCD by one of its members, Mexico.[12]

Wide-ranging debates on general disarmament have become a thing of the past. Only partial measures are discussed, and no reference is made to the complex problems of nuclear disarmament. On the other hand, the number of problems exclusively negotiated by the major powers or based on their joint documents has steadily increased. The evolution of negotiations on these lines has often given rise to statements such as this:

I have already repeatedly stated how obviously the disarmament negotiations have been handled by the super-powers as in substance bilateral, even when done within an international framework. This preoccupation of theirs with each other rather than with the world has led them to use two different tactics, depending on whether the game is played between the two of them alone or between both of them against the other nations.[13]

It also explains why the results of the disarmament negotiations seem to lead nowhere. Pressing topics of general and immediate concern for international peace and security such as thermonuclear issues have gradually receded into the background, while a systematic attempt is made to focus attention on problems which may arise in the future. While recognizing the value of such attempts in improving the international climate, we cannot deny that they touch only secondary, future concerns and are often hypothetical. Included in this category are the Treaty on the Antarctic, the Treaty on Principles Governing the Activities of States in the Exploration and Use of Outer Space, including the Moon and the Celestial Bodies, the Treaty on the Prohibition of the Emplacement of Nuclear Weapons and Other Weapons of Mass Destruction on the Sea-bed and the Ocean Floor and in the Subsoil Thereof, etc. In other words, the danger of war is being sought at the poles, on the moon, on other planets and on the ocean floor, while one loses sight of the fact that explosive materials have been heaped and piled on our own planet and are ready to cause a world disaster.

At present, there is a kind of hierarchical order of disarmament negotiations depending on the topics approached. The SALT negotiations restrict complex strategic problems to bilateral debates, Mutual Force Reduction (MFR) discussions, concerned with Central European problems, are confined to inter-bloc relationships, and the CCD, occupied with the secondary problems already mentioned, comes last among the forums.[14]

The apparently multilateral framework of the CCD has tacitly accepted certain privileged institutions such as the system of co-chairmanship based on an East-West division of the world. The verbatim proceedings of the CCD debates, and many of the papers submitted there, bring out the anachronistic nature of such conventions. The CCD is practically one of the last bodies, in the area of international negotiations, still preserving such structures: neither the Conference on Security and Cooperation in Europe, nor the many conferences of the non-aligned countries, nor the negotiations on the law of the sea and other international negotiations have preserved structures of this kind. An increasing body of expert opinion has repeatedly emphasized that the system of co-chairmanship stands in the way of participation by the People's Republic of China and France in the CCD's debates and thus constitutes an obstacle to universal disarmament.[15]

Current disarmament problems cannot be considered in isolation from the growing interest in a new international economic and political order. That is why numerous states, in expressing their views on the Special Session of the United Nations General Assembly on Disarmament, have urged an improvement in the present CCD structures, machinery and organization. The necessity of re-examining the value of the system of co-chairmanship was particularly stressed, if the CCD is not to become a debating club aloof from the real problems of disarmament.

A quantitative analysis of the negotiations conducted by the CCD in the 1962–76 period clearly brings out the growing marginality of its negotiating capacity. One of the first indicators is the pace of the negotiations, which has been uneven during the whole period surveyed. Findings indicate that the CCD has been gradually losing both its intensity

Year	Sessions[1]	Public meetings	Pages of verbatim records
1962	14 March to 7 September	82	3 462
	26 November to 20 December	13	500
1963	12 February to 21 June	52	1 827
	30 July to 29 August	9	293
1964	21 January to 28 April	31	1 007
	9 June to 17 November	40	1 115
1965	27 July to 16 November	17	478
1966	27 January to 10 May	29	775
	14 June to 25 August	23	57ᶜ
1967	21 February to 23 March	10	163
	18 May to 14 December	60	617
1968	18 January to 14 March	24	342
	16 July to 28 August	14	285
1969	18 March to 23 May	21	390
	3 July to 30 October	33	696
1970	17 February to 30 April	21	421
	16 June to 3 September	25	450
1971	23 February to 13 May	22	424
	29 June to 30 September	28	328
1972	29 February to 27 April	16	334
	20 June to 7 September	24	309
1973	20 February to 26 April	19	284
	12 June to 30 August	23	338
1974	16 April to 23 May	12	196
	2 July to 22 August	16	215
1975	4 March to 10 April	11	236
	24 June to 28 August	22	380
1976	17 February to 22 April	17	287
	22 June to 3 September	23	341

1. Private meetings and meetings of working groups of experts not included.

of involvement and its capacity to negotiate its defined objectives.

Calculating only the public meetings—that is the verbatim records on a 'per annum' basis—and taking into account the sessions held in the same year, the following situation may be observed.

Some points require special emphasis. First of all, we do not consider the method of calculating the average pace of negotiations to be a relevant one. The CCD's capacity to negotiate is better reflected in the intensity of its activities. In the first three years of its existence, from 1962 to 1964, the CCD held a large number of meetings every year: 95 in 1962; 61 in 1963; 71 in 1964. The total number of meetings in 1962 was never repeated in the whole history of the CCD; the number 71 appeared only once more—in 1967 during the NPT negotiations. After that period, the pace slowed down and the CCD appeared to be a body whose vital functions were being discharged with greater and greater difficulty. The 1969–71 period witnessed about 50 meetings per year. The number came down to 40 meetings a year after 1972 and declined further in the following years. Initially, the normal pace was of three meetings per week. This was subsequently reduced to two in a process of gradual erosion of the CCD's functioning, in terms of both tasks and capacity.

Secondly, the CCD negotiations progressively lost content. To illustrate that phenomenon, in the light of the quantitative analysis, we point to another indicator; the number of speakers during the working sessions. During the first year, in 1962, there were 635 interventions in 95 working meetings, including the first meeting for the organization of the work, which meant an average of seven speakers per meeting. That was the situation during the period when the total number of participants was only seventeen states. At present the CCD membership is almost double that figure. But how often do the members intervene in its deliberations?

In 1974, the number of speakers was 109, or an average of almost 4 per working session; in 1975, it was 164, giving an average of about 5 speakers per working session. More than that, a number of working sessions were held without a single speaker taking the floor. The first such session was recorded on 1 June 1967. We have recorded twenty-seven such speaker-less working sessions during the period June 1967–August 1976.

Problems related to the role and competence of the states in contributing to disarmament

The functioning of the disarmament negotiations machinery has created an understandable feeling of pessimism about its outcome. However, there is another phenomenon: that of the experience gained by the participants and their growing awareness of their ultimate purpose as well as their present limitations. The very ineffectiveness of the CCD and the lack of tangible results from the SALT and MFR negotiations may actually stimulate new initiatives. Our investigation of the CCD documents and our contacts with the representatives of different states participating in the negotiations, including political highbrows,* have made us appreciate the value of unorthodox and radical approaches which deserve support for formulating pragmatic solutions to difficult technical problems. It is our firm conviction that participation of all states—on an equal footing—is the latent force which can be turned to better results in changing the present trends. The inability of the CCD to reach conclusive decisions does not, in any way, constitute a judgement on the competence of its members to comprehend the issues involved and submit proposals offering solutions. From a survey of its proceedings, we have identified three distinct categories of documents considered by the CCD. These are:

Papers on procedures concerning different decisions or proposals made by the co-chairmen or members of the committee regarding the activities of the CCD, the implementation of better procedures and the organization of work, the existing connections with the United Nations and the draft reports addressed to the General Assembly and to the Disarmament Commission;

Working papers of the committee, including documents, memoranda, draft treaties, etc., scientific papers on subjects under negotiation, surveys and summaries of papers on special problems and comparative analyses of different draft treaties before the CCD;

Other papers without direct reference to the CCD framework, e.g. opening addresses, exchange of notes between the participating states, declarations by some international organizations, press coverages, etc.

* On the occasion of the research work undertaken by the author for the Ford Foundation on 'Comparative Positions of Various States Participating in the Geneva Disarmament Negotiations, 1962–75'.

During the period 1962–76, the respective share of various documents was as follows: papers on procedures, 119; working papers, 310; other papers, 92.

For our point of view the most interesting ones are the working papers submitted to the CCD, excluding the draft treaties submitted by different states, of which only a small fraction were actually concluded. Looking for the working papers with a really scientific background and forming a solid basis for negotiations, we found the highest frequency of these in the second phase of the CCD activities, after 1968. A total of 30 such papers were submitted during the 1962–68 period, their numbers going up in the later years as follows: 1969, 20; 1970, 30; 1971, 24; 1972, 24; 1973, 20; 1974, 10; 1975, 17; 1976, 30; 1977, 17. Total: 1969–77, 192.

These trends provide a strong argument in favour of the potential of the CCD to offer competent expertise on the complex disarmament issues. Among the subjects covered by the working papers were:

Nuclear disarmament problems; delivery systems limitations, cut-off of fissionable material, supervision of various decisions banning or limiting nuclear armaments.

Total ban of nuclear tests; checking methods for underground tests ban, seismic events and surveys, detection of small nuclear tests, etc.

Reduction of military budgets of states.

The problem of non-proliferation, including the amendment submitted by states during the NPT negotiations.

The problems of bacteriological (biological) weapons.

The problems of chemical weapons.

The problems of the sea-bed.

Nuclear-free zones.

Complementary disarmament measures and the problems of conventional weapons.

The problems of new technology and weapons systems of mass destruction.

The democratization of disarmament negotiations.

Soviet-American relations in strategic fields.

In all, twenty-five out of the thirty-one CCD members were authors of a large number of working papers. In our view, this fact itself goes to prove the competence of the participants to negotiate and their growing awareness of their responsibilities. As noted in a CCD document, 'Whatever other criticism may have been levelled against it, the CCD has at least kept its reputation as a serious expert body for the consideration and negotiation of disarmament agreements.

The meagreness of the tangible achievements of the CCD can be attributed to several factors, such as inter-bloc competition, international tensions, conflicting strategic interests of negotiating powers, and national preferences for bilateral or bloc-to-bloc negotiations. Sometimes, immature proposals which are straightforward propaganda have been forwarded. On other occasions, rational and feasible ideas expressed at the CCD have not moved on even to the discussion stage. Many times proposals initially ignored have been taken up during later negotiations and have, sometimes, been agreed upon either within the CCD framework or outside it.

The present international order is facing several mutually related developments. The continuation of the world economic crisis has intensified the struggle for a partition of the world, for new zones of influence and zones of interest and for positions of domination by different states and groups of states. In this struggle all kinds of weapons are being used, peaceful and non-peaceful, economic as well as military. The continuation of the arms race and its acceleration are contributing greatly to the aggravation of this state of affairs. It constitutes an immense obstacle to the normalization of international life which is necessary if the crisis is to be overcome and world economic and political stability to be improved. It is necessary, therefore, to emphasize that progress in the field of disarmament is intimately related to the promotion of a new international economic and political order. Radical changes in the structure and pattern of international relationships and the establishment of a new international economic order will facilitate a breakthrough in the current deadlock in the domain of disarmament, which, after all, is the common concern of all states irrespective of their size and position in the prevailing hierarchy of power.

Notes

1. It is worth emphasizing that the last report of the Club of Rome proposes 'a review of some of the major problem areas relevant to the creation of a new international order', and that it lays stress on the arms race. 'We must begin our review of the world's major problems with the competitive armaments race since this, more than any other, carries the very real threat of the destruction of virtually all life on our planet'.—Jan Tinbergen (co-ordinator), *Reshaping the International Order*, p. 25, New York, E. P. Dutton, 1976.

2. *The Military Balance* in its 1970–71 and 1977–78 issues the following estimated figures: Intercontinental missiles of all types belonging to the United States and the Soviet Union: 85 (1960) and 4,096 (1977).
3. See Cecil L. Hadson Jr and Peter H. Haas, 'New Technologies: The Prospects', *Beyond Nuclear Deterrence: New Aims, New Arms*, London, Macdonald and James, 1976.
4. Seymour Melman (ed.), *Disarmament—Its Politics and Economics*, p. 49–50, Boston, The American Academy of Arts and Sciences, 1962.
5. Hedley Bull, *General and Comprehensive Disarmament in the Strategy of World Order*, Vol. IV, p. 270–71, New York, World Law Fund, 1966.
6. William Epstein, *The Last Chance: Nuclear Proliferation and Arms Control*, p. 3, New York, Free Press, 1976.
7. Arthur H. Dean, *Test Ban and Disarmament, the Path of Negotiation*, p. 12, New York, Harper and Row, 1966.
8. Ibid., p. 23.
9. Ibid., p. 13.
10. Canada submitted a number of such relevant working papers. See ENDC/19/Rev.1; ENDC/36; ENDC/79.
11. Arthur S. Lall, *Negotiating Disarmament, ENDC. The First Two Years 1962–64*, p. 41–2, New York, Center for International Studies, Cornell University, 1964.
12. CCD/394.
13. Alva Myrdal, *Armaments and Disarmament in the Nuclear Age*, p. 227, Stockholm, SIPRI, 1976.
14. Excerpt from the statement of the Yugoslav representative at the CCD, Ambassador Lalovic: 'Fifteen years have passed since its founding, the Committee has still not become what it should—by its nature and the logic of things—be: a negotiating body in the full sense of the word. The dimension is still underdeveloped. Actually, the Committee becomes a negotiating body only when the two Co-chairmen submit for its consideration the agreed text of some international agreements.... On the other hand, to be quite candid, we see no particularly persuasive reason for circumventing the Committee this time, too, and conducting negotiations outside its framework, and also for failing to inform it of the course and results of talks.... The members of multilateral body in the disarmament fields . . . should not be excluded from any round of negotiations. . . .'—CCD/PV 757, p. 22 and 24.
15. For example, the statement made by Ambassador Garcia Roble of Mexico: 'It has proved axiomatic that as long as the system of the Co-chairmanship of the super-powers is maintained, there is not the remotest possibility that France and the People's Republic of China will participate in the work of CCD.'—CCD/PV 728, p. 32.

Determination of strategic interests

Swadesh Rana

A strategy has been broadly defined as a plan to gain maximum advantage from resources that are insufficient to provide complete security for the nation and to serve all its positive ends.[1] Viewed thus, strategic considerations constitute the most obstinate single obstacle to disarmament. Claiming that 'arms competition or force matching is natural to normal relations between rival powers',[2] strategic planning in the United States is concerned with ascertaining whether the Soviet Union is politically hostile but militarily contained or politically responsible but gaining military advantages. The Soviet strategic analysts resent the undifferentiated linking together of the American and Soviet strategic interests and insist that without the tremendous effort of the Soviet Union in the field of strategic armaments the world would have witnessed an imposition of the Pax Americana.[3] They argue that while the United States has used its military might to maintain the status quo, the Soviet Union is committed to being on the right side of history through its proclaimed policy of anti-colonialism and anti-racialism.

Stripped of their doctrinaire and ideological trappings all the three commonly shared strategic goals—retaliation, pre-emption, and deterrence—require continuous efforts to prevent the acquisition of any advantage to the rival. Arms procurement policies in pursuit of strategic goals are constant exercises in matching numbers with payloads, payloads with accuracy, accuracy with manoeuvrability and all these with target possibilities. Reductions in the number of weapons are not easy to attain, primarily because the classic economic argument of choosing the most cost-effective from a number of alternatives does not generally apply to military procurements. Defence economists admit that:

Men who have fought in wars where they saw that some particular small qualitative advantages yielded a great edge in combat are going to have a most understandable bias towards high performance, and hang the costs.[4]

The deterrent framework and strategic interests

Even when any actual reduction in the large number of existing low-performance weapons is effected in favour of a smaller number of high-performance weapons, the exercise can hardly be considered a disarmament measure unless one believes that the purpose of disarmament is to deter the use of weapons and not their possession. The deterrent habit weighs arms-control measures in terms of their impact on strategic capabilities and resists any attempts at reducing the level of deterrence itself.

Although the American and Soviet pronouncements about their respective deterrent capabilities have given it a contemporary relevance, the idea that an awareness of the adversary's overwhelming power deters conflict predates their strategic interaction. Participating in the British fleet redistribution debate, caused by the serious German naval efforts in 1904, Admiral Sir John Fisher, the First Sea Lord, described the essence of the theory of deterrence when he said:

My sole objective is PEACE in doing all this! Because if you rub it in both at home and abroad that you are ready for instant war with every unit of your strength in the first time and intend to be 'first in' and hit your enemy in the belly and kick him when he is down and boil your prisoners in oil (if you take any) and torture his women and children then people will keep clear of you.[5]

The German role in the two world wars did not discredit the doctrine of deterrence; it merely emphasized the need to make it more effective. Within a little over three decades after the Second World War, more than one major military power claims to have built up effective deterrents. Claiming a near monopoly of strategic thinking and defence planning, American analysts believe that their strategic 'triad' effectively deters a direct Soviet assault on the United States: even if one of its three strike forces, the land-based, the airborne, or the seabased, were to be fully destroyed by a Soviet first strike, the other two would inflict unacceptable damage to the Soviet Union. The NATO planners claim that most of the customarily cited options available for Soviet military operations in Europe have been prepared for. These include: (a) a general attack on NATO's central region with armoured strike divisions forming the first several echelons; (b) *blitz-kriegs* against the exposed and possibly isolated northern or southern flanks; (c) military probes or provocations.[6]

The Soviet deterrent is built primarily around the concept of the automaticity of global nuclear warfare, described by Sokoloskii as follows:

A world war, if the imperialists initiate it, will inevitably assume the character of a nuclear war with missiles: i.e. a war in which the nuclear weapons will be the chief instruments of destruction, and missiles the basic vehicle of their delivery to target.

Besides projecting the image of the destructiveness of nuclear weapons, in strategic, operational and tactical missions in which 'entire countries will be wiped from the earth', the Soviet Union also claims readiness for 'small-scale local wars which the imperialists might initiate' in order to achieve 'a rapid victory over the enemy'.[7]

Since the primary objective of deterrence is to instil in the adversary a fear about its vulnerability, the deterrent ability involves an inevitable element of demonstration. It is not enough to possess a deterrent unless your adversary knows about it. On the face of it, the official spokesmen of the United States appear somewhat more unwilling to talk of the formidableness of their deterrent than their Soviet counterparts, but their reluctance to divulge details does not entirely conceal their confidence in their capacities.

Besides emphasizing the automatic quality of nuclear warfare and reacting sharply to any downgrading in the American estimates of Soviet military capacity, the Soviet Union issues repeated reminders of its own war-fighting capacity in terms reminiscent of Khrushchev's reaction to McNamara's assessment of Soviet power in the early 1960s. Khrushchev had said:

They frighten us with war, and we frighten them back bit by bit. They frighten us with nuclear arms and we tell them 'Listen, now only fools can do this, because we have them too, and they are not smaller than yours. So why do you do foolish things and frighten us?' This is the situation and that is why we consider the situation to be good.[8]

Based upon the writings of Lieutenant-General Zavylov, Major-General Milovidov, Marshal Sokoloskii, Major-General Marshal Grechko and other Soviet authorities, the American strategic analysts insist on drawing a subtle distinction between the war-fighting and war-avoiding concerns of the American and Soviet strategic thinking respectively. Soviet strategic analysts also repeatedly stress that their views on the essence of war and the views accepted in the capitalist states' doctrines are diametrically opposed. In the context of arms-control negotiations, however, both American and Soviet strategic preoccupations have a similar impact. Conceived in a strategic framework, which resists the acquisition of any advantage to the adversary, arms-control negotiations become an exercise in communicating threats, assessing capacities, and adjusting strategic priorities. The United States and its NATO partners increase military expenditures in anticipation of negotiated reductions and introduce the most advanced weapon systems to gain 'greater latitude in maintaining relative superiority by providing a broader use base for continued qualitative improvements'.[9] The Soviet Union sees to it that neither SALT I nor SALT II should have any discernible impact on overall Soviet postures, activities or plans relative to the further development and possible utilization of nuclear weapons. Strategic considerations compel arms-control negotiations to put ceilings, which appear out of sight, on weapons that are yet to be produced, for a war that is hardly ever likely to be fought.

In an unsparing criticism of both the United States and the Soviet Union for their attitude towards nuclear arms control, Professor Alan Geyer, head of an American non-governmental organization called the Council for the Non-Proliferation Treaty (NPT), told the NPT Review Conference in Geneva:

The harsh fact is that the United States and the USSR, in the name of detente, nearly destroyed the NPT at Geneva. If these superpowers had been willing to announce a test ban moratorium or even a token reduction in their nuclear arsenals, or a simple pledge not to attack non-nuclear treaty parties with nuclear weapons, or a willingness to help poorer countries beat the costs of technical nuclear safeguards, the conference could have strengthened the fragile international regime against nuclear spread.

Claiming that bilateral agreements between the Soviet Union and the United States had done more harm than good, William Epstein, retired Director of the United Nations Disarmament Division, disclosed that the 1974 American-Soviet treaty, putting a 150-kiloton limit on underground nuclear tests, had actually raised and not lowered the threshold, because more than 80 per cent of the tests conducted since 1945 had been under that level. The Soviet Union agreed to discuss ceilings on warheads only after having found a hard-target killing successor to the SS–9 and SS–11. The Americans expressed willingness to negotiate the ICBMs only after they had perfected the technology of their ICBMs. All this was done in deference to strategic considerations of avoiding a war which, both the Soviets and the Americans claim, will leave few survivors if it occurs. 'While convergence of the American and Soviet social systems is unlikely in the foreseeable future, and many issues will continue to divide the two superpowers, both have a common interest in avoiding situations that could lead to a nuclear conflict', insist the American officials. 'Soviet retaliatory capability deters the west from starting a war except possibly in the case of a mad man', claim the Soviet officials.

When confronted with the apparent anachronism of preparing for a war which they want to avoid, the decision-makers usually leave it to the academicians to find intellectually acceptable explanations of the dynamics of the arms race. In a pragmatic analysis of 'what drives the arms race?' Colin Gray identifies the following candidates:

Interstate action-reaction processes (a fairly mindless view); action-reaction process between and within armed services; bureaucratic politics (something of a portmanteau candidate); the character of political/social systems; electoral politics (in the United States, of course!); organisational momentum; technological innovation; industrial production line follow-on imperatives; the military industrial complex; and the nature of the capitalist system.[10]

All these factors, either singly or in combination, provide sensible explanations about strategic reservations to arms-control measures. But in using these explanations to offer radical correctives to the arms race there is a general tendency to overlook the as yet unresolved problems of cause and effect, symptom and disease, aberrations and normal international behaviour. Describing dedicated disarmament enthusiasts as old-fashioned, high-minded idealists, Lawrence Whetten says that such men believe that 'conflict, arms race, crisis and war are abnormal features on the landscape of history'. They hope that 'somewhere around the corner, is *the* agreement that will terminate the disease of arms competition'. To quote Lawrence Whetten:

This belief, let it be proclaimed, is false. Limited arms control agreements, for limited political ends, can and often should be signed. But the transnational arms control community cannot, by its endeavours, devise agreement packages that will write *finis* to the competitive character of international politics.[11]

Strategic interests and national security concerns

If strategic considerations, involving the constant matching of insufficient resources with maximum national security, have made disarmament into an exceedingly elusive goal for those with relatively larger resources, it should not be difficult to ascertain their impact on those nations where resources are more scarce and security concerns more immediate. The abundant and growing literature on the resource scarcity of four-fifths of the United Nations member nations needs little elaboration except to emphasize that 70 per cent of the world population is surviving on merely 30 per cent of the world resources. As for the immediacy of their national security concerns, it should be pointed out that while the two most heavily armed adversaries—the United States and the Soviet Union— have never gone to war with each other on their own soil, the 200 or so military conflicts since the Second World War have occurred in the developing countries.

The overwhelming response of the developing countries to the strategic priorities of the heavily armed developed world is a mixture of envy and despair. Even in disapproving the tremendous resource wastage of military expenditure by the industrialized world, they tend to demonstrate an element of longing for it. In a response typical of this phenomenon, K. Subrahmanyam analysed the strategic priorities of India by writing:

No one in this country has made any analysis of the cost of postponed economic decisions on account of our preoccupation with various security crises. Perhaps a slightly higher order of defence outlay and a greater attention to the management of our security would have yielded better results on the economic front as well.[12]

Preoccupation with various security crises, involving five military conflicts on the national frontiers within a little over two decades of attaining independence, is not exclusive to the Indian experience. Even a random survey of the developing countries indicates that an overwhelming majority of them have been involved in one or more of the following security crisis situations: (a) adversary relationships with neighbours; (b) hostile internal groups threatening secession, insurgency and military coups; (c) personal insecurity of national leaders; (d) pervading sense of 'national nakedness' after the departure of the colonial power; (e) adverse strategic environment related to the interaction of conflicting major power interests.*

At least twenty countries, among the forty randomly selected in December 1979, make hostile pairs involved in an adversary relationship; as many as thirty-six have faced secessionist, insurgency or uprisings; almost two-thirds of those experiencing the above two situations show evidence of the original crisis being intensified or extended beyond its origins owing to external involvement. The phenomenon of personal insecurity of national leaders is more marked in Africa than in Asia. The sense of 'national nakedness' is particularly noticeable among those countries where no national militia existed during the colonial period. The classic example of adverse strategic environment is South Asia, where an incipient détente relationship among erstwhile adversaries has changed into one of increased security preoccupations owing to the region becoming strategically important for major military powers.

Out of the forty developing countries surveyed, fifteen are spending more than 20 per cent of their national budget on military expenditure, ten are spending more than 10 per cent, only two are spending less than 5 per cent and the rest vary between 5 and 10 per cent. Disarmament enthusiasts, mostly from the industrialized world, refer to this phenomenon as the process of getting stark naked in order to get armed to the teeth; they consider a reallocation of the scarce resources absolutely imperative for the survival of the developing world. Disarmament critics, mostly from the

* The author conducted the survey for a United Nations commissioned study on disarmament and development.

developing countries, produce massive evidence to demonstrate the enormity of the contrast between the comparative military spending of the developed and the developing countries as a share of the global total and protest that the most heavily armed are trying to disarm the unarmed.

In the absence of strategic analysis about the developing countries, whose strategic thinking consists mostly of a set of ad hoc responses to crises situations, there are hardly any attempts to suggest that scarcity of resources does not detract from but adds an urgency to the strategic factor in the disarmament policies of the developing countries, particularly when they have been involved in one or more of the security crisis situations mentioned above. There cannot be a more convincing illustration of this phenomenon than a simple reproduction of the perceptions of the national leaders in their own words. From the hostile pairs like India-Pakistan, Egypt-Israel, we have selected the following three statements, among the many made by Prime Minister Jawaharlal Nehru of India, Prime Minister Bhutto of Pakistan and President Nasser of Egypt respectively.

Describing the second five-year plan of India as a 'defence plan' Nehru defined defence as 'defence forces plus your industrial and technological background plus thirdly the economy of the country and fourthly the spirit of the people'. In according a higher priority to defence over other considerations, Nehru explained to the National Development Council of India, in January 1963:

Maybe a few things might be slowed down or otherwise. But by far the greater part of our plan itself is essentially for defence so that it is neither correct nor justifiable to draw a line and say this is defence expenditure and this is developmental expenditure as if they were two separable things.[13]

Insisting that 'all European strategy is based on the concept of total war; and it will have to be assumed that a war waged against Pakistan is capable of becoming a total war', Bhutto wrote in his book *Myth of Independence*:

Pakistan's security and territorial integrity are more important than economic development. Although such development [sic] and self-reliance contribute to the strengthening of the nation's defence capability, the defence requirements of her sovereignty have to be met first.[14]

After having signed an agreement for the supply of arms from the Soviet bloc in exchange for Egyptian cotton, Nasser told Kenneth Love of the *New York Times* that much as he regretted giving armaments priority over social expenditure he had been left with no alternative.

'I cannot defend Egypt with schools and hospitals and factories and what will be the use of them if they are destroyed?' said Nasser.[15]

For the crises-ridden developing countries facing hostile internal situations like secession, insurgency and conflicts of ethnic, tribal or communal origins, 'Development, often an intangible concept, has proved to be an elusive goal. Order, in contrast, is both more tangible and, so it seems, more necessary.'[16] In looking for devices to bind together an essentially fragmented society, many national leaders inevitably end up by establishing hard-handed security forces which invariably obliterate the distinction between the functions of the police and the military as recognized in the industrialized world. A conversation between President Keita of Mali and President Kennedy of the United States portrays the former as explaining how his first need after independence was for a new DC-3 aircraft and a few armoured jeeps for his police. He is reported to have said that he found himself responsible for a piece of territory which called itself a nation. The people had to feel that the government could make its presence felt in every part of the country and that it had instruments to effect its authority.[17]

The concern for survival as a nation is translated into near obsessive preoccupation with the survival of national leaders in cases where the leaders become conscious that the scarcity of resources and fragmentation of society is making underdevelopment a continuing experience. As the euphoria of nationalism gives way to mass despair of unfulfilled social expectations, remaining in power becomes a precarious endeavour forcing the ruling leaders to shift their attention from developmental strategies to survival itself. One of the primary concerns of the Organization of African Unity (OAU), established in May 1963, was to protect the African presidents from possible assassination attempts by their countrymen or outsiders. The murder of President Olympio of Togo, in early 1963, was so much on the minds of those who framed the OAU Charter that they included in it an explicit proclamation of 'unreserved condemnation, in all its forms, of political assassination as well as of subversive activities on the part of neighbouring states or any other states'. This twin concern for the personal security of the national leaders and subversion against the state acquires added significance when it is noted that as many as four, out of the seven, OAU Charter principles are addressed to the sovereign status, territorial integrity and non-interference among states. Not even one of the seven fundamental OAU principles mentions development.[18]

The sense of 'national nakedness'[19] is a near universal phenomenon among the developing countries during the immediate aftermath of independence from a colonial power. The countries inheriting national militia from the colonial army prize their inheritance: those without it hasten to create them. The near-reflex act of creating a national army, as one of the first priorities of a newly independent country, is somewhat like the human practice of getting dressed before going out. What you wear and how you wear it are unimportant as long as you wear something.

The biographies about and autobiographies by reputed national leaders from the developing countries, including Jomo Kenyatta of Kenya, Kenneth Kaunda of Zambia, Julius Nyerere of Tanzania, Kwame Nkrumah of Ghana, Ahmed Sukarno of Indonesia, Patrice Lumumba of Congo—to mention a few—are replete with expressions of apprehensions about their national security concerns being stretched beyond their immediate territorial frontiers owing to the clashes among the geo-strategic interests of the major military powers. These apprehensions cannot be summarily dismissed as fabricated élite alibis for inaction on national development fronts. There are obvious limits of time frame and credibility in persistent projection of national-security concerns for non-performance in the developmental field and vice versa. Even after detracting the propaganda value of customary references to the legacies of colonialism and imperialism, the Third World leaders are merely acknowledging realities when they talk about the problems of confronting a hostile environment created by the strategic interests of major military powers. In a forthright analysis of Malawi's security problem President Banda described it thus:

We can take it for granted that in any war against South Africa and Rhodesia, the General Staff of these two countries would order the occupation of strategic centres in Malawi, Zambia and

Congo Kinshasa in order to deny anyone else from using these centres as springboards against them. . . .

Germany has at least twice invaded Belgium in order to get at France, and in that way at Britain. On the other hand . . . Britain has always fought in the Low Countries—Belgium, Holland—in order to prevent any other country from using [them] . . . as a springboard against herself. As a result, Belgium also has at least twice been the major battlefield of Europe.

To me . . . it is most frightening—indeed horrifying—to think that one day . . . Malawi might become part of a larger, bigger Belgium of Central Africa. . . .[20]

Very few developing countries like Malawi have opted for a dialogue with their hostile neighbour to buy immunity from a possible strategic occupation of their national territory. Many more, as in the Gulf area and the Horn of Africa, have allowed themselves to be sucked into the military effort of the major strategic rivals in their neighbourhood. An overwhelming majority of them, however, have shown marked preference for remaining aloof in a possible clash of strategic interests of the major military powers. And for most of them a worrying development is the direct extension of major power strategic interests into Third World conflicts.

On the basis of systematic research, a study by the Brookings Institution in the United States identified 215 incidents since the Second World War when American forces were used as a political instrument. Recommending that armed forces should not be used for political purposes abroad, except under very special circumstances, the Brookings study, nevertheless, concluded that 'demonstrative uses of the armed forces can sometimes be an effective way—at least in short-term—of securing United States objectives and preventing foreign situations inimical to United States interests from worsening'. While no comparable study on the use of Soviet forces has been carried out, it is obvious that, in the post-Viet-Nam period, the Soviet Union has shown a greater willingness than the United States to demonstrate its war-fighting capabilities in Third World conflict situations, as in Angola in 1975 and the Ogaden region in 1977. The Ogaden conflict involved not only the largest peacetime airlift of Soviet technicians and armour to a Third World country but also witnessed a new Soviet weapon never before observed. The Somalis described it as a 'moving castle'; eyewitnesses reported that it was a highly mobile armoured vehicle mounted with a 73-mm gun, an anti-tank missile and a heat-seeking anti-aircraft missile. The direct Soviet military involvement in Afghanistan has the awesome potential of affecting the arms procurement policies of all the countries bordering South-West Asia.

The United States has begun to insist that it needs innovations in its strategic postures to meet conflict situations outside NATO's original mandate. Talking about the need to change NATO's 'European character into a global one', in January 1978, General Alexander Haig referred to situations 'on our flanks or on the periphery which the Soviets might exploit as targets of opportunity'.

We must be armed with regional military capabilities which could be employed as deterrent forces to prevent the escalation of Third World dynamics into major conflict, said General Haig, adding that there was no substitute for 'inplace ready forces'.[21] A little over a year after General Haig's statement, his successor, General Bernard Rogers, disclosed, in June 1979, (a) that the United States army was drafting plans for a 'quick-strike' force of 110,000 troops to respond to crisis in the Gulf or other hot spots outside NATO; (b) that the force called the Unilateral Corps would consist of the 82nd Airborne and other established units that are not committed to fighting a NATO war; (c) that the Unilateral Corps would be a 'go anywhere' force rather than one specifically targeted on the Gulf or any other area.[22]

The official United States reluctance about how and when the United States would or should use its 'quick-strike' forces has been paralleled by abundant contingency analysis in the American academic community. One such contingency analysis prepared by Guy Pauker, for the Rand Corporation, anticipated the following two situations which may confront the American decision-makers in the not too distant future.[23] To quote from this study, 'Military Implications of a Possible World Order Crisis in the 1980s', these are:

1. A possible breakdown of the global order as a result of a sharpening confrontation between the Third World and the industrialized democracies;
2. Situations of 'system overload' caused by exponential growth of population, incessant demand for energy and other natural resources, cumulative pollution of the planet's atmosphere and oceans, and the incapacity of

obsolete forms of government to deal with the complexities of global interdependent industrial civilization. Warning that the Third World movement has many similarities with the growth of trade unionism in the West in the nineteenth century, Pauker anticipates that the United States:

cast by history in a role of world leadership . . . would be expected to use its military force to prevent the total collapse of the world order or, at least to protect specific interests of American citizens in the absence of an international rule of law.

All the considerations mentioned by Guy Pauker, and many more, make South Asia extremely vulnerable to any clash of strategic interests among the major military powers. It is located at the apex of the Indian Ocean littoral, which accounts for more than half of the conflict-ridden countries of the developing world. It is also situated at the feet of the two heavily armed and ideologically motivated rivals—the Soviet Union and China—whose adversary relationship has acquired a third dimension after the repeatedly stated American interest in co-opting China as a quasi-ally for the United States. South Asia has an arm stretched into the highly volatile Gulf area producing 37 per cent of the world's oil, without which the industrialized world cannot afford its present level of prosperity. It also has a foot in the strategically crucial Malacca Straits which separate the Pacific from the Indian Ocean region, which produces sizeable percentages of the global total of strategic minerals: 90 per cent of the rubber, 70 per cent of the tin, 28 per cent of the manganese, 32 per cent of the chromium, 16 per cent of the iron ore, 12.5 per cent of the lead ore, 11.5 per cent of the nickel, 10 per cent of the zinc and 30 per cent of the antimony, besides the world's largest known reserves of thorium and non-negligible reserves of titanium.

Scientists involved in the law of the sea negotiations have calculated that the Indian Ocean sea-bed contains large deposits of nodules—manganese, nickel, cobalt, copper, molybdenum, etc. Just one square mile of sea-bed could produce as much as 30,000 tons of manganese, 3,600 tons of aluminium, 2,300 tons of cadmium, 17,000 tons of nickel and 650 tons of copper. Manganese nodules alone may fetch about $1 million a square mile. The resource-starved Indian Ocean littoral and hinterland countries consider access to these resources vital for their survival, however it is defined, in developmental or national security terms.

Their strategic interests in the large, and not yet fully ex-
ploited, resources of the Indian Ocean region have a quanti-
fiable economic dimension which they find threatened by
the increasing military activity in the Indian Ocean.

Not surprisingly this aspect of the resource potential
of the Indian Ocean region receives little publicity in the
deployment plans of the powers interested in strengthening
their naval presence in this area. Soviet interests are customarily ascribed to the general need of the Soviet navy for
warm waters and the specific Soviet anxiety for a presence
in the Arabian Sea to acquire the ability to build bases near
the exit from the Gulf to the Straits of Hormuz. Three
plausible strategic interests are associated with the growing
American inclination towards a permanent presence in the
Indian Ocean. Firstly, it is a response to developments in
the Indian Ocean region, particularly its north-western
sector and to the situation in Iran after the Shah's departure,
Pakistan after Bhutto's execution, the Middle East in general
after the Egypt-Israel Treaty and the Horn of Africa after
the conflicts between Somalia and Ethiopia and the two
Yemens. Secondly, it reflects a growing debate within the
American administration about the Navy's role in the
strategic triad concept, where the Air Force and the Army
are believed, by some defence planners, to have received
greater attention recently as compared to the Navy. The
choice of an ocean for deployment is thus inextricably linked
to the Navy's role and the type and number of ships it wants
to build. Thirdly, it is an expression of American anxiety
to acquire quick-strike capability in areas which fall outside
NATO's theatre of operations.

Any increase in the military activity of major powers
either in and around the Indian Ocean or in the continental
vicinity of South Asia will have a directly adverse impact
on the security concerns of the South Asian countries.
Unlike the Middle East, where the two major adversaries have
settled down to a detente relationship built around rival
deterrent capabilities, supported by the United States, the
hostile pairs in South Asia continue to be involved in situations of strategic uncertainty extendible from one hostile
pair to another. Afghanistan feels compelled to increase its
military effort in response to any strengthening of Pakistan's
arsenals, which Pakistan insists are indispensable to face
the Indian threat, which India believes is non-existent

so far as Pakistan is concerned. India projects its military requirements in terms of the defence preparedness of China, whose main strategic concern, its leaders say, is not with India but with the Soviet Union. The Soviet leadership weighs its strategic requirements against American military capabilities. In no other region of the world are hostile pairs involved in the kind of strategic situation prevailing in South Asia today. Any set of arms-control measures proposed by the South Asian leaders, inevitably, acquires a global dimension which may sound utopian to outside powers but has an immediate relevance for the national security concerns of the countries in this region.

Notes

1. Robert J. Art and Kenneth N. Walz, *The Use of Force: International Politics and Foreign Policy*, p. 24, Boston, Little Brown and Company, 1971.
2. Lawrence Whetten (ed.), *The Future of Soviet Military Power*, p. 5, New York, Crane Russak and Company Inc., 1976.
3. See V. D. Sokolovskii, *Soviet Military Strategy*, Englewood Cliffs, N. J., Prentice Hall Inc., 1963, Chapters I and III.
4. Roland N. McKean, *Issues in Defence Economics*, p. 6, New York, National Bureau of Economic Research, 1967.
5. See Art and Walz, op. cit., p. 168.
6. See Lother Ruel, 'The Soviet Threat to Western Europe: An Example of Theater War Capabilities', in *The Future of Soviet Military Power*, op. cit., pp. 157–73.
7. *Soviet Military Strategy*, op. cit., pp. 47–79.
8. Khruschev's speech at Maritsa, Bulgaria, on 15 May 1962, quoted in *Soviet Military Strategy*, op. cit., p. 43.
9. Lawrence Whetten, in *The Future of Soviet Military Power*, op. cit., p. 10.
10. Colin S. Gray, *The Soviet-American Arms Race: Interactive Patterns and New Technologies*, Santa Monica (California), Rand Corp., Chapter II.
11. Colin S. Gray, 'The Racing Syndrome and the Strategic Balance', in *The Future of Soviet Military Power*, op. cit., p. 39.
12. K. Subrahmanyam, *Defence and Development*, p. 28, Calcutta, Minerva Associates, 1973.
13. Quoted in *Defence and Development*, op. cit., p. 20.
14. Zulfikar Ali Bhutto, *Myth of Independence*, p. 152, London, Oxford University Press, 1969.
15. Quoted in Anthony Nutting, *Nasser*, p. 105, London, Constable and Co., 1972.
16. Gerald A. Heeger, *The Politics of Under Development*, New York, St. Martin's Press, 1974, Chapter I.
17. Quoted in W. W. Rostow, *Politics and the Stages of Growth*, p. 392, London, Cambridge University Press.
18. See Ali Mazrui, in David Gwyn, *Death Right of Africa: Idi Amin*, pp. 228–32, Boston, Little Brown and Co., 1977.
19. Ali Mazrui, op. cit. pp., 233–40.
20. See Philip Short, *Banda*, p. 293, Boston, Routledge and Kegan Paul, 1974.
21. See *U.S. News and World Report*, op. cit.
22. See *International Herald Tribune*, 23–24 January 1979.
23. Guy Pauker, *Military Implications of a Possible World Order Crisis in the 1980's*, Santa Monica, The Rand Corp., 1977.

Armament dynamics and disarmament*

Editor-in-Chief of the
Bulletin of Peace Proposals
and Director of the
International Peace Research
Institute, Oslo (Norway)

Marek Thee[†]

Dynamic versus static perspective

For years, the international community has been preoccupied with the rising rate of armaments on the one
hand and the failure to halt the arms race on the other.
The missing link, it is becoming clear, is to be found in the
armament dynamics, which have acquired a momentum of
their own, resisting social control. A prime prerequisite for
effective disarmament strategies is an understanding of the
contemporary armament dynamics.

First, we need to find the right perspective and method.
As in many other fields of social and political research, the
crucial choice is between a dynamic and a static approach.

The basic facts of current armaments are well known.
Since the beginning of the Cold War, and despite détente,
the arms race has grown steadily in intensity and, by today,
has become a highly alarming global phenomenon. In the
last three decades, world military expenditures in constant
prices have more than trebled; the nuclear stockpile has
escalated, surpassing more than a million times the explosive
power of the Hiroshima bomb; the arsenals of strategic and
tactical nuclear weapons contain tens of thousands of
warheads, far exceeding the number of imaginable targets;
the sophistication and destructiveness of both nuclear and
conventional weapons have reached levels unparalleled in
history. By whatever indices—military expenditures, the
nuclear stockpile, number of missiles and nuclear warheads,
nuclear megatonnage or killing capacity—the world military
potential has surged to an overkill capability that can destroy
all life on earth.[1]

Though the realities of the arms competition are self-
evident, we somehow tend to think about armaments in

* Paper prepared for
the International
Workshop on Disarmament,
Centre for the Study
of Developing Societies,
New Delhi,
27–31 March 1978; and
for the Conference
on Disarmament, World
Council of Churches,
Glion, Switzerland,
9–16 April 1978.

† The author is indebted
to Susan Hoivik, Oslo,
and to Asbjorn Eide and
Sverre Lodgaard, PRIO,
Oslo, for reading the
manuscript and
commenting on it.

essentially static terms. We too often associate the current
arms race with conventional arms competitions of regular
increment and temperate pattern, in other words a race
which may be dangerous but need not end in hostilities.
Moreover, pointing to the 'deterrent effect' of nuclear
weapons, many political figures and official spokesmen
explain away the current arms race as a stable race which,
unlike the unstable race in the Richardson tradition, does
not necessarily lead to war.[2] The result is a false sense of
security, which contributes to the apathy of the general
public in relation to questions of armaments and disarmament. While the arms race is intensifying, the level of awareness of the dangers ahead is decreasing.

To understand contemporary armaments, we have to
see the process as a whole, in its dynamic development.
We have to take account of the current military environment,
but more so of the speed of innovation, replacement and
deployment of new weapons. It may well be that the rapid
rate of change and the revolutionary progression in military
technology are more perilous even than the temporary state
of affairs in armaments. The consequences here may be
incalculable.

This chapter discusses some aspects and regularities in
the contemporary armament dynamics. Our concern is
mainly with the East-West conflict configuration and the
arms race between the two pre-eminent world military
powers: the United States and its NATO allies on the one
hand, and the Soviet Union and the Warsaw Pact allies on
the other—a race which also fuels armaments and militarization in the rest of the world.[3] In conclusion, some
remarks are added on action for disarmament.

A new reality

There is a new reality in the contemporary arms race not
comparable with anything in the past. Static notions of the
arms competition, even the memory of the vigorous races
before the First and Second World Wars, help to obscure the
entirely new environment and dynamics underlying the current arms race.

Firstly, the arms race today is no longer a competition
in quantities only, but predominantly a race in modern

technology—in product improvements and sophistication. Implicit in this is a rapid rate of weapon modernization, which continuously introduces new variables into the military contest and constantly disrupts presumed conditions of strategic stability. Moreover, the complex nature of contemporary armaments and the technological advances on a broad front of weapons systems make it almost impossible to evaluate progression and shifts in the balance of forces. This balance evades exact measurement and invites subjective and arbitrary judgements, leading to worst-case analysis and over-reaction.

Secondly, with technology becoming the focal point in armaments, the dynamics of the arms race have changed profoundly. From a customary step-by-step arithmetic augmentation, the race has moved into an exponential curve—steep, fast and unpredictable.

Thirdly, the magnitude and proportion of the destructive power of modern arms have reached unprecedented levels. This is primarily due to second- and third-generation improvements in nuclear weapons. New technology has also amplified both the operational efficiency and the destructive power of conventional weapons to an extraordinary degree.

Fourthly, socio-political and economic motives for the arms race have grown stronger in response to the transformation of the industrial society, the changed role of the state, the centralization of authority, the abundance of means, the explosion of technology, broader and stronger corporate constituencies behind armaments, and the polarization of the international community.

Yet another new dimension to the contemporary arms race, with its vertical escalation in weapon modernization and destructive capabilities, is a horizontal proliferation of global dimensions. The pace-setters here, again, are the Soviet Union and the United States, followed by other industrial powers like France, the Federal Republic of Germany, the United Kingdom and to a lesser extent by countries like Czechoslovakia and Poland. Weapons are exported and sold both for strategic-political and economic reasons. One basic motivation for weapons exports is the need to sustain an economy of scale in the armaments industry and to support large military research and development establishments in the major arms manufacturing countries.

The political and economic effects are considerable.

Modern weapons are found in all corners of the world, feed-
ing local conflicts and rivalries. In the Third World, supersonic aircraft are now part of the conventional equipment in
twenty-one countries, and surface-to-air missiles in eighteen
countries. Seventy-five developing countries are among the
importers of major weapons.[4] Armaments have become a
status symbol, an indication of rank, power and authority
in the international community. They are widely used as instruments of politics and diplomacy.[5] The standards, in political
behaviour as well as in weapon modernization, are set by the
major powers; and the horizontal spread of arms, now mainly
visible in conventional weapons, is moving fast to include
nuclear weapons as well.[6] At the same time, there are
enormous social and economic costs in the waste of human
and material resources and in the distortion of development
priorities.

The harmful implications of the armament dynamics are
obvious. Those concerned with arms control issues as well
as scientists have been warning of the possibility of cata-
strophic developments.[7] They have called for a halt to and
reversal of the present trends. Yet the dominant response
among arms control negotiators is still a 'peace through
strength' posture. Rather than try and build peace on a
lower level of armaments, the prescription is to 'win' the
arms race. The outcome is a vicious circle of arms accumulation and acceleration of the armaments race.

Theorems of the arms race

A number of theorems try to explain the motivation, causation and dynamics of the arms race. According to the specific
approach, emphasis may be put on the political, economic,
technological or psychological aspects and on various elements
of given situations and structures. Most current are five sets
of explanations:[8]
1. Imperial and national rivalries, power politics and expan-
   sionist schemes.
2. Security dilemmas caused by aggressive and rapacious
   policies of neighbours or other powers.
3. System competition and ideological or religious enmity
   (Cold War crusades).
4. Profit or other vested interests of industry, the military,

the state, the bureaucracy and the technological establishment.

5. The technological momentum caused by pressures of science and technology, their impact on the art of warfare and weapon modernization.

In real life, we find that combinations of some or all of these factors determine the outcome of, and act as stimulants to, the arms race. Such a complex and broad phenomenon as the current arms race cannot be adequately explained in terms of one or two stimulants only. In different contexts and circumstances, the prime causation may be attributed to a specific set of determinants, but to some extent all the above factors are present in most of the situations.

Obviously, there are also restraining factors. In a dialectical way, we find these factors within parallel political, social, economic, technological and psychological parameters. Among the constraining factors are political rationality, resistance to violence, economic curbs and expediency, strategic caution and prudence, ethical inhibitions and moderation, or the very limits of current technological capabilities. It is certainly important to keep in mind these constraints, especially when attempting to devise strategies for arms control and disarmament. However, in dealing with the current arms race we must also remain aware of the asymmetry between the driving and restraining forces, and turn our attention first and foremost to what stimulates armaments. Today, the driving forces behind armaments are overwhelmingly stronger than the elements of restraint.

Basically, the motives behind the arms race may be reduced to two main categories: the externally and the internally induced. This classification is useful for designing basic paradigms of the arms race on the one hand and for developing measures for its control on the other. Although elements and extensions of both these categories can be found to varying degrees in all the five groups of stimulants, and though both categories tend to interact and overlap, the first three groups may essentially be classified as external inducements, and the last two as internal. The 'external' pattern is mostly associated with the internationally animated action-reaction model of inducing and energizing the race, while the 'internal' pattern is mainly related to socio-economic and self-sustaining models rooted in the structures and operation of the war machine, and the reinforcing behaviour of particular internal factors.

Over the last century and especially after the Second World War, with the growth of the industrial society and the advent of the second technological revolution, the trend moved from mainly internationally induced to predominantly internally energized arms races.[9] The recent acceleration of the arms race despite détente and the lessening of international tension, and despite the conclusion of a number of arms-control agreements, may serve to confirm this trend. Its explanation lies in the growth of the corporate constituencies with vested interests in military production and strength, and in the powerful impetus given to armaments by the technological race. The outcome is a momentum which takes less account of external factors and gains a life of its own.

Contemporary armament dynamics

Current armament dynamics are characterized by four dominant features: (a) the high intensity of the action-reaction and over-reaction impulses on the international level; (b) the threat postures inherent in the dominant military-strategic doctrines and their autistic reinforcement; (c) the role, size, structure and mode of operation of military research and development, or the technological momentum; and (d) the coalition of economic, military, political and technological forces.

These different features can be related either to the material base or to the political and ideological super-structures in society, and the way they interact. Together they form the structural framework, environment and climate which set the pace for the armament dynamics.

The action–reaction–over-reaction pattern

Historically, the mutually stimulating action-reaction pattern is the most frequent explanation of the arms race phenomenon. Driven by contest over territory and wealth, by security dilemmas, ideological fervour, suspicion and fear, pairs of contending nations or alliances steadily increase their armaments. In the process, they not only react to the real moves of the adversary, but also raise the stakes in response to imaginary moves which they perceive as measures or intentions of the opponent to bolster his military strength in order to achieve supremacy. The final outcome is frequently an over-response by both sides. A chain reaction of spiralling armaments is set in motion.

To date, with the focus less on quantities and more on technological advances, the action-reaction effect is much stronger and wider than in the past. The two main traditional assumptions of the action-reaction theory were: (a) that an increase in a nation's armaments is positively proportionate to the opponent's armaments expenditures; and (b) that the rate of armaments acceleration is negatively proportionate to the level of existing armaments.[10] Because of the technology race, both these assumptions are losing their validity. The technology race generates a propensity to reach far into the future, with a view to meeting expected breakthroughs by the adversary. By means of advance planning, it tries to match the long lead-times required for the development of new weapons. Such postures naturally stimulate over-response—a reaction out of proportion to real challenges. Consequently, over-reaction becomes a permanent condition. At the same time, the rate of innovation in technology produces a continuous dissatisfaction with the levels of armaments already attained. Despite an awareness of its escalation effects, both the United States and the Soviet Union are constantly engaged in improving the development and deployment techniques of new and more advanced weapon systems, like the intercontinental ballistic missiles, new generations of nuclear warheads, the multiple independently targetable re-entry vehicles (MIRVs), laser-guided weapons, etc.[11]

A vital ingredient of the action-reaction dynamics is the atmosphere of excessive secrecy surrounding security and military affairs. This practice has been tightened up in the post-Second World War period, as attested by the mushrooming activities of the various intelligence services. Introduced as a matter of principle and accepted by mutual agreement as a rule of behaviour, secrecy generates a propensity to 'worst-case' analyses, or contingency planning based on pessimistic assumptions, about adversary intentions and capabilities, which exaggerate the actual intelligence

assessments. Worst-case analysis, in fact, means the insti-
tutionalization of over-reaction. Secrecy undermines confidence and breeds mistrust. It also sanctions hawkish moves
to close the 'weapon gaps' by accelerating the arms race.
This was the case with the famous 'bomber gap' in the
mid-1950s and the 'missile gap' in the 1960s in the United
States.

Since the Second World War, the action-reaction dynamics
have been reinforced by ideological polarization and socio-
political systemic confrontation. Much of the prevailing
atmosphere of suspicion and fear is fed on the 'iron curtain'
mentality, which produces exaggerated enemy images. In
such a climate, the armaments curve reacts nervously to any
crisis situation and knows only one direction—upward—with
no chance of its ever returning to its starting position. The
dynamics generated by action-reaction-over-reaction have
intensified in direct proportion to the increase in international
polarization—systemic, political and ideological. One of the
most deplorable corollaries has been a climate which facili-
tates the misuse of the action-reaction pattern to mobilize
public opinion behind the arms race.

A relatively new aspect of this phenomenon is the change
from a bilateral to a triangular constellation, with China
entering the arms race as a potential superpower. Such
triangular dynamics tend to have a more energizing effect
than bilateral competition. It seems plausible that if a party
in the arms race has to take account of not one but two
adversaries, reaction and over-reaction will increase accordingly. The threat from the third opponent serves as a catalyst
for the race between the two other antagonists. It was the
triangular dynamics between the Soviet Union, the Western
powers and Nazi Germany which exploded into the Second
World War. It was also the triangle dynamics between the
Soviet Union, the United States and China that contributed
to the protraction of the Indochina war.[12] Thus, considering
the growing role of China in international affairs, as well as
the sensitivity of military relations between China and the
Soviet Union on the one hand, and of relations between
China and the United States on the other, we may assume a
further intensification of the action-reaction effect and its
increasing impact on the current arms race.

Military doctrines, threat postures and autistic pressures

The discussion of the political and ideological climate in contemporary international relations, in its military context, leads to a central concept in current armament dynamics: the autistic effect. 'Autism' refers to the hardening, in specific circumstances, of hostile impulses and motives into obstinate and persistent attitudes. Such a process becomes self-sustaining and impervious to changes in the environment as well as to possible alterations of the postures of the adversary. An in-depth study of the behavioural consequences of the contemporary international polarization has revealed that autism—self-reproduced enmity—plays an important role in the current arms race.[13] Influenced by the doctrines of deterrence and the threat system as reflected in the balance of terror, autistic pressures or bilateral autism reinforce political antagonism and the rush to armaments.

The doctrine of deterrence has a special place in contemporary armament dynamics. Devised to fit the emergence of nuclear weapons, its main assumption is that the foe can be held in check by the threat of nuclear retaliation. It thus requires a constant increase of armaments, so as to be able to inflict ever greater damage on the enemy. Consequently, the doctrine of deterrence has become a compelling motivation for moving up the armaments ladder. Presented to the general public as a device to preserve peace, deterrence has meant in fact the establishment of a threat system, a constant perfecting of the tools of war, and the perpetuation of a state of continuous war preparation. As nuclear arms have improved and have been made more operational, the concept of retaliation has been widened, finding reflection in ever more refined war strategies. It first started with the crude massive retaliation threat, moved on to the concept of Mutual Assured Destruction (MAD) which made the populations of large cities hostages to nuclear attack, and finally to counterforce strategies directed mainly against targets of military significance.

No other element in contemporary international relations has had a greater impact on armaments than the doctrine of deterrence. By urging ever higher levels and more sophisticated armaments for retaliatory strategies, deterrence locks the contending parties in an open-ended arms race.[14] It both stimulates military R&D and the war industry to ever greater efforts and tends to perpetuate enmity.

It is in this context that autistic pressures become evident. Threats, originally directed to the adversary and meant to deter his military potential, turn inward and generate security fears and a quest for stronger retaliatory power. External threats enter the internal security debate mainly as a legitimization for armaments. In the process, preoccupation with the enemy fades into a self-centred and inner-directed security psychosis, laden with enemy images, and materializing in an urge for more arms.

The consequences are far-reaching. The traditionally tension-producing postures of 'peace through strength' harden and petrify. No level of armaments seems satisfactory. In the Strategic Arms Limitation Talks (SALT), though the talk is of 'parity', the race is for superior strength and strategic superiority. Growing military capability by one side is interpreted by the other as political and military intent, and the race for strategic superiority becomes a permanent condition.[15] In fact, at the centres of power, strategic superiority is believed to have an essential political utility. The National Security Adviser to President Carter, Zbigniew Brzezinski, has put it thus:

I don't consider nuclear superiority to be politically meaningless . . . The *perception* by others or by oneself of someone else having 'strategic superiority' *can* influence political behaviour. In other words, it has the potential for political exploitation even if in an actual warfare situation the differences may be at best or at worst on the margin . . .[16]

The race for strategic superiority is also one of the reasons for the failure of SALT to halt strategic armaments. Despite arms control negotiations, it is becoming evident that we have now reached a stage where the pursuit of strategic superiority and, indeed, efforts to achieve first-strike capability have become the focal point of the arms race.

New technology and military research and development

The achievements of nuclear physics and the second technological revolution are essential to the current race for strategic superiority and first-strike capabilities. It must be emphasized, however, that the pursuit of new technological breakthroughs in nuclear armaments involves great risks. We are experimenting and manipulating with unknown forces. In the past, the search for improved weapons could proceed by trial and error. Today it is not possible to test fully the effects and consequences of nuclear explosions.

This aspect of the arms race has been stressed in a recent study by the United States National Academy of Sciences which states that many discoveries on the possible effects of nuclear explosions have been made not through deliberate scientific inquiry but by accident and chance.[17] The most striking example cited is the recent accidental discovery that nuclear explosions could destroy the ozone layer in the stratosphere which helps to protect all life on earth from ultraviolet radiation. A report by the United States Arms Control and Disarmament Agency adds:

We have come to realize that nuclear weapons can be as unpredictable as they are deadly in their effects. Despite some 30 years of development and study, there is still much that we do not know. This is particularly true when we consider the global effects of large-scale nuclear war.[18]

Despite warnings from the concerned scientific community,[19] the technological armaments competition continues unabated and contributes to the arms race. The very size of the venture points to the magnitude of the effect. Military research and development (R&D) absorbs today the talents of about half a million scientists and engineers around the globe, 85 per cent of this effort being concentrated in the United States and the Soviet Union.[20] The present size of military R&D is a post-Second World War phenomenon, reflecting the shift in the arms race from quantity to quality. Whereas before the Second World War military R&D consumed less than 1 per cent of armaments expenditures, it now absorbs 10–15 per cent. Investments in military R&D have increased four to five times faster than the general rate of growth of global armament expenditures. Given that current world military spending reaches the sum of $400 billion annually, we may deduce that military R&D has a global budget of $40–80 billion yearly—three times as much as funds spent on official aid for developing countries.[21]

Exact data on military R&D expenditures are few and are not available from the Soviet Union at all. We may, however, take the rough data from the United States as reflecting global trends. The American federal research and development draft budget for the financial year 1979 amounts to $27.9 billion, out of which about 50 per cent is devoted directly to defence, $3.4 billion to space research (remote sensing techniques, air traffic control systems, nuclear safety, etc.), and $10.7 billion to civilian related projects with the focus on basic research and energy with possible military significance.[22] These figures confirm the estimate of the Stockholm International Peace Research Institute (SIPRI) that military R&D 'absorbs more than one-half of the world's most highly qualified physical and engineering scientists'.[23] Given the Soviet efforts to catch up with and overtake the United States in military technology, we may assume that Soviet spendings and human engagement in military R&D are at least comparable, if not equal, to the American venture.

American investment in military R&D is indicative of the main directions in the technological race. The two main items in the financial year 1979 budget are devoted to major strategic and tactical weapons, *inter alia* the development of high-energy laser technology,[24] the development of the Trident submarine and missile, and the long-range cruise missiles—all considered crucial for attaining first-strike capability.[25] According to United States Secretary of Defense Harold Brown, the defence budget for the 1979 fiscal year covers ninety-three weapons systems earmarked for procurement, and an additional thirty, considered as high-value projects, still in the research and development stage.[26] While the investment in strategic weapons would point to a race for first-strike capability, the parallel development of tactical weapons—at a cost of $5 billion in the military R&D budget—including new generations of miniaturized nuclear warheads such as the neutron bomb, multi-role missiles, tank, helicopter and tactical aircraft systems—would indicate a race for the increase of effective warfighting capabilities, both nuclear and conventional.

Historically, we seem to be at a turning point that is similar, albeit on a higher spiral, to the revolutionary change in military technology that occurred in the late 1950s and early 1960s with the launching of the Sputnik, the development of intercontinental ballistic missiles, the nuclear-powered strategic submarine, the supersonic bomber and the high-speed re-entry vehicles. These technological breakthroughs radically changed the strategic scene, making nuclear weapons more operational and extending their reach to all continents, including the national territories of the United States and the Soviet Union. Today, the perils loom even larger. Both the cumulative improvement in military technology of the last decade and the new weapons systems developed, produced and deployed or in the development stage increase the nuclear warfighting capabilities and make first-strike capabilities a thinkable proposition.

An important aspect in the operation of military R&D is what may be called the 'Frankenstein drive': an autonomous impulse which McNamara defined as having 'a kind of intrinsic mad momentum of its own'. In fact, we can easily identify four constant trends which govern the work of the military R&D. These may be described as: the impulse to technological competition; the stabilizing and invigorating effects of the long lead-times; the follow-on imperative and growth propensity; the block-building and cross-fertilization effect.

The impulse to technological competition derives from the very size, expansion and goal-setting of military R&D. Military research has spread into a large number of industrial enterprises, laboratories, universities, special research institutes and centres of learning. As modern warfare covers all aspects of human life and invades all environments—land, sea, space, jungles and deserts—military R&D too has penetrated almost all scientific disciplines—the natural, social, medical and behavioural sciences. It is only natural that the hundreds of thousands of scientists and engineers dispersed in thousands of research plants, and working on parallel problems, should be competing among themselves in inventing, developing and perfecting new arms and weapons systems. Moreover, in order to stimulate results and achieve optimum efficiency, 'healthy' competition is encouraged by the authorities through the allocation of funds, the structured rivalry between different services (army, air force and navy) and various laboratories, and the procurement policy.[27]

Thus, competition in military R&D is no casual phenomenon. It is a built-in structural feature of the armament dynamics. The rivalry within the military R&D network is partly comparable to the competition in other socio-economic dynamics, where prestige, material interests and group pressures are vital. However, the scientists' motivation has

additional incentives in scientific curiosity and the importance attributed to their work. Secondly, competition is
tougher both because of the size of the venture and because
the end-product can never be allowed to fall below the highest
technological standards. By definition, new weapons must
be better and more efficient than the previous generation
and, of course, better than those in the hands of the adversary.
Certain standards of cost-efficiency must also be kept to.
Although military R&D is probably one field where economic factors play a minimal role, there are instances where
the abundance of new weapons systems with similar applications poses problems of competition in production and
deployment. Such a case was the recent rivalry in the United
States between the B–1 bomber and the long-range cruise
missiles. The choice fell on the cruise missiles, and Secretary
of Defense Harold Brown indicated cost-effectiveness as the
crucial criterion for the selection.[28]

The outcome of this competition is a race on the national
level which reinforces the race on the international level. In
fact, researchers in the military R&D network are more
often preoccupied with the better-known exploits of fellow-
researchers in rival institutions in their own country than
with the less-known achievement of the adversary's military
R&D. Consequently, the autonomous internal impulsion of
the race tends to exceed the international momentum.

One may also point to the extremely detrimental effects
of the commanding role of military R&D in science and
technology on national and international development. It
not only absorbs the best scientific and technological talents,
and represents a waste of human and material resources
but also distorts priorities in research and development. It
twists the direction of research and corrupts a field of scientific activity which is essential for human development. The
spill-over effects into civilian fields are negligible in comparison with the investments.[29] The loss incurred is particularly great considering the development requirements of
the Third World. Science and technology are diverted from
real human needs and harnessed to the perfection of the tools
of war.

A second trend is linked to the long lead-times needed
for the development of modern arms. It takes up to ten years,
or more, from the initial stages of discovery to the mastering
of technology and the production of new weapons systems.

This has several consequences. First, it assures stability, constancy and continuity—both for military R&D and the armaments momentum. Secondly, long lead-times intertwine with bureaucratic inertia, infusing additional vigour into the armaments process. It is difficult to withdraw from a commitment to a specific weapons system once an initial investment has been made and a decision taken. Thirdly, long lead-times influence the very decision-making process in armaments, by exerting pressure for early decisions in order to pre-empt the adversary and make the new weapons available in time. The technological imperative influences both judgements about a given situation and the choice of arms. Fourthly, long lead-times also produce impulses to improve the efficiency of military R&D. As the race in technology aims to close—and paradoxically to widen—the technological gap between the contending parties, there is an urge to shorten the lead-times for the development of new weapons. This, in turn, stimulates the internal dynamics of military R&D and the arms race as a whole.

In the context of the long lead-times in military R&D, we may also point to an important side-effect: namely, the harmful impact on arms control. While arms-control negotiators discuss the limitation of known existing weapon systems, military R&D, protected by secrecy, proceeds with the development of new weapons which undermine both the negotiations and the accords concluded. The pace of weapons innovation generally moves faster than the pace of arms-control negotiations, and as certain categories of arms become obsolete, agreements controlling them become irrelevant. Thus, in addition to being a driving force behind armaments, military R&D also obstructs arms-control and disarmament negotiations.

A third trend is the 'follow-on' imperative—the urge to go ahead and expand. Focus on qualitative improvement of weapons makes it vital to maintain and expand military R&D. Preserving or obtaining a lead in technology is crucial for maintaining military establishments and the power hierarchy in the international system. The more advanced the technological race, the greater the reliance on military R&D. The perfection of one weapons system requires a follow-up by a new one, the development of offensive arms requires response in the development of new defensive weapons, and vice versa. Since the highly specialized manpower mobilized for military R&D must be retained and protected, entire enterprises have to be kept on a constant footing of readiness and alertness. Moreover, the involvement in ever-new research projects calls for a steady extension of facilities and for increasing manpower. Thus, military R&D tends to swell and grow and, in turn, tends to invigorate the arms race. Military R&D has grown to become a material force in itself. Its capabilities and readiness count high in the balance of power. As a technological, military and political asset, military R&D has become an instrument of diplomacy, adding force to negotiating positions.

A fourth trend is what Kosta Tsipis has named the building blocks of weapon development, or the cross-fertilization effect of R&D.[30]

Quite often a major military system grows out of the maturing of several seemingly unrelated technologies—the building blocks—which, when pulled together, form a new and often unexpected system or make technically possible a system envisioned years before.[31]

Many projects moving initially in different directions meet later to develop a new system, as was the case with strategic reconnaissance satellite programmes.[32] The great variety of research projects and the mass of scientists involved generate a high cross-fertilization of ideas and projects. At the same time the building-block generates armaments pressures which evade control. In his *Origins of the MIRVs*, Herbert York has emphasized this aspect of the building-block dynamics:

Programmes evolving from many independent and seemingly unrelated purposes and decisions, cannot be controlled or stopped by directly confronting them. They can only be slowed or stopped by slowing or stopping the arms race as a whole.[33]

This is but one indication of the complex problems of bringing military R&D under control.

Destabilizing effects, arms control and irrationality

The race in military technology has exerted a destabilizing effect on the world military balance. Each new discovery, in offence or defence, contributes to instability because it adds advantages to one side in the race, often seeming to indicate the intention to strike first. From a more general perspective, the technological race promotes instability in two ways: by material advances, and by the psychological effect. Material advances in technology tend to destroy whatever stability in the balance of forces may be apparent, while the psychological effect contributes to intensifying the race. The psychological effect reinforces responses stimulated by secrecy—worst-case planning and over-reaction. The higher the spiral and the more complex the technological architecture, the more difficult it is to judge and control the balance and the more shaky are the prospects for stability.

The race in military technology augments and amplifies elements of uncertainty in the military environment. As it spreads and acquires global dimensions, it also adds fuel to local conflicts and regional arms races, thereby contributing to the growth of international tension.

From the point of view of arms control, the effect of the race in military technology is devastating. Arms control cannot keep pace with technological progress. The technological race wrecks the main purpose of arms control, which is to arrive at some military stability through a deliberately achieved balance in armaments. Faced with the arms-control failure because of the interference of technology, some arms controllers think that stability may be achieved only by adjusting to the highest level of technological weapon perfection. Yet, obviously, this is a prescription for an even more fierce race in military technology and for the intensification of the arms race.

The focus on high military technology interferes with arms control in an even more immediate way. It corrupts the very negotiating process, stimulating techniques in the talks themselves which contribute to hastening the armaments dynamics.[34] Efforts to achieve quantitative limitations in armaments generate pressures for qualitative compensation. While the negotiators are trying to agree on a ceiling on numbers, innovations which make even lower numbers of weapons more efficient and destructive are being introduced. This practice has gone hand in hand with another device—the bargaining chip method. This consists in the development, parallel to the negotiations, of new weapons systems; systems which supposedly force the adversary's hand during the talks, but are eventually absorbed into the military inventory.

This was the case with the MIRVs, which were first developed as a bargaining chip in the SALT negotiations but ended up finally as a key strategic weapon in the arsenals of both the United States and the Soviet Union.

An effect similar to the quantitative/qualitative compensation is achieved by the passage from simple first-generation testing methods to more advanced techniques. Thus, the 1963 Partial Test Ban Treaty pushed nuclear tests from the atmosphere to the underground, and the 1974 Threshold Test Ban Treaty was tailored for a continuation of the tests at a lower threshold but with better techniques. Finally, confronted with different force structures and levels of equipment in the Soviet Union and the United States, the SALT negotiations succumbed to reconciling the specific military requirements of both military establishments by accepting ceilings which made allowances for the actual force levels and the existing weapon programmes of both parties. Thus, under pressure of technology, arms control turned into a collaborative exercise in mutual armaments.

The current stalemate in arms control reflects the dilemmas created by the explosion of military technology. Writing in 1975 on the subject of the quantitative arms race, Harvey Brooks postulated that 'a limitation of the rate of technological progress in weapon systems is emerging as a central problem for the future of arms control'.[35] Today, the problem remains unsolved, and the accelerated rate of military technological innovation further exacerbates the crisis in arms control.

No element in contemporary armament dynamics has assumed such a central position, with such a profound impact on the arms race, as military R&D—the core and nerve centre of the race in technology. Military R&D is the mainstay and most energizing factor in the arms race. It operates in a way which makes armament dynamics organically tied to economic and productive structures, to the military establishment, to the state bureaucracy and to the second technological revolution. As a dynamic force, military R&D defies social control and tends to become ungovernable.

An air of irrationality and absurdity underlies the hasty and nervous exertions of military R&D. There is little rationality in the accumulation of overkill capabilities and the deployment of ever more advanced nuclear arms around the world. Europe is a case in point. Its nuclear arsenals grew erratically as newly perfected warheads were made available by military technology. The latest in line is the neutron bomb. Foe and friend alike fall victim to the terror of the robot-like military R&D production line. The very pace of the arms race is largely decided within the military R&D network through the sheer autonomous technological drift. Military R&D, it must be evident, thus becomes the major challenge to genuine disarmament.

The military-industrial-technological-bureaucratic complex

The autonomous internal armaments drive impelled by military R&D finds powerful social support in the alliance of the military, industrial, state bureaucratic and military scientific-technological establishments. It was Dwight D. Eisenhower who in his farewell presidential address drew attention to the new phenomenon of the 'military-industrial complex' as a mighty influence in society:

This conjunction of an immense military establishment and a large arms industry is new in the American experience. The total influence—economic, political, even spiritual—is felt in every city, every State House, every office of the federal government . . . In the councils of government, we must guard against the acquisition of unwarranted influence, whether sought or unsought, by the military-industrial complex. The potential for the disastrous rise of misplaced power exists and will persist.[36]

These were not casual observations. They reflected a deeply felt reality and a growing anxiety for the possible consequences, not only for the rise of armament pressures but also for the democratic fabric of the society. In the context of the Indochina adventure, these words had a prophetic ring. 'We must never let the weight of this combination endanger our liberties and democratic processes', Eisenhower had emphasized.[37] Professor George Kistiakowsky, President Eisenhower's Special Assistant for Science and Technology, notes in his memoirs that the President 'had talked to me more than once about his concern with what the speech called "the military-industrial complex"'.[38] Eisenhower was unhesitatingly in favour of basic academic research, but, as Kistiakowsky reports, he 'feared only the rising power of military science'.[39] As research became central to the technological revolution—Eisenhower warned—we must also be alert to the 'danger that public policy could itself become the captive of a scientific-technological élite'.[40]

Though Eisenhower spoke about the 'military-industrial complex', he was evidently concerned not only about the alliance of the military and industry behind armaments, but also about the role of the state political bureaucracy in 'every State House, every office of the federal government', and the 'position of power captured by the military-scientific-technological élite'.

Thus, in identifying the internal social forces behind armaments—'the web of special interest', in Eisenhower's words[41]—we may speak of the military-industrial-technological-bureaucratic complex (MITBC). This is a formidable power, based on organic unity between the strongest elements in the material base of the society, and the most relevant force in the political and ideological superstructure. For reasons of profit, professionalism, status, personal and group interests, diplomatic utility and so on, all four establishments have developed a vested interest in military strength, and they promote it by separate and co-operative undertakings. Their horizontal reach in society has spread constantly since the Second World War, and their vertical influence on the decision-making process has grown sharply with the explosion in military technology in recent years. It is not necessary to study the inside stories of governments, such as the one provided by *The Pentagon Papers*, to pinpoint the facts. We know too well that armaments, force structures and power politics have a decisive influence on the formation of governments, external and internal politics, and the way our world is governed.

The military-industrial-technological-bureaucratic complex is by no means an exclusively Western phenomenon. The lack of available studies concerning the Soviet Union does not mean that such social forces do not exist there.[42] It only reflects the official Soviet attitudes to social sciences in general and free research in military affairs in particular. Certainly, the MITBC in a society with state-owned industry and the prevalence of the state in all spheres of social and economic life operates differently from a society with privately owned industry and different socio-political structures. The functioning, procedure and form are not the same. Yet the motivation springs from similar roots, the inner dynamics move on similar lines and the effects are the same.

Considering the socio-economic structural differences between East and West, the broad dominance of the state and the regimentation of society in the East, we may even ask if the MITBC in the Soviet Union is not a stronger influence than the parallel corporate constituencies in the West. Without detailed study and research, it is difficult to give an answer. There is, however, one fundamental element in the structure of the Soviet economy and state management which may allow some tentative conclusions. Official economic theory and practice in the Soviet Union, as well as in China, keeps to the orthodox Stalinist teaching which asserts that heavy industry, the mainstay of defence production, must have absolute primacy, prevailing over other industrial branches, including light industry and the production of consumer goods.[43] This basic structure in the socio-economic model, however large the share of civilian production in the heavy-industry sector may be, is highly indicative of the role of military affairs in the management of the state as a whole. It provides at least circumstantial evidence for the preferential position of military production in the state economy. To this we may add that military-industrial, technological and bureaucratic interest groups are well represented, indeed prominently, in 'every city, every State House and every office of the Federal government'—to use the Eisenhower formulation—at all levels of the party and government hierarchy, in the Soviet nomenclature. It may be difficult to ascertain where their main influence lies—with the generals, the bureaucrats, the technocrats or the men in industry? But it is harder to deny that they carry important weight, or even dominate the decision-making processes, judging from the composition of the leadership in the party and state bodies and organizations, and from a simple reading of the East European press.

In the context of the special position of the MITBC in the councils of the state, and its influence in politics, economy and social affairs, a number of broader societal and systemic problems emerge. Considerable evidence points to processes which generate malfunctions in society and structural deformations of a fundamental nature both in national and international life. Eisenhower was concerned, and rightly so, with the impact on liberties and the democratic processes.

With military interests winning prevalence in state affairs, there is strong reason to fear that participation in and democratic control over public matters will diminish and authoritarian trends will increase, at the cost of basic human values of peace, the sanctity of human life and non-violence.

Parallel problems are posed by the seizure of controlling positions by the military in science and technology. The socio-economic consequences are wide-reaching. Acquiring the higher competence in modern technology, the military demands not only a decisive voice in the choice of arms, but aspires also to predominance in determining priorities in other crucial spheres of economic activity and human development. This is most evident in the Third World, where, in the wake of the world arms race, militarism and militarization have spread alarmingly.

There are other economic, social and political consequences. One, of basic significance, is the waste of resources. Another is the global proliferation of arms promoted by the pursuit of economies of scale. Yet another is the gravitation of investments away from civilian projects and into military production because of attractive conditions like profit incentives, lower public control, state support, elimination of rational economic calculus. Finally, under the pressure of the different corporate MITBC constituencies, basic human needs are degraded, the system becomes rigidified by a growing bureaucracy and loses the flexibility to respond in a human way to human affairs. Many other instances of critical detrimental effects of the MITBC impact on national and international affairs could be mentioned. They have in common one crucial effect: all of them sustain and accelerate the armaments dynamics and the arms race.

Some proposals for action on disarmament

Approaching the problem of disarmament, we should realize the magnitude of the challenge. As this analysis has shown, we confront not only powerful socio-political forces with a vested interest in armaments, but we also have to face active structural blockages with a life of their own, not at present subjected to democratic control, and with a coherence and tenacity defying surveillance and human direction. A corollary of this armaments momentum is that, while the nuclear powers may want to avoid nuclear disaster, they are caught by forces which they themselves unleashed. There is tension between the declared aims of avoiding war and the dynamics of armaments. To overcome these barriers and prevail over both the political, bureaucratic and economic interests and the technological drift is no easy assignment.

Whatever we may do to promote concrete disarmament measures, the major long-term task is an educational effort to raise the general awareness of the predicament caused by the arms race. To be effective such an effort must be based on real knowledge and insight into the complexities of armaments—their material realities, dynamics and implications. The whole process must be exposed by continuous effort. The aim should be to reach as wide an opinion as possible, to clarify the issues involved, to stir the public ethical self, and through a process of awareness induce people and nations to come out actively against armaments and for disarmament. The insight gained in this learning process may be decisive for choosing the right programmes of action, priorities and ways to genuine and comprehensive disarmament.

While we should continue to address ourselves to policy-makers—not least as part of the educational effort for the benefit of both the politicians and the public—the main assault must be on armament promoters of whatever profession or status.[44] Without the support of such an opinion, simple appeals to governments bear little weight. All this presupposes an action-oriented strategy which, while taking into consideration specific interests of various segments of the national and international community, can bring together large pressure groups, political forces and broad coalitions in a common struggle for disarmament.

Objective conditions certainly seem favourable. The overwhelming majority of people—of all classes, sexes and professions, as well as whole nations—are definite losers in the arms race. This includes even those temporarily drawing profits from armaments. Thus, informed debate and reason should be able to stimulate action for disarmament on the part of all working people, whose human conditions are deteriorating, and of all human beings who despise violence and cherish peace and freedom.

In such an educational and mobilizing effort, we may build on the whole range of constraints—material and spiritual—which prompt a stand against armaments and the arms race. Let us first consider the appeal to human rationality. On many grounds—costs, waste, perils—the arms race is highly irrational. It is also counterproductive. The rule, confirmed by experience after the Second World War, is that the accumulation of increasingly sophisticated arms designed to increase security has in fact weakened and reduced this security. Even the safety of the Soviet Union and the United States became more vulnerable by the introduction of intercontinental missiles and the increase in precision, range and reliability of modern weapons systems.[45] Sooner or later, such systems become the property of both sides in the arms race, making the world a more dangerous place than ever.

A second set of inhibitions to the arms race is moral and ethical. The theory of a 'just war' becomes at least questionable, at a time when the very survival of humanity is at stake. Conventional arms with nuclear powers of destruction and the perfection of nuclear arms to suit conventional scenarios blur the dividing line between the two types of weapon. The danger that any conventional conflict between the big powers would escalate into nuclear catastrophe becomes a near-certainty. The search for security on a lower level of armaments, for a non-violent and peaceful resolution of conflicts, becomes mandatory.

Within the framework of moral inhibitions, special attention should be given to the social responsibility of scientists.[46] Because of their deeper insight and superior inside knowledge, because of their key role in military R&D and their better grasp of the far-reaching implications of their work, the awakening of the scientific community to social and moral responsibility is of crucial importance today. The adoption of a code of conduct for scientists and engineers, including a sort of a Hippocratic oath, is long overdue.[47]

As far as general strategies for disarmament are concerned, our analysis would point to a distinction to be made between the external and international stimulants of armaments on the one hand, and the political and technological aspects of the arms-race dynamics on the other. As we have seen, the centre of gravity of the arms-race dynamics today lies in internal, autistic and technological pressures. We should certainly not ignore the complex political interaction and mutual stimulation on the international level, but should support every effort to reduce these tensions, to infuse political will for disarmament, and press for genuine measures to reduce both conventional and nuclear armaments. The best framework for such actions was set by the United Nations approved goal of general and complete disarmament.[48] There exists at the same time a real need to re-think critically the arms-control experience of recent years, which has meant a turning away from disarmament towards co-operative, balanced armaments.[49] However, to draw on our analysis, high priority must also be given to the autistic and technological forces behind armaments. A limitation of their impact would influence the most critical factors of armament dynamics to date.

It is implicit in this approach that efforts at disarmament must start at home. Reduction of international tension has little chance of success, if left to forces of action-reaction and over-reaction. To clear the political atmosphere we have also to do our homework. This requires subduing and eliminating the autistic tension-generating pressures linked to deterrence theories, excessive secrecy, *para bellum* postures and enemy images which lock us in structured enmity and feed the arms race. Such internal effort, of course, must not proceed in national isolation, but must go hand in hand with parallel efforts in nations tied to the arms race. Human solidarity in a conscientious national and international movement for peace is a prerequisite for success in action for disarmament.

Finally, central to disarmament efforts is action to check military R&D, to freeze its potential, and bring about its gradual dismantlement within the framework of general and complete disarmament. This is a tall order, but unless it is attacked with vigour, burgeoning technology may undercut all attempts at disarmament.

Various approaches have been proposed: budgetary cuts, non-use and non-development accords, controlled limitation of test activities, conversion to civilian use or mobilization of social control. None of these proposals is watertight. But if tried together, they should yield some positive results. The international community especially is now well armed, not least thanks to the achievements of modern technology, to impose 'strict and effective control' as actually postulated in the 1961 Agreement between the Soviet Union and the United States on Principles for Disarmament Negotiations (the Zorin-McCloy Agreement) endorsed by the United Nations.[50] The Zorin-McCloy accord concretely foresaw the establishment of an international disarmament organization within the United Nations framework to undertake this task. At that time, the tools for non-intrusive control were perhaps still too weak for effective action. But today methods of satellite, electronic, physical and chemical surveillance abound.[51] The major powers, in fact, make use of these methods for their own intelligence. The problem is to internationalize these capabilities and transform them into a common fund of knowledge in order to check the arms race and military R&D. The time is ripe for the creation of an International Agency for a Satellite Surveillance, Control and Verification System to make disarmament work.

Disarmament efforts following the Second World War have been foiled by the technology race and have got lost in the wilderness of arms control. In the meantime, the dynamics of armaments have increased greatly. To halt these dynamics is today the major criterion for genuine disarmament.

Notes

1. See 'World Armaments and Disarmament', *SIPRI Yearbook 1977*, Stockholm, SIPRI, 1977.
2. See John F. Lambelet, 'Do Arms Races Lead to War?', *Journal of Peace Research*, Oslo, Universitetsforlaget, Vol. XII, No. 2, 1975.
3. See Marek Thee, 'Militarism and Militarization in Contemporary International Relations', *Bulletin of Peace Proposals*, Vol. VIII, No. 4, 1977.
4. See *SIPRI Yearbook 1976*, pp. 16–20, Stockholm, SIPRI, 1976.
5. See Barry M. Blechman and Stephen S. Kaplan (Eds.), *The Use of the Armed Forces as a Political Instrument*, Washington, D.C., The Brookings Institute, 1976.
6. See Sverre Lodgaard, 'The Increase in International Nuclear Transactions', *SIPRI Yearbook 1977*, pp. 29–51, Stockholm, SIPRI, 1977.
7. See Barnard T. Feld, 'The Consequences of Nuclear War', *The Bulletin of the Atomic Scientists*, June 1976, and Carl von Weizsäcker, 'The Avoidance of Atomic War', *World Issues*, December 1976.
8. For a detailed table of armament determinant models, see R. Curnow et al., 'General and Complete Disarmament, A System Analysis Approach', *Futures*, Vol. VIII, No. 5, October 1976.
9. See Klaus Jurgen Gantzel, 'Armaments Dynamics in the East-West Conflict, An Arms Race?', *The Papers of the Peace Science Society (International)*, Vol. XX, 1973.
10. See Anatol Rapoport, 'Richardson, Lewis Fry', *International Social Science Encyclopedia*, Vol. XIII.
11. See George W. Rathjens, 'The Dynamics of the Arms Race', *Scientific American*, April 1969.
12. See Marek Thee, 'The Indochina Wars. Great Power Involvement —Escalation and Disengagement', *Journal of Peace Research*, Oslo, Universitetsforlaget, Vol. XIII, No. 2, 1976.

13. See Dieter Senghaas, 'Towards an Analysis of the Threat Policy in International Relations', *German Political Studies*, London, Sage Publications, 1974.
14. See 'The Perniciousness of the Policy of Nuclear Deterrence'. 25th Pugwash Symposium, Kyoto, *Pugwash Newsletter*, Vol. XIII, No. 2, October 1975.
15. See J. David Singer, 'Threat Perception and the Armament Tension Dilemma', *Journal of Conflict Resolution*, Vol. II, No. 1, March 1958.
16. Zbigniew Brzezinski in an interview with Jonathan Power, *International Herald Tribune*, Paris, 10 October 1977.
17. National Academy of Sciences, *Long-Term Worldwide Effects of Multiple Nuclear Weapons Detonations*, Washington, D.C., 1975.
18. United States Arms Control and Disarmament Agency, *Worldwide Effects of Nuclear War . . . Some Perspectives, A Report*, Washington, 1975.
19. See declaration by the Pugwash Council at the conclusion of the 27th Pugwash Conference, *Pugwash Newsletter*, Vol. XV, No. 1–2, October 1977.
20. See Randall Forsberg, *Resources Devoted to Military Research and Development*, Stockholm, SIPRI, 1972.
21. See Ruth Leger Sivarth, *World Military and Social Expenditures 1977*, Virginia, WMSE Publications, 1977.
22. Eugene Kozicharow, 'Real Growth Emphasized in U.S. Research Funding', *Aviation Week and Space Technology*, 13 February 1978.
23. *SIPRI Yearbook 1977*, Stockholm, SIPRI, 1977, op. cit., p. 3.
24. Writing in 1975, Harvey Brooks considered research in high power lasers as aiming at 'possible exotic ballistic missile defences'. See Harvey Brooks, 'The Military Innovation System and the Qualitative Arms Race', *Daedalus*, Summer 1975, and also Paul J. Nahin, 'The Laser BDM and other Radiant Energy Weapons: Some Thoughts', *IEEE Transactions on Aerospace and Electronic Systems*, Vol. AES–13, No. 2, March 1977.
25. E. Kozicharow, op. cit.
26. *Aviation Week and Space Technology*, 30 January 1978.
27. See Samuel H. Day, 'The Nuclear Weapon Labs', *The Bulletin of the Atomic Scientists*, April 1977; Robert F. Coulam, 'Inter-Service Weapon Rivalry', *The Bulletin of the Atomic Scientists*, Chicago, June 1977; Judith V. Reppy, *The Independent Research and Development Program of the Department of Defense*, Peace Study Program, Cornell University, Occasional Paper No. 6, March 1976; Robert Lindsey, 'Domestic Arms Race Pits Livemore vs. Los Alamos', *The New York Times*, 31 July 1977.
28. See Harold Brown, 'Background for the BI Bomber Decision', *Bulletin of Peace Proposals*, Oslo, Vol. VIII, No. 4, 1977, p. 350.
29. See Seymour Melman, 'Twelve Propositions on Productivity and War Economy', *Armed Forces and Society*, Chicago, Inter-University Seminar on Armed Forces and Society, Vol. I, No. 4, August 1975.
30. Kosta Tsipis, 'The Building Blocks of Weapon Development', *The Bulletin of the Atomic Scientists*, Chicago, April 1977.
31. Ibid.
32. Herbert York, 'The Origins of MIRV', *SIPRI Research Report No. 9*, Stockholm, SIPRI, 1973, p. 23.
33. See Herbert York and G. Allen Greb, 'Strategic Reconnaissance', *The Bulletin of the Atomic Scientists*, April 1977.
34. See G. W. Rathjens et al., *Nuclear Arms Control Agreements: Process and Impact*, Washington, D.C., Carnegie Endowment for International Peace, 1974, and Jane M. O. Sharp, 'MBFR as Arms Control', *Arms Control Today*, April 1976.
35. Harvey Brooks, op. cit., p. 75.
36. Dwight D. Eisenhower, *Waging Peace, The White House Years 1956–61, A Personal Account*, p. 616, New York, Doubleday & Co., 1965.
37. Ibid.
38. George B. Kistiakowsky, *A Scientist at the White House*, p. 425, Cambridge, Mass., Harvard University Press, 1976.

39. Ibid.
40. Ibid.
41. Dwight D. Eisenhower, op. cit., p. 615.
42. See Vernon V. Aspaturian et al., 'The Military-Industrial Complex USSR/USA'. Special issue of the *Journal of International Affairs*, Vol. XXVI, No. 1, 1972; David Holloway, 'Technology and Political Decision in Soviet Armaments Policy', *Journal of Peace Research*, Vol. XI, No. 4, 1974; David Holloway, 'Soviet Military R&D: Managing the Research Production Cycle', in John R. Thomas and Ursula Kruse Vancienne (eds.), *Soviet Science and Technology*, Washington, NSF, George Washington University, 1977; Egbert Jahn, 'The Role of the Armaments Complex in the Soviet Union', *Journal of Peace Research*, Oslo, Vol. XII, No. 3, 1975.
43. The Soviet defence industry consists of: Ministry of Defence Industry (conventional weapons), Ministry of Aviation Industry (aircraft and aircraft parts), Ministry of Shipbuilding Industry, Ministry of Electronics Industry and Ministry of Radio Industry (electronic components and equipment), Ministry of Media Machine Building (nuclear weapons), Ministry of General Machine Building (strategic missiles) and Ministry of Machine Building (ammunition). See David Holloway, 'Soviet Military R&D', *Soviet Science and Technology*, Washington, op. cit., p. 229.
44. See Marek Thee, 'Speaking to Policy-Makers', *Bulletin of Peace Proposals*, Oslo, Vol. VII, No. 2, 1976, pp. 161–2.
45. See Herbert York, 'The Ultimate Absurdity', *Bulletin of Peace Proposals*, Oslo, Vol. VII, No. 1, 1976, pp. 61–3.
46. See Marek Thee, 'The Scientist's Role in Society', *Bulletin of Peace Proposals*, Oslo, Vol. III, No. 4, 1972, pp. 367–70; Nils Petter Gleditsch, 'Six Arguments Against Research for the Military', *Bulletin of Peace Proposals*, Oslo, Vol. VIII, No. 2, 1975, pp. 172–5.
47. See 'Science and Society', *Bulletin of Peace Proposals*, Oslo, Vol. III, No. 4, 1972, pp. 339–55.
48. See Statement by the Disarmament Study Group of the International Peace Research Association, March 1978, *Bulletin of Peace Proposals*, Oslo, Vol. IX, No. 2, 1978.
49. See Marek Thee, 'Arms Control, The Retreat from Disarmament', *Journal of Peace Research* (Oslo), Vol. XIV, No. 2, 1977.
50. United States Arms Control and Disarmament Agency, *Documents on Disarmament 1961*, Washington, 1962, p. 441.
51. For the table of surveillance/verification possibilities, see Owen Wilkes, 'Military Research and Development: Problems of Control', *Bulletin of Peace Proposals*, Oslo, Vol. IX, No. 1, 1978, pp. 8–9.

Militarism in developed and developing countries

Peace activist in the United Kingdom and Council Member of War Resisters International

Michael Randle

When the delegates to the United Nations discuss disarmament they disagree about many things. They represent, after all, governments of widely differing character. Yet there are two fundamental things on which all of them generally agree: that universal disarmament is a desirable objective and that it is something which, alas, must be indefinitely postponed.

In part, their admission that the ultimate goal is at present unattainable reflects a realistic appraisal of the persistent obstacles. While these need not be minimized, it should be said that some of them are the result of a particular approach to disarmament—one which views it coming about as a result, and virtually only as a result, of bilateral or multilateral agreements. Given this approach, one can, indeed, envisage at the best some limited measures such as an agreement not to proceed with the development of a certain new weapons system or to curtail the magnitude of the global arms race. To dismiss such partial measures of arms control as worthless exercises would be a hasty conclusion. At critical moments they may make the difference between peace and war and may, thus, buy more time in which to take more radical measures. Are they sufficient in themselves? There is little reason to think so.

The arms race has become a dynamic process. Not only is militarism spreading to new areas but the sophistication and destructive power of the technology have increased many times over, making the current arms race qualitatively different from any preceding it. Given that, and the intensification of social and economic problems it engenders, it is hard to believe that partial and piecemeal agreements will be enough. The sober reality is that without radical departures in the approach to disarmament nuclear war is likely. Even if this disaster is avoided, tens of thousands will die as a result of the constant diversion of human and material resources from more constructive purposes. Yet there is nothing inevitable about this process; it is not a law of nature that thousands should go hungry so that others can be suitably equipped with weapons to shoot them or to blow up the world.

Militarism as a historical phenomenon

Historically, militarism has been associated with stridently aggressive regimes such as Prussia under Bismarck, Germany under Hitler, Italy under Mussolini, but there is a good case for interpreting militarism in a broader sense. Regimes which differ very much from these, and from one another, have also come to be dominated by the dynamics of military expansion. This phenomenon of the expansion of armies and armaments—not simply their existence—is the major concern of this paper. To quote Marek Thee,

Under the term 'militarism' I subsume such symptoms as the rush to armaments, the growing role of the military (understood as the military establishment) in national and international affairs, the use of force as an instrument of prevalence and political power and the increasing influence of the military in civilian affairs.[1]

The ideological dimension of militarism represents the emphasis on discipline and regimentation and the assumption that the use of armed force is a key component in the solution of social and political problems. This paper also considers the related and overlapping process of militarization which pertains to the last part of Marek Thee's formulation and which he elaborates as 'the extension of military influence to civilian spheres, including the economy and socio-political life'.

It is easy to identify a close association between militarism and the evolution of the nation-state. The nation-state is now such a ubiquitous institution that there is a tendency to accept it as a given fact of the natural order. It has not always been so. In many parts of the world it is still a comparatively recent phenomenon. As it has evolved, particularly in Europe over the past few hundred years, it has come to be characterized by its degree of centralization and by its claim to the monopoly of armed force within the territory over which it has jurisdiction. Flags, uniforms, armies, military anthems—how many national anthems are *not* marching tunes?—these are some of the things that are intimately and perhaps inextricably linked with it. Not all the states are equally militaristic, but the association of the state with the military and with facets of military ideology may suggest the limits to what can be expected from disarmament initiatives at the level of governments.

The industrial revolution, the creation of the state bureaucracy, together with professional armies and police forces and the introduction of conscription, starting with Bonaparte's *levée en masse*, are the milestones in the evolution of the military and state power. Today the destructive efficiency of advanced weapons in conjunction with electronic computing, triggering and guidance systems, has meant a decreasing importance for manpower in the military establishments of some industrialized countries. The United Kingdom ended conscription in 1962 and, following the end of the Vietnamese war, the United States has ended the draft. In most European countries the period of military service has been successively cut, and there are legal provisions for conscientious objection. Yet, many European countries retain it, and newly independent states have shown no distinct distaste for conscription. Moreover, in those countries that have abolished it there are powerful voices demanding its return.

Conscription is important not only because it is the mechanism through which a large proportion of the world's regular armed forces, estimated at 22 million in 1977,[2] are raised but also because it performs an important educational—or rather mis-educational function. It exposes young people to the military ethos and subjects them to its discipline. In many countries conscripts are also placed on military reserve and subjected to periodic refresher training so that the discipline and influence are renewed. Here then is a powerful socializing agent that functions to spread and consolidate militarism. It is so widespread, and so readily accepted as a prerogative of the state, that even many of its opponents focus their attention on the human right of conscientious objection rather than demanding the abolition of this system of forced labour.

Industrialization provided the material basis for a quantum leap in the level of militarism in the late nineteenth and early twentieth centuries and led, among other factors, to the two most destructive wars in history. The conditions under which industrialization took place, that is harsh discipline and low wages at home and imperialism abroad, required the expansion of the military. Even today a few major powers provide the sinews of global militarism. In the period 1960–75 the Soviet Union and the United States accounted for two-thirds of the total world military outlays. The next tier of military powers—China, the Federal Republic of Germany, the United Kingdom and France—accounted for another 15 per cent. The two superpowers in conjunction with these second tier powers continue to account for 80 per cent of current world military outlays.[3]

The two superpowers also dominate the field of military research and development, estimated globally to cost $25 billion a year, and employ half a million scientists and engineers for the purpose.[4] That militarism—as defined above—is a dynamic process, rather than a static one, is shown by the fact that however one measures the size of the military establishment the total military expenditures, expenditures on research and development, arms transfers, numbers in the armed forces, numbers engaged in the military industries, the number and destructive power of weapons—one sees the same picture of expansion. This expenditure and commitment of resources to militarism have damaged and distorted the economies of the major powers and of other industrialized nations. Most of the studies in this area have examined the case of the United States and Western powers, where the data are more readily available, but it is reasonable to suppose that there are many parallel effects, making allowance for the different social and economic structure, in the Soviet Union and Eastern Europe.

Before listing some of the features and structures of militarism, a word of caution is necessary. There is a temptation to regard militarism as an institution in itself and to pay too little attention to the social, economic and political events which give rise to it or interact with it in a variety of ways. Some of these factors constitute, in themselves, obstacles to disarmament and need to be dealt with in detail. This paper assumes that the backdrop to world militarism is the struggle between the major powers (including China), the network of military alliances, the domination by the two superpowers of a number of less powerful countries for their own strategic and economic purposes—and the struggle of these countries to free themselves from such domination—and more generally the unequal and exploitative relationship that persists in many aspects between the industrialized and de-developed countries.*

Militarism in the industrialized countries

Against this background, this paper considers some aspects of militarism in industrialized countries that might impede the process of disarmament.

War-related production in a number of Western economies is linked with the expanding high technology, and its effect on the overall economy is out of proportion to its relative size. A sudden decline in war production is bound to have an immediate impact on several key industries. This is not to say that a changeover to peace production is impossible, or that it would not be beneficial, but it is at this point a complex process and involves more radical structural changes in the economy than at any previous period, including the periods of demobilization following the two world wars.[5]

The structural links between military production and foreign arms sales are especially important for the second-tier arms producers such as France, the Federal Republic of Germany and the United Kingdom. Foreign sales help to offset the high research and development costs and give the producers the benefit of longer production runs. But economic factors probably do play a part even in the case of an industrial giant like the United States. American arms-export policy has undergone a major shift towards arms sales as opposed to military aid.[6] The phenomenal increase in arms trade with a number of oil-producing states in recent years has been a definite boon to arms exporters in commercial terms, which does not entirely explain their vigorous interest in the Gulf region. It is not only armaments as such that are involved in military transfers; they often include such related equipment as vehicles, communication systems and so on. Sometimes major construction work such as the building of roads and bridges is also involved. Additional

* I prefer the term 'de-developed' to 'developing' because, while it too suggests an oversimplified picture, it comes nearer to indicating the historical process that has been involved.

contracts accrue to the supplier country, besides arrangements for servicing and maintenance which tie the recipient country to the supplier over a long period. The armaments business extends beyond weapons production and covers a whole range of industries.

A growing number of multinational companies, based in the United States or other industrialized countries, and their subsidiaries have started to produce arms or components for arms, in de-developed countries, through arrangements like licensing and co-production.[7]

The electronics revolution in the manufacturing industry has a destabilizing effect on the balance of power among major military spenders. Things are changing so fast that there is no longer any certainty that a given stalemate in deterrence will last. Thus, precision-guided rockets together with detection and surveillance devices might make a first-strike attack feasible. The secrecy with which this work is surrounded, coupled with the speed at which it is progressing, has quickened the tempo of escalation.

With the expansion of internal security forces by para-military units and the tightening of security laws and procedures, there has been an explosion in the technology of surveillance, data-storage and riot control. By now, there is clear evidence to show that major military powers have been indulging in systematic work on methods of extracting information from suspects. The export of this type of technology, and the training of police and military forces for security and counter-insurgency operations in the consolidation of repressive regimes, is an important aspect of the spread of militarism to new areas.[8]

The stationing of sophisticated weapons in any region entails a preoccupation with internal security. Thus, the proposed stationing in depth of mini-nukes in Europe would inevitably involve a further expansion of the surveillance activities, including intricate devices for reading and controlling people's minds.[9]

The prospects for disarmament are substantially affected by these developments. First, because they move governments in an authoritarian direction and make it less likely that they will be prepared to take any creative risks for peace; and secondly, they help to insulate governments from those popular pressures from below which might persuade them to take a different course.

Militarism in de-developed countries

Turning to the de-developed nations, the striking thing is the rapid increase in military spending and the spread of military and authoritarian regimes. While the rate of increase in military spending for the world as a whole is 2.6 per cent, that for the de-developed nations is 10.3 per cent.[10] Similarly, in the period 1965–74 the military expenditure of the industrialized nations as a percentage of the GNP declined from 7.22 per cent to 5.77 per cent, whereas in the de-developed nations it rose from 4.36 per cent to 5.33 per cent.[11]

The spread of military rule is still more alarming; over 40 per cent of de-developed countries have come under military rule since 1956. Of these, the largest group have a right-wing character and tend to be pro-Western in orientation; a second group have populist or leftist leanings and are likely to be non-aligned internationally; a third and smaller group have a definite Marxist commitment. Whatever their political complexion, however, military regimes are unlikely to show much enthusiasm for programmes of disarmament. An analysis of how this situation has arisen is beyond the scope of this paper, which simply points out those aspects which relate to global militarism.

Some expansion of armies was almost inevitable with the passing of the colonial era and the creation of new states with their own national armies. However, the precariousness of national unity in territories where national boundaries were carved out at random by the colonial invaders has frequently encouraged a very militant nationalism. Border disputes and civil wars have also occurred. In the Middle East, the Arab-Israeli conflict has led to a major build-up of armies and armaments, and this fact tends to inflate somewhat the overall figures for military expenditure in the de-developed world. Nor, even aside from that, is the rate of military expansion at all uniform. In Latin America, for instance, in the early 1970s six countries—Argentina, Brazil, Chile, Cuba, Peru and Venezuela—were responsible for 85 per cent of the total arms purchases of the region.[12]

Global militarism influences this situation in many ways. There have been several instances of direct or indirect intervention by major military powers to undermine a government whose economic policy or political stance was unacceptable to the intruders. External intervention in a number of local disputes has resulted, in several cases, in escalating the conflict beyond its original purpose and area. Strategically placed countries have received abundant military supplies. The creation of forward defence areas has produced an acute internal imbalance between the strength of the military and other social institutions. This has frequently paved the way for a military take-over. In other cases nominal civilian governments have come to rely heavily on the military.

The diversion of resources for military purposes generally exacerbates social tensions, causing a cut-back in both productive investment and programmes of social welfare and reconstruction. Furthermore, the import of arms tends to create a long-term dependency on the supplier. Meanwhile, as the social crisis deepens, the military becomes stronger and may eventually step in to restore order and impose discipline. Where they do so under such circumstances, the social crisis does not end. Rebellion, guerrilla warfare and widespread unrest ensue, followed by intensified repression. If the military are able to impose discipline on the population and the work-force in particular, a favourable climate may be created for foreign investment under some kind of dependent capitalist development. Its main beneficiaries are an élite at home and foreign interests, while the conditions for the majority of people actually deteriorate. This corresponds to the situation in many countries in Latin America where middle-class elements have sought an alliance with the military, partly to check the power of the traditional oligarchy but chiefly to control more radical social forces.[13]

While right-wing military rule and repression predominate and are associated with capitalist modes of production, some of the left-wing military regimes have also unleashed a reign of repression and terror. This may be facilitated by supplies of weapons from socialist countries. Weapons systems are not neutral pieces of hardware; they require a particular type of social institution for their operation. In the case of the major weapons systems developed in the industrialized countries, they call for a disciplined, hierarchical social institution such as the conventional armies for which they were designed. Thus the tendency—at any rate when de-developed countries, in the process of remoulding their institutions, import such weapons—is to import with them a social system.[14] It must be admitted that the armed forces did play a historical and sometimes decisive role in many instances in ending colonial rule or foreign intervention. However, the rapid expansion of the military and military budgets today is more likely to be a source of impoverishment and dependence for the de-developed countries. The problem needs to be tackled at its source in the industrialized countries, which promote a system of economic exploitation and provide the technology of militarism and repression.

Having said that, one must add that the picture is not uniformly bleak. If the arms race has promoted militarism, it has also provoked its opposite. The past twenty years have seen anti-war movements of a new vigour and radicalism in some of the industrialized countries. While these have declined in recent years, there are occasional signs of their revival. The activities planned in connection with the United Nations Special Session on Disarmament were one such indication. The convening of the Special Session itself showed an awareness, especially among the non-aligned countries, of the gravity of the problem. An international mobilization for survival has been formed comprising individuals and organizations from many countries who will press for radical measures, including the abolition of nuclear weapons. Moreover, a growing number of young men are refusing military service on grounds of conscience, and an international collective resistance to conscription has been formed. In the Federal Republic of Germany, for example, following a law introduced in August 1977, simplifying the procedure for registering as a conscientious objector, the number of conscientious objectors rose from an average of 2,500 a month to a peak of 10,563 in November. The law was set aside the following month by a constitutional court. Nevertheless, the number of objectors in February 1978 was 25,000, and about half of these took part in a nation-wide strike to oppose a plan that would require them to live in barrack conditions. Internal repression is also being answered by radical dissent and resistance. This is not confined to any particular part of the world but exists, to some degree, in all societies which deny the freedom to organize and campaign for social and political change.

It is the forces from below which are the main hope for progress in disarmament. If bilateral and multilateral agreements to disarm continue to elude the governments, it is the people who have to organize a demand for action, including, if necessary, unilateral disarmament.

Notes

1. Paper prepared for the Pugwash Symposium on 'Militarism and National Security', Oslo, 21–25 November 1977. Reprinted in *Bulletin of Peace Proposals*, Oslo, Vol. VIII, No. 4, 1977.
2. Ruth L. Sivard, *World Military and Social Expenditures*, New York, Institute for World Order, 1977.
3. Ibid.
4. Ibid.
5. See for instance some of the contributions. See Seymour Melman (ed.), *The War Economy of the United States*, New York, 1971.
6. American military aid fell from a high point of $5.7 billion in 1952 to under $600 million in recent years. But in the same period arms sales rose, reaching $1 billion for the first time in 1966, averaging $1.8 billion, in the early 1970s, and reaching $4 billion in 1975. For figures see Leslie H. Gelb, 'Arms Sales', *Foreign Policy*, New York, December 1976.
7. See Ulrich Albrecht, 'Arms Trade with the Third World and Domestic Arms Production', *Instant Research on Peace and Violence*, No.1–2, 1976. One example Albrecht gives is of an anti-aircraft gun produced in Switzerland which incorporates an electronic guidance system made mainly by low-paid Indian women.
8. See Michael T. Klare, *Supplying Repression*, New York, Field Foundation, 1977.
9. See Peter Lock, 'In Memoriam: Constitutional Rights and the Liberal State. A Worst Case Analysis in Peace Research', *Instant Research on Peace and Violence*, Vol. VIII, No. 3–4, 1977. The spread of nuclear power technology, because of the risk of its by-products being used for military purposes, has similar implications.
10. *SIPRI Yearbook, 1976*, Stockholm, SIPRI, 1976.
11. U.S. Arms Control and Disarmament Agency. *World Military Expenditures and Arms Transfers: 1965–74*. Washington, D.C. 1975.
12. SIPRI, *The Arms Trade with the Third World*, London, Pelican Books, 1975.
13. See Jose Nun, 'The Middle Class Military Coup', *Imperialism and Underdevelopment*, Monthly Review Press, 1970.
14. See Mary Kaldor, 'The Significance of Military Technology'. Paper presented at the Pugwash Symposium on Problems of Military-oriented Technologies in Developing Countries, Feldafing, 23–26 November 1976. Reprinted in *Bulletin of Peace Proposals*, Oslo, Vol. VIII, No. 2, 1977.

Ways of overcoming obstacles to disarmament

The arms race and the role of education

Director of the Corporación Integral para el Desarrollo Cultural y Social (CODECAL), Bogotá (Colombia), and Vice-President of the World Council on Curriculum and Instruction, and of the Peace Education Commission of the International Peace Research Association

Jaime Diaz

Violence in the world

As a result of research studies conducted over recent years, a distinction has come to be made between physical or direct violence and indirect or structural violence. Usually it is direct violence that first comes to mind when reference is made to the need to halt the arms race. Nevertheless, structural violence is its fundamental cause: the violence of an unjust economic and political system, whether within a country or at the international level, produces armed violence. Starving people are driven to despair and violence when they see no other way of bringing about a real change in their situation.

The former type of violence has—at least in Latin America—a fundamentally repressive character: arms are a necessity for weak governments in order to stifle protest, criticism and armed revolutionary movements or demonstrations by the civil population. Hence the violation of political and civil rights and the declaration of the state of emergency, whereby legal guarantees are suspended. But the fundamental cause is the violation of the economic rights of the underprivileged mass of the population. The very governments that should be protecting human rights are thus their main violators, aiding and abetting those who wield economic power, in spite of their statements in support of such rights.

All this results in a state of war, as it were, between government and people, reflecting the whole problem of social and economic groups, in a chronic state of war themselves.

Repression, nevertheless, does not eliminate the reasons for that state of war; it merely suppresses its outward signs for a certain length of time—for how long, we cannot tell—while, paradoxically, it exacerbates the state's underlying causes.

Everything is liable to explode at any moment. We are justified in referring to the 'escalation of violence', when we can see that one kind of violence leads to another.

Forms of violence

Violent protest by the people finds its expression in attacks, guerrilla warfare, the kidnapping of persons and the hijacking of vehicles or aircraft. Repressive violence, legitimized by the declaration of a state of emergency, takes the form of unjustified imprisonment without trial, subsequent questioning and the manipulation of justice.

Violence among countries at the world level is closely bound up with the desire by certain countries to dominate others, or to maintain such domination. Arms become necessary for attack, control and defence.

Injustice at all levels provides the main background for all forms of violence and for the enormous volume of funds expended on the armed forces and on military equipment. Warmongering can, then, never be countered unless at the same time injustices are remedied.

Obstacles to peace

The fundamental obstacle to enduring peace is, then, according to the above observations, the state of poverty—destitution even—of a large part of the world's population, and the political exclusion that is bound up with it. This situation should not be regarded simply as a set of circumstances affecting a large number of individuals, but as a poverty-generating system within countries and beyond national borders. Advantage should be taken of the most recent social studies in order to formulate a strategy which, instead of seeking economic benefits, is designed to serve, first and foremost, the underprivileged population groups throughout the world.

It is within the context of that system that the economic relations between the rich and poor countries are situated. They are based on the exploitation of raw materials to supply sophisticated industries the products of which are exported to the poorer countries at very high prices, resulting in the only too familiar consequences for the balance of trade.

International military aid agreements, in fact, strengthen technological dependence through the war machine. Such aid often reflects complicity, in military terms, between the government that provides it and the government that receives it, with a view to stifling expression of the people's needs. It is a matter of government versus people.

The arms-manufacturing countries preach peace while they furnish the implements of war in which they are basically interested for economic reasons. They have already built up an economic system which has to be nourished by means of warfare in other countries, the purchasing countries. Directly or indirectly, customers must be pushed into war so that a large volume of sales will result. All this forms part of a system of hypocrisy and lies which seems to be acceptable in international relations. Technological rivalry among the major world powers has become a means of dissuading possible attack and a permanent incentive to the arms industry, providing constant justification for the incredible sums that, either directly or indirectly, are allocated to the military budget.

In Latin America, low salaries, the lack of basic services such as health and housing, together with spiralling prices, constitute the most important obstacle to peace. The sluggishness or inefficiency of governments and the lack of resources needed to solve social problems foster despair and strengthen the conviction among many that only through violence can justice and peace be achieved.

Attention should be drawn, furthermore, to the dissemination—one could say in an organized and deliberate form—of violence and war, reflected in the exportation of the ideology of violence through literature and films and in a growing systematization in the organization of the war machine, in which training for combat is a very important factor. For many people, military service has become the only way in which they serve their country on an organized basis over a relatively long period of time. Military service is based on hypotheses or, rather, on dogmas which should be thoroughly reviewed. It is inconceivable that the force and energy of young people should continue to be squandered in the name of their country, and the blood of their forefathers, in order to strengthen the war machine, when their generosity and capabilities could be devoted, with their countries' resources, to solving urgent and fundamental problems. Modern military service reflects the ideology of a practice born of historical circumstances that have long been superseded. Religion has contributed, whether consciously or otherwise, to the justification of militarism. In Latin America, the armed forces have often appointed the Virgin Mary as their 'General'. There are archbishops and cardinals who hold military rank. Even if these are no more than honorary titles, the significance of such a situation cannot be disregarded. The fact that the Church carries out its pastoral duties in respect of the armed forces by itself becoming, as it were, a part of the army through its chaplains and, thus, subject to military discipline creates serious ambiguities. It may well be asked if undertaking the spiritual care of soldiers requires that one must also become a soldier.

The school is child and mother of the warfare ideology. It reproduces the ideology that nourishes it. The educational structure is designed to serve the purposes of competition and struggle among individuals. Its organization has been inspired by military discipline for a long time. A veritable warfare ritual has been developed in connection with national festivities and patriotic symbols. Study of the history of one's own country or of neighbouring states is focused on the wars and the victories which constitute something to be gloried in and an example to be followed. Every act of domination *vis-à-vis* another country is justified; injustices become, almost by miracle, heroic gestures to be celebrated. History is relative to the country that makes it. As long as history is used as a means of justifying any event that will redound to the credit of the country concerned, it will be impossible to recognize mistakes and see the future through different eyes. Citizens cannot continue to be unwavering defenders of the past of their countries. There are other ways of expressing a love for one's own country. This is closely bound up with the meaning which one unconsciously attaches to what is termed 'patriotism'. National anthems, marches and flags, etc., all serve this form of patriotism. But would it not be worthwhile examining in depth the implications of traditional patriotism in order to create another kind, more in keeping with a universe in which we would be citizens, not merely of one country, but of the whole world, and in which co-operation could replace rivalry and domination?

In general, it can be said that the agents of education, whether family, school or non-formal education is involved, lack awareness of the problem; they often act, unwittingly, in an inconsistent way. They need both active support and the means for influencing children and students against war and for peace in the context of education. All this, together with a climate of increasing aggressiveness, particularly in larger cities, constitutes an obstacle to peace.

The place of education

It is necessary to take account of the educational influence, not only of the school, but also of the family and the mass media, political parties, unions and civic organizations and religious groups.

It is not only a matter of changing programme content and historical assessments, but of creating or developing new attitudes in keeping with the type of society we want. It will be necessary, as stated in the Recommendation concerning Education for International Understanding, Co-operation and Peace and Education relating to Human Rights and Fundamental Freedoms, adopted by the General Conference of Unesco in 1974 to 'further the appropriate intellectual and emotional development of the individual' by 'combining learning, training, information and action', to 'develop a sense of social responsibility and of solidarity with less privileged groups . . .' and 'to acquire a critical understanding of problems at the national and international level' (paragraph 5). In order to achieve this, it will be necessary for education to include 'critical analysis of the historical and contemporary factors of an economic and political nature underlying the contradictions and tensions between countries, together with study of ways of overcoming these contradictions' (paragraph 14). In fact, it is not just a question of knowledge, but of the ability to contribute to eradicating 'conditions which perpetuate and aggravate major problems affecting human survival and well-being . . .' (paragraph 18).

In other words, the aim must be to produce citizens of a new type: not passive beings whose policy is *laisser-faire*, or who confine themselves to discussion, but individuals who will exercise their responsibility in regard to the functioning of society, in thought and deed; who are not simply content to exist but who think of others; who do not merely accept one existing state of affairs, but who become increasingly capable of transforming their society, starting with their immediate surroundings.

Within the logical context of what has just been stated concerning the major obstacle to peace, the role of education should be to help transform the present system that generates war into one which will make justice and, hence, peace, possible. What has to be done, to quote the Recommendation concerning Education for International Understanding, is to change society 'so that human rights are applied in practice' (paragraph 33).

Social education, in the sense of education designed to serve man in his role as a member of society, thus becomes the main aspect of any type of instruction. It will, then, be necessary to consider alternative societies and to have the possibility of choice. Man has organized society. It is man's task, then, to change it. It should be possible to do so lucidly. Technical education, designed to serve economic interests and based on a man-nature relationship, has taken pride of place. Technical education is necessary for the purpose of transforming nature, but, at the same time, it is part of social education; it is, consciously or not, at the service of a society. The neutrality of science is a myth that should be exposed. All science is related to the society it serves.

Social education cannot disregard the global dimension of current problems. Nowadays, a national approach is quite inadequate. The international character of our lives is a fact. This new education, directed towards justice and peace and not war, demands changes in attitudes, in values, approaches, the emotional milieu, contents and methods in conjunction with a policy for effective action for change, which is neither repressive nor military, but pacific. The task is enormous, and it has to be tackled on a long-term basis. The historical moment for transforming the future is already here.

What we can do

Betty Reardon makes some important suggestions in the next chapter of this book. There are, however, a number of particular points to which attention should be drawn.

If we are to tackle the root-cause of these obstacles, we shall have to bring about a fundamental change in the military policies of governments, so that the provisions of agreements and declarations are translated into practice. We have already pointed out the lack of coherence which is so evident today. It is important to identify and study ways and means of putting into effect, according to specific situations, the recommendations and resolutions which concern disarmament more directly, and to make such means widely known.

In particular, the Unesco Recommendation concerning Education for International Understanding (1974) is a document of which all teachers at the different levels should be aware and the application of which they should ensure. So far, however, very little has been done. It can be said that, here again, governments very often lack coherence, although a number of measures, already applied in certain countries, could provide a basis for realistic solutions.

It is important that people are informed about their government's actions and decisions concerning military matters, as well as about expenditure for military purposes at national, continental or worldwide level, and the consequences that may be expected if present trends continue. At the same time, pressure in favour of disarmament must be brought to bear through governmental or non-governmental channels. It has to be borne in mind that disarmament is not an isolated issue and that it should be viewed against the background of the whole current economic and political structure. The question is not, therefore, one of merely reducing military expenditure and allocating the savings achieved to development in other areas of the world but, at the same time, of taking a decisive step forward in order to replace the present world scheme of things by a new international order.

Measures should be taken to ensure that social education is given its rightful place. Accordingly the man in the street (and not merely an élite) should be provided with the basis for forming critical judgements, so as to be able to participate fully in the life of the community. It is particularly necessary to review social studies, especially history and civics, so that they may become the means of education for peace and not for war. In order to ensure coherence in regard to values as experienced and the actual subjects taught in the curriculum, all the elements within the school that contribute to the diffusion of a warfare ideology must be identified with a view to the 'demilitarization' of education.

Experience concerning non-violent action for change (known in Brazil as *firmeza permanente*) should be turned to account and applied more widely as a significant contribution to the peaceful transformation of society and as an example of the new possibilities offered to us. This experience has been developed mainly outside the school. Much can be done for the cause of peace by the considerable number of people who, because they have never attended school, have not become victims of the present school system.

Obstacles to disarmament education*

Chairperson, Consortium
on Peace Research,
Education and Development
(United States of America);
Executive Secretary, World
Council for Curriculum and
Instruction

Betty Reardon

Introduction

In this essay, 'disarmament' refers to those processes which are intended to lead from the present system of armed nation-states, each charged with its own defence (the war system), to an international system in which nations need not be armed nor be responsible for their own defence, having assigned the security function of the international community to some form of global authority charged with peacefully resolving disputes and defending the rights of the member states (a peace system). 'General and complete disarmament' refers to the goal of reducing arms among nations to only those necessary to maintain domestic order, a goal virtually synonymous with 'a peace system' in which institutions appropriate for conflict resolution, peacekeeping, and the defence of the rights of nations and persons have been established collaterally with the reduction of arms. 'Arms control' refers only to efforts to prevent an increase in the volume of arms production and/or their development. 'Arms limitation' refers to agreements among armed states to maintain and not go beyond a specific level of weaponry, in terms of volume and destructive capacity. It should be noted that arms limitation and arms control assume no basic change in relationships among and between states, nor in the international security system, whereas disarmament, particularly general and complete disarmament, assumes a major change in the international political system. It is towards achieving such a change that education for disarmament should be directed.

'Disarmament education' is used here to mean education for the promotion of general and complete disarmament. The objectives of such education should be: (a) to enable people

* This essay is revised
and abstracted from
a longer study conducted
under a contract with
the Peace Education
Commission of the
International Peace
Research Association.

to understand the four concepts defined in the previous
paragraph; (b) to acquire some knowledge of what will be
required to achieve successful results under the rubric of
each concept; (c) to appreciate actual differences between
the 'limitation/control' and 'disarmament' concepts, especially as regards the changes in relationships among states
and the new global institutions which will be required to
replace the former concepts with the latter. Education for
disarmament should also prepare citizens (a) to understand
the purposes and operations of these global institutions,
(b) to participate in their planning, and (c) to support governmental endeavours to bring them into being. Disarmament
education should be presented from a global perspective;
it should comprise such subjects as arms and security,
conflict resolution, the functions of conflict, and the means
of protecting human and national rights through diverse
institutions at all levels, particularly the global level. A focus
upon the economics of the world community, especially as
regards the conversion of much of the world's present productive capacity from military to peaceful uses, is also crucial
to such education, as are other measures towards arms
control and disarmament such as denuclearized zones, test
bans, and no-first-use agreements. In short, disarmament
education must deal not only with armaments, but also with
conflict, human rights, economic development, and policies
for structural change.

In general

Obstacles to education for disarmament, some of which
arise because of the meaning and nature of disarmament
education itself, fall into three general categories: political,
perceptual and pedagogical.

Political obstacles

First and foremost among the political obstacles is the international system itself, which recognizes the right of all
nations to arm in their own defence and to use armed force
in the pursuit of their own interests. Although conventional
and customary international law has declared the use of
armed force for aggressive or repressive purposes to be

unacceptable, this has not significantly influenced the behaviour of most nations. Indeed, conflicts of economic interest, of ideology, and of the quest for dominance and power have intensified the constant threat and frequent use of armed force. The risks increase day by day—including, clearly, the nuclear risks—and the reality of minor violence certainly is not decreasing. The true tragedy, however, is that mostly these political realities tend to be viewed as an inevitable part of the human experience and as a natural phenomena beyond the powers of ordinary mortals to deal with constructively. The political intricacies of extricating ourselves from this state of affairs are seen as so complicated and complex as to defy the human imagination.

From this perspective, the political problems are as much problems of attitudes, of acceptance, and of lack of creative imagination as they are problems of power politics and political structures; and as such they are essentially educational problems which should be the concern of educators. In any event, they most certainly indicate the special political responsibility which educators have for the achievement of a disarmed world—even though, as is well known, this responsibility entails some political risk, there being few if any societies in which the sovereign right of states to arm may be publicly questioned with impunity.

Perceptual obstacles

Although the political obstacles may seem the most severe, and the pedagogical the most challenging, it actually is the perceptual obstacles that are the key to both educational and political action. What educators and political leaders need to understand is how people perceive the need for, and functions of, systems of security which depend on weaponry, particularly the present highly destructive and technologically sophisticated weaponry. In response to a recent survey of peace educators concerning their perceptions of the major obstacles to disarmament, the three frequently mentioned as most severe were fear, militarism and ignorance.*

Fear

* This poll was taken by the author during the period November 1976–March 1977.

Fear of disarmament was high on most lists, the fear coming from three related subsidiary fears: first and foremost, fear of the economic consequences of disarmament, of unemployment, and of economic dislocation in particular; second, fear of 'the enemy' and of being defenceless in a world in which one party or several, but not all, might be disarmed;* and finally, but less clearly articulated, fear of the unknown. People in general seem to have difficulty in envisaging a disarmed world, and therefore fear what they cannot describe to themselves as a reasonable set of living circumstances. Circumstances under which persons and nations would not need arms to defend themselves seem incomprehensible to most people.

Militarism

Another important perceptual obstacle frequently mentioned was the militarism of most societies, in which good citizenship consists of obeying authority and being punished for 'disloyalty'. The belief that social order depends upon obeying military authority is almost as widespread as is an equation of dignity with strength or strength with violence. These ideas, it was noted particularly by the teacher educators, are reinforced by present methods of recording and teaching history. People educated by the public authorities usually equate support of the military with patriotism and virtue, and dissent therefrom with lack of patriotism, treason, ignorance or naivety—a notion relating to the general distrust of others and the disbelief that all parties in the international war system ever would disarm. The educators also pointed to a close relationship between not only the concepts of military strength and 'national security' but also the concepts of personal identity and 'national security'. The preservation of the nation preserves one's identity, and the military provides a symbol of that identity together with a symbol of selfless (even ultimate) sacrifice in the public—hence the personal—interest. Some of the educators also noted a widely held, even if erroneous, belief that human beings are rational and that they are or would be rational and restrained in their use of weapons.

Ignorance

Most of the educators also identified ignorance as a major obstacle. In general, they reported, people lack sufficient and

* Closely related to this particular fear was the lack of trust of other nations, particularly (but not exclusively) nations in competition or conflict with one another. Some even noted hatred as part of this fear, especially of political, racial, religious or national groups.

appropriate information to perceive possibilities for disarmament. They attributed it to an emphasis on war as opposed to peaceful alternatives in history courses and, most especially, to negligible teacher training on questions of war, peace, and disarmament, and minimal coverage by the media of major issues related to arms control and disarmament. In general, the peace educators lamented the lack of understanding regarding arms control and disarmament and the widespread belief that the problems of arms control and disarmament are, in the main, too technical for the average citizen to comprehend. This widespread ignorance, some asserted, made it possible for 'the military-industrial complex' to exploit its knowledge and sophistication about weaponry, to maintain its specific interest in continued weapons production, and to exercise an inordinate influence over both public policy and public information. Some of the educators believe that there is a lack of public interest in these issues which may account for ignorance, but most felt that this lack of interest is due primarily to the failure of the media and political leadership to present disarmament issues in a manner comprehensible to most citizens.

Pedagogical obstacles

Pedagogical obstacles to education for disarmament, which stem from the political and perceptual, fall into the affective as well as the cognitive domain. Indeed, the affective may be even more crucial than the cognitive in the whole area of teaching and learning for a disarmed world.

The affective domain

The perceptual problems have high emotional content, which is often avoided because of the discomfort such perceptions usually cause. We know, for example, that it is not natural for human beings to seek to confront their own fears. Yet, unless this is done sensitively and constructively, there is little hope of moving on to content and the analysis that is required to understand the technical and political problems of disarmament. Educational programming in this area must recognize that such fears exist. It must work constructively to enable people to deal with these problems and, if not to overcome them, at least to explore the true reasons for the fears. For example, education should help people explore whether their fear of loss of security as a consequence of disarmament really stems from ignorance of alternative security systems or from the normal and all pervasive fear of change, or from reservations about the strange, the new, the alien and the inexperienced. For, if the latter is true, then affective learning has even greater importance than we assume. A word of optimism, however, is warranted by the fact that part of the education of every small child involves helping him (through life experience and by developing confidence in others such as parents and teachers) to overcome fears of abandonment, failing, and various other 'natural disasters' which we all learn are more or less subject to our own behaviour. By the time they walk and talk, people come to understand that they themselves have some responsibility for their own security and that others care for their welfare. Thus, we must realize that lack of self-confidence and distrust of others is a major obstacle to education for a warless world. Learning designed to create confidence and trust must, therefore, be an integral part of disarmament education.

Closely related to fear is the emotion of hatred of an enemy who threatens our security, our life and our identity, and who does so because of values and behaviour which appear less than 'civilized' because they are different from our own. Disarmament education should try to overcome such hatred by seeking to eradicate irrational prejudices, be they cultural or ideological, from all educational materials and practices. The misguided belief that inculcating such prejudices creates loyalties to one's own culture or nation poses a major problem for the kind of education we hope to develop, a problem which can never be overcome unless systematic efforts to root out the prejudices are undertaken by all educational systems. It is absolutely essential, as is noted in the 1974 Unesco recommendation, that Member States formulate policies for the improvement of international understanding and for overcoming the misconceptions and cultural ignorance which often permit the toleration of injustice as well as the nurturing of fear of the enemy, which in turn nurtures the arms race.[1] If, according to the guiding principles of the recommendation, education is presented from a global perspective, students will come to understand that the human species has a common planetary destiny, that we have more in common than differences, and that respect for other people, their cultures, civilizations, values, and ways of life is absolutely essential to the preservation of the species, its cultural diversity and its physical survival.[2] In recognizing that interdependence militates against the continued acceptance of nationalistic forms of education (which reinforce hatred, prejudice and consequently continued maintenance of the arms system), the Unesco recommendation has pinpointed a major source of the affective obstacles to disarmament education.

Thus, the most essential correction to the emotional obstacles of fear, hatred, and prejudice is a fundamental respect for human life and dignity in keeping with the principles of the Universal Declaration of Human Rights. The absolute core of all social education, all learning environments, must be a fundamental commitment to the dignity of the human person and an insistence that full human rights for everyone be respected by all persons and governments. Further, it cannot be overemphasized that the most fundamental human right, the right to life, cannot be pursued without peace. War, the indiscriminate consumer of human lives, is in direct contradiction to the principles of human rights. Disarmament education should illuminate this contradiction and 'stress the inadmissability of the recourse to war'.[3]

The cognitive domain

In the cognitive area of factual knowledge, the most severe obstacles are lack of general information and disregard of particular areas of information.

Perhaps most obvious is the general lack of attention to a systematic interpretation of either the world political system or the world ecological system. By and large, there still is a compartmentalized, linear and chronological organization of most social education. Students—indeed most citizens—fail to understand the systemic nature of the human social order, particularly at the global political level. As a consequence, they do not comprehend that each nation is but one component of a total system, that its actions and reactions are affected by the other components, and that unilateral—even bilateral or multilateral—actions are of necessity severely limited and almost always inadequate to the achievement of any single objective throughout the world political system.

Conspicuous also is the limited attention given in formal educational curricula to international institutions and organizations. There is little information presented about the United Nations, and virtually nothing is taught about United Nations efforts in the area of disarmament. Indeed, the substantive study of disarmament as such has almost no place in the required, even optional, curricula of schools and universities throughout the world. It appears that the only people who are well informed or who have a minimal comprehension of the concepts of disarmament and arms control are those who develop a special interest on their own. Since disarmament, as previously mentioned, has been presented as a highly technical and politically sensitive subject, it is scarcely found in most educational settings. Most of the full courses currently offered are in a few research centres and graduate schools.

One cognitive obstacle, made more lamentable because there are no technological obfuscations to prevent consideration in curricula and private discussions, is the paucity of information on alternatives to the arms system, both actual and historical as well as proposed and potential. Just as the concept of disarmament is hardly known to the general public, so are the concepts of non-violent processes for social change and conflict resolution unknown. The ever-growing field of scholarship on non-violent as well as less radical alternatives to the arms system is, however, rich in substance and should be included in the knowledge base of contemporary social education. Although it may appear that these alternatives represent too great a threat to the established orders, it should be noted that all such proposals are not built upon the reallocation or re-ordering of power. Some simply advocate different modes of exercising power and of enforcing existing authority. There is a wide range of alternatives to armed force stemming from various philosophical, political, and ideological bases which can and should be considered to limit the arms race and to avoid the potential destruction it threatens.

In particular

Obstacles at the elementary level

When we look at specific obstacles to disarmament education within particular educational settings, it seems almost ironic that so large and technical a problem as disarmament is perhaps most seriously impeded by the educational experience of the very young, sometimes even before their entry into elementary school. In part, the problem is affected by their lack of opportunity to have cross-cultural experience or to understand life-styles different from those of their immediate family and culture. Even more serious, however, is the socialization process which enforces a belief that the child's own culture is preferable if not superior to most or all other cultures.

With few exceptions, socialization seems also to foster the notion that every culture group is competitive with other groups and must struggle against them to achieve fulfilment and survival. This enforcement of the concept of competition as the route to fulfilment and recognition can be seen unfortunately even within families, with children frequently competing for the attention of their parents or for other benefits coming from special recognition. Of course, blame for such competition is not to be laid only at the feet of the parents. It must be directed also to societies in general, most of which place a higher value on some persons than on others, thereby encouraging competition and ultimately nurturing beliefs in force, aggression, and other competitive modes for self-assertion and identity. Such forms of behaviour provide a psychological base for the acceptance of the competitive nation-state system and of the psychological, social and political environment which makes the arms race possible. To be sure, there is more often than not a conscious effort on the part of parents and teachers to discourage violent behaviour among children. But sufficient attention has not been given to the discouragement of other forms of competitiveness. The high value placed on 'winning' and on being 'the best' or 'the strongest' often contributes to the acceptance of force. The larger social order constantly reinforces the lesson that force and violence are effective and acceptable means for achieving goals, especially when imposed against those who are 'different'.

It must be noted, however, that these circumstances are not equally pronounced in all societies. Noteworthy, for example, are the Tasaday, a Stone-Age people living in the Philippines according to a co-operative ethic, a loving people who have no word for 'war' in their language. Clearly, if such societies represent the human species in its 'natural state', there is reason for hope. But it is not only the 'primitive' societies that provide us with the hope needed to sustain risk. Among some cultures which put a higher premium on tradition and human relations than on 'modernization' and 'efficiency', group co-operation is a strong socializing force, and individualism and competition as practiced in 'modern industrial' societies are viewed as anti-normative. Mexican-American children, for example, have had difficulty in the strongly competitive, individualistic American school system. These children are taught by their traditions to co-operate with those in their ethnic group and to put a higher value on family and community than on self. Indeed, the dominant system which has often categorized them as 'slow learners' could learn much from these children about the techniques of peace and community building. Other examples could be cited, but these two are sufficient to make the point.

Also worth noting is the phenomenon that the highest degree of competitive socialization exists in those societies which are the most active in the arms race. These societies also exhibit a virtual inverse ratio between individualism and self-confidence.[5] That is, the more individualistic a society in its drive to pursue its own aims irrespective of others within the system, the less confident it is of being able to pursue those interests without having recourse to force and extensive weapons systems. This circumstance should be closely examined in formulating educational programmes intended to socialize young people to a disarmed political system. Unless the close relationship of early socialization to the character of the social order is understood, it is highly unlikely that we can develop education appropriate to the achievement of a disarmed world. This is not to say that all societies which have instituted co-operative ethics within their formal education system are not involved in the arms race. Some schools in some countries put high emphasis on teamwork among children in work and play activities while simultaneously carrying out military exercises, with children learning the military ethic of co-operation to compete against those who hold different ideologies or who belong to different political systems. Their need, however, is to extend the co-operative ethic to the global level, to equate friendship and interdependence with global co-operation, and, perhaps above all, to develop comprehension of the negative consequences of competition, particularly when the competition results in armed combat or preparation for armed combat.

Another significant obstacle is that, in early years, the educational system encourages the development of national identity and national loyalty. Though a positive form of human development in and of itself, within the context of a highly competitive nation-state system, this larger (national) identity and loyalty commonly assumes a competitive character relative to others in the world. People identify most strongly when they are in a competitive relationship and when differences rather than similarities are emphasized. In other words, although transcendence over ethnic differences is encouraged within nations, the process of transcendence has not been sufficiently extended to cultures and political ideologies beyond the given nation-state. In times of actual or cold war, this national identification to the discredit of other nations or systems is most pronounced, and it is extremely difficult to overcome when hostilities and competition have ceased in the formal sense.[6]

In this same respect, a very important influence on the socialization of young children (particularly in urban industrialized areas, although to be expected in other parts of the world with the rapid introduction of transistor radios) is the media. All pre-literate persons, but especially children with limited social experience, are profoundly affected by visual and oral messages and images projected through the media. Much of this effect is contrary to international understanding, peace and human rights. In the United States, for example, young children are given prejudicial views of the people of Japan and Germany through the telecasting of films produced during the Second World War to rally the American people against their 'enemies'. In addition, the media apparently affect children's attitudes toward violence. Although there is still some controversy over the effects of the media on the acceptance and development of violent behaviour, there is a growing belief among educators, largely as a result of observing immediate behavior, that the media encourage admiration for and emulation of violent behaviour. Many also believe that the media have a negative impact on the ability of children to comprehend the real human consequences of violence, the facts of death and destruction and the true nature of war. Because many countries, especially those in the process of capitalist industrialization, are importing some of these same television programmes and films (and using many of the slick media techniques), this condition can be considered to be incipiently, if not actually, global.

Obstacles at the secondary level

It is at the secondary level of schooling that more formal citizenship or social education is usually provided. In the years from approximately 13 to 18, young people learn about the operations of their government, the philosophy and ideology which inform their governmental processes, and the positions their governments take in the world political system. It also is at this stage that they move from the general patriotic legends of their nations to a somewhat more detailed and sophisticated acquaintance with their national histories. Thus, the nationalistic aspects of education, begun at the elementary level, are reinforced in the education of adolescents.

It is important to note in this connection that it is the adolescents (and not always the late ones) who usually make up the major portion of the fighting forces of nations, and that young people go from secondary schools into the armed forces. Thus, one of the functions of secondary education, particularly of boys, has been to educate for the support of and service in the military. Some analysts believe that the extreme emphasis on competitive sports, particularly body-contact sports among adolescent boys, has been an important contributing factor to the acceptance of military service, i.e. a sort of pre-military training. Outbreaks of violence at football matches support this opinion, as does the infamous 'Soccer War'. In recent years, professional athletes in the United States who have reflected upon the social consequences of some of these sports have come to advocate new forms of physical education which eliminate competition, particularly games which are competitive with outside groups from other schools or nations where the 'otherness' is a reason for competing with and winning over the opponent. For years, of course, there have been observations among such former imperial powers as the United Kingdom that the extreme discipline of boys' secondary schools, together with their training on the sports field, provided the military efficiency which made possible the building of empire.

In addition, some schools at the secondary level, particularly in the United States, encourage actual formal conscription into a pre-military service (such as the Junior Reserve Officer Training Corps) which gives young people recreational and financial rewards for devoting time to the study of military techniques. There is, in fact, a growing movement among those concerned with peace to prevent the conscription of young Americans into ROTC, at least at the secondary-school level if not at the university level. The most systematic efforts are being made in Japan and in the United States by the Committee on Militarism in Education.[7]

Perhaps the most important obstacle is the curriculum itself. The extreme nationalism of the study of history has been researched and found to have given a distorted view of the behaviour of nations, particularly as regards nations which have been at war with each other.[8] Prejudice and ethnocentrism seem more strongly reflected in history and social education texts than in others. Further, history at the secondary level emphasizes wars, and only rarely the story of avoided wars or of events in which there has been a peaceful resolution of conflict. Such history reinforces the attitude that war is inevitable, to be expected as a continuous part of the human experience, and that there are few if any alternatives to war for playing out international competition in the pursuit of national goals. Furthermore, although there is a growing effort among global and peace educators to introduce such subjects as conflict resolution, peacemaking, and alternatives to violence, these subjects are as yet very limited, often looked upon with great suspicion as unpatriotic or the devious plots of a competing or enemy state. In secondary schools throughout the world, there is lamentably little information provided about other cultures, about the world in general, and about human rights, peace, and disarmament in particular.

In countries once under colonial control, the information taught during the colonial period about the indigenous cultures was very limited, even distorted. Young people usually were taught more about the history of the colonial power than of their own people. Such nations must now build completely new curricula to teach their own national experience and this need has sometimes prevented the newly independent countries from giving adequate attention to other parts of the world. An ethnocentrism, similar to that of the colonial period, has yet to be overcome. While there are some efforts at multi-cultural education from a global perspective, for the most part these efforts are still far too limited. A truly diverse cultural education from a global perspective is required as a basis for international understanding and as a climate in which disarmament education will or can be pursued.

In sum, secondary education is too parochial and ethnocentric for the purpose of achieving a disarmed world. Further, it contains several obstacles to that objective in the competitive, militaristic and nationalistic forms of social education.

Obstacles at the university level

The major barriers to disarmament education at the university level are lack of resources for innovative education and research, and the limitations of academic tradition.

Although there is a rapidly growing peace education and research movement in the universities of some countries, resources available for the support of these efforts are scant in the extreme. Only a very small fraction of the per cent of resources available to the scholars and researchers working on behalf of the weapons industry and the military establishment is used for peace research and education. War research and development outstrips many thousands of times the work in peace research and development. For many years, the universities have been used as the sites of research (particularly engineering, physics and nuclear research) that has contributed and continues to contribute to the development and refinement of weaponry, both conventional and nuclear as well as chemical and biological.[9] For the most part, this activity has been funded by governments, with some funds coming from private foundations as well. Except for a few countries such as the Federal Republic of Germany, the Netherlands and Sweden, governments have not offered resources for peace research and peace education. The differential in universities between the amount of resources going into war research and development and peace research and development is, in microcosm, a reflection of the percentages of resources which go to military as opposed to social needs in general.

Another serious barrier is the entrenchment of traditional disciplines, which have paid little or no attention to peace and disarmament questions. Many scholars still view these issues as narrow segments of one discipline, and some assert that any inquiry into such subjects is advocacy rather than scholarship (in contrast to the research into weapons systems and the like, which is seldom viewed as advocacy of the arms race). Thus, the practitioners of peace research and development and disarmament studies who require insights from and research by all of the disciplines, both scientific and behavioural, find it difficult to pursue their inquiries and teaching within the traditional pattern and curricula of the universities. Notwithstanding these obstacles, a few universities have established peace-studies courses and departments which are innovative and interdisciplinary, often forming constructive linkages among and between other departments, even those with a strong traditional bias. But it should also be observed that even within peace-studies departments there is as yet insufficient emphasis on arms and security issues.[10] Until all peace-studies programmes admit the necessity of including the subject of disarmament in their programmes, even this field will not be adequate to the needs of education for a disarmed world.

A further obstacle is the role of the university in professional and vocational training. Since the war establishment far outstrips the peace establishment, opportunities for employment in the peace field and in the disarmament area are too limited to make, as is commonly required, the vocational argument for spending resources on this kind of education. Efforts are being made to identify a whole range of professions in the peacemaking area—from peacekeeping (a form of soldiering) to mediation, arbitration, and other kinds of skills relevant to conflict management, in general, and the pursuit of social justice and human rights, in particular.[11] But these professions are not yet widely known or practised, and information is not yet sufficiently available to have real influence on university course offerings. Vigorous though these efforts have been, they are still dwarfed by education for the arms system. Military scholarships and training are frequently provided at universities, in addition to opportunities in most countries to attend national military academies. In some countries, scholarships are given to young men who commit themselves to a certain period of military service following the granting of their degrees. This influences the type of education they receive, so that at the university level there are far many more offerings in military science than in peace science or in inquiries into alternatives to arms for achieving disarmament.

Obstacles in the non-formal educational settings

The purpose of most non-formal educational programmes is to meet immediate needs, particularly of adults and usually within a limited geographical setting. Very often the needs are community development needs. There is, therefore, a legitimate preoccupation in such programmes with understanding the immediate environment and its potential for development, and with nurturing very specific skills for transforming that environment into one appropriate for a human community. Because of the pressure of immediate needs and because of limitations on resources, however, only a few of these non-formal educational programmes for community building have addressed themselves to some of the wider issues of global problems and to the relationship of the immediate social system or setting to the other components of the global social system. Among the most notable efforts making these linkages are those being conducted by the organization CODECAL in Colombia[12] and the programmes projected by the Southeast Asian Global Community Education Project, the first phase of which is being developed in the Philippines.[13] Each of these programmes reflects a systematic attempt to relate issues and problems of the local setting to the global system, and to provide education that can enable participants to take some part in formulating opinions and positions relative to world politics.[14]

Although it is defensible to expend resources primarily on local concerns and needs in non-formal educational programmes, it is nonetheless questionable to exclude such global issues as the arms race from them. Concentration on local objectives as exclusive goals serves to disenfranchise persons in these local areas who do not participate in the large global community and who have little or no say in the formation of global political policies, such as those relating to disarmament. Further, it is people in these settings who are most in need of the resources which many assert could be effectively converted to social and economic development, were arms expenditures to be reduced. These same people are the victims of the gross disparities in the distribution of the world's wealth which is a conflict root and potential cause of armed struggle.

Non-formal education for adolescents and children tends to be offered in two instances: when formal schooling is not available, or when formal schooling is inappropriate or irrelevant to the behaviour or learning style of the students or the values of their parents. The latter case, which produces alternative and independent education, can sometimes be an advantage. More often it is an obstacle to education for disarmament, because what is appropriate or relevant, even from the point of view of some students, has often been defined in terms which are much too personal to confront major societal issues adequately. Further, all people (and youngsters are no exception) tend to be interested in what they already know something about. Since information about disarmament, its consequences, and the problems of achieving it is so limited, youngsters are not likely to request such courses, nor express interest in them. This same obstacle, resulting from lack of general information, is to be found also in adult education programmes.

Obstacles in adult education

In the three most frequently practised forms of adult education, there is at present little place for education about disarmament. Adult education is for the most part either enriching or compensatory, or in the more formal settings oriented to advanced training in technical and professional skills. When programmes are compensatory, they reflect the offerings of the normal curriculum of the established school system, and do not focus any notable attention on arms policy. With minor exceptions, the same condition prevails in the vocational and professional training programmes. However, in vocational training through the armed forces there are opportunities to consider arms policy, albeit mainly for purposes antithetical to disarmament. Ordinarily, vocational training through the armed forces deals with methods for the use of arms, the repairing and maintenance of arms, or training for a military vocation. On the other hand, many technical skills which are not arms related, some of which could be used in the conversion of technology to peacetime uses and a fully disarmed world, are also taught. It is to the credit of some institutions and some military educators that observations and analyses about these alternatives are sometimes, even if infrequently, made. It should be noted, too, that for many, especially the poor, a military training is the only avenue to technical training.

A further obstacle in the vocational area applies to social learning in general, and not just to peace and disarmament in particular. Far too few vocational educational programmes deal with the social need for and consequences of the skill being learned, its relevance for the total life pattern of a person, or its role in a lifelong educational process. For the most part, the only exceptions are in programmes now being developed in alternative technology and low-resource-consumption industrial projects; projects often designed by persons having a larger social vision and who are motivated to achieve a society characterized by non-violence and social justice. One should also note, however, that there are some cases in which intermediate technology is seen as a step towards more 'sophisticated' technology and to more highly resource-consuming industries. Much of our present vocational education is aimed at training people to participate in the large-scale use of resources to maintain the arms system.

In those adult education programmes classified as 'enrichment' (or, in more direct terms, recreational), or even those classified as 'continuing education' (which may have some direct bearing on the way people live or make a living), there is little, if any, consideration of subjects dealing with global issues and far fewer with peace education. The notable exception to this norm is the 'folk high schools' in some Western European countries where courses on world problems or international relations are sometimes offered, and in a few continuing education programmes in the United States organized by the extension divisions of universities where similar programmes are offered.

Courses in the European 'folk high schools' (for example, the Vasterhaninge Folk High School in Sweden) are somewhat better than those in the United States. They tend to be more globally oriented than courses in the United States, which, in contrast, tend towards the traditionally narrow foreign-policy perspective. They are often concerned with the inequalities between the industrial and developing countries and, therefore, can be said to deal with the conditions necessary for peace. Most do not, however, confront directly such causes of war as the arms race, nor do they examine in detail the effects of military spending on the development process. While folk high schools have taken some steps forward, they still have a long way to go to fulfil the objectives of disarmament education. Furthermore, such courses are attended, for the most part, by persons who are already motivated by a desire for peace and concerned with human rights. Individuals who are not yet aware of the severity of the problem—those who are probably most in need of such education—rarely elect to take such courses. This implies a failure on the part of adult education programmes to offer adequate guidance to students in their programme choices, as well as a lack of imagination in creating courses intrinsically interesting to persons who might not already be motivated about reversing the arms race and strengthening prospects for peace. Both of these shortcomings are serious obstacles to adequate adult education about disarmament.

Lifelong learning is becoming more significant in educational programming and development in most countries of the world. It is crucial that such programmes be reviewed and adequate attention be given to the development of disarmament-related curricula and activity. Citizenship 're-education' of adults should be as widespread as citizenship education for adolescents.

Conclusions

Much of the responsibility for the serious lack of attention given to disarmament in our various educational processes thus may be seen to lie within our educational systems and programmes themselves. However, this responsibility must be said to lie ultimately in political leadership (or, more accurately, in the failure of such leadership)—in the major influences on public attitudes and in the main sources of public information, namely, governments and the media. The most serious obstacle to disarmament and to disarmament education is the all too pervasive failure of political leadership to communicate and elaborate upon the concept of general and complete disarmament and to present it as one option to be pursued within the realm of arms policy.

The full recognition and application of the guiding principles outlined in the 1974 Unesco recommendation,[15] which calls for 'a global perspective,.an understanding and respect for various cultures, awareness of global interdependence', and most important of all, 'decision-making based on free discussion and value judgements based on rational analysis of relevant facts and factors', would go a long way towards counteracting—even gradually altering—this state of affairs. These guiding principles cannot be fulfilled without attention to the issues and problems of disarmament, and the ethical and civic aspects of education called for in the recommendation. They constitute, in essence, a call to make education an instrument for transition from a war to a peace system. Only through a 'critical analysis of the historical and contemporary factors of an economic and political nature underlying the contradictions, which are the real impediments to understanding true international cooperation and the development of world peace', will disarmament and the peace system be attained. Only through such measures can education help to achieve 'the true interest of peoples and their incompatibility with the interests of monopolistic groups holding economic and political power which practice exploitation and foment war'.[16]

The moral, civic, cultural, scientific and technical elements of international education must focus clearly on the varied and crucial issues of disarmament. Questions concerning the ethical acceptability of weapons of mass destruction and the arms trade must be explored, together with such issues as the civic responsibility of citizens to question governmental policies that encourage arms development and arms trade. How secure is a nation in which acute human needs go unfulfilled because of enormous expenditure of resources on weapons production? Should the scientific and technical expertise of the human family be used to so great an extent on the perfection of weaponry and on techniques of warfare? Learners in all environments, citizens of all societies must be able to reflect constructively on these and similar questions, and to offer responses which can help bring about the structural changes needed to move the world from the war system to a peace system.

Notes

1. See Unesco, *Recommendation Concerning Education for International Understanding, Co-operation and Peace and Education Relating to Human Rights and Fundamental Freedoms*, 1974, No. IV–9.
2. Ibid., No. III–4b.
3. Ibid., No. III–6.
4. J. Nance, *The Gentle Tasaday*, New York, Harcourt Brace, 1975.
5. J. Galtung et al., *Educational Growth and Educational Disparity*, University of Oslo, 1973 (a study prepared for Unesco).
6. B. Reardon, 'Beyond Nationalism: Education and Survival', in D. Allen and J. Hecht (eds.), *Controversies in Education*, Philadelphia, W. B. Saunders Co., 1973.
7. For information write Committee on Militarism in Education, Box 271, Nyack, New York 10960, United States.
8. J. Nelson, *Nationalistic Education*, a paper presented at the National Council for the Social Studies Convention in Washington, D.C., in November 1976.
9. 'Between War and Peace: The Quest for Disarmament', *Bulletin of Peace Proposals*, Oslo, Vol. VI, No. 3, 1975.
10. Factual data on this subject as it relates to North America are contained in a report of a survey carried out for Unesco by the Consortium on Peace Research, Education and Development (COPRED). The method used in the COPRED survey was statistical sampling, whereas the study on which this essay is based was done in a more ethnographic manner. For the COPRED survey, write Executive Director, COPRED, Bethel College, North Newton, Kansas 67117, United States; or write Unesco, Division of Human Rights and Peace, 31, rue François-Bonvin, Paris 15e, France.
11. Systematizing this information, and publicizing the possibilities for professions in peace, is one of the objectives of the National Peace Academy Campaign in the United States, which seeks to establish a university-level, educational institution of equal alternative importance to the military, naval, and air force academies run at government expense. National Peace Academy Campaign, 122 Maryland Avenue N.E., Washington, D.C. 20002, United States, William Spencer, Executive Secretary.
    Some progress towards clarifying the concepts of what would be involved in such an educational institution's programme and purpose has been elaborated by the International Peace Academy with headquarters near the United Nations in New York. The IPA programme, which has been carried out in various parts of the world, has undertaken the training of conciliators, peacekeepers, and peacemakers who return from this training to public service in many nations. Future graduates of IPA may serve in a world authority set up for peacekeeping and disarmament purposes within the United Nations or under its auspices. For further information concerning the Campaign, write International Peace, Academy, 777 United Nations Plaza, New York City 10017, United States, General Indar Rikhye, Director.
12. For information, write to the Corporación Integral para el Desarrollo Cultural y Social, Apartado Aereo 20439, Bogotá, Colombia.
13. The Philippine model is co-ordinated by Dr Ludivina, Chief Research Officer, Department of Education and Culture, Quezon City, the Philippines.
14. In both programmes the core concepts are the universality of human dignity and the equality of persons, with emphasis on human rights. The programmes attempt to build a sense of cultural identity and unique character among the Colombian and Philippine participants, while simultaneously engendering a sense of their place in the world and the potential contribution they can make to a peaceful and just world order. The learning experiences incorporate concepts of peace as these operate in families and local communities as well as on the global level, and learners are encouraged to take up responsibility for the development of

peaceful relations in all spheres of human relations, at both 'micro' and 'macro' levels. Both programmes emphasize also the equal participation of women and men in the process of building peace, and therefore incorporate the exploration of 'feminine values' as related to peace and of the present limited degree of women's participation in policy-making related to issues of war and peace.

15. Unesco, op. cit. (note 4).
16. Ibid.

The role of public opinion in overcoming psychological obstacles

Secretary General of the
World Veterans Federation
and President of the Bureau
of the Special NGO
Committee on Disarmament
in Geneva

Serge Wourgaft*

War veterans have experienced armed conflict and witnessed the sacrifices made to ensure the survival and, ultimately, the independence and security of their respective countries. They are deeply concerned with the promotion of international understanding and the establishment and maintenance of peace in the world. They are also profoundly anxious to safeguard man's integrity, dignity and full development. They believe that achievement of these aims is closely linked with a curtailment of the arms race with a view to achieving steady progress towards disarmament.

Two important events in the work being carried out for this purpose in Europe, the main theatre of the first and second world wars, were the All European Meeting of War Veterans, Resistants and Victims of War for Peace, Security, Co-operation and Friendship held in Rome in November 1971 and the European Symposium of War Veterans on Disarmament held in Paris in November 1975. The Rome meeting, organized on the initiative of national war veterans' organizations, brought together, for the first time in history, those who had fought side by side or against each other. The participants represented different political backgrounds and came from every corner of Europe. They unanimously adopted an appeal setting out principles for encouraging co-operation in Europe. These are reflected in the Final Act of the Conference on Security and Co-operation in Europe, which stressed the importance of making progress towards disarmament.

The European Symposium of War Veterans on Disarmament met in Paris on the initiative of four international organizations, namely the European Confederation of War Veterans, the International Confederation of Former Prisoners-of-War, the International Federation of Resistance Movements and the World Veterans Federation. It brought

* The author wrote
this chapter on behalf of
the World Veterans
Federation.

together European war veterans from every walk of life. It examined the contribution that war veterans might make to slowing down the arms race and encouraging disarmament. The symposium expressed particular concern about the psychological obstacles that hampered achievement of these aims.

This chapter elaborates on the ideas discussed at the symposium in November 1975 in the light of subsequent developments in Europe. At the same time, it extends the scope of its reflections to other regions of the world. Lastly, it makes some proposals concerning the ways and means of surmounting the obstacles it identifies.

The large-scale slaughter and destruction in the First and Second World Wars, the emergence of weapons of mass destruction, particularly atomic weapons, the probability of even more deadly weapons systems being developed and the possibility that a mere accident or error may plunge the world into an irreparable chemical, bacteriological or nuclear disaster emphasize the need to replace armed conflict by dialogue and conciliation among nations. This new awareness is reflected in developments in international relations during the last few years. The progress made in international co-operation will, however, remain precarious and inadequate as long as the only guarantee of peace is based on the necessarily unstable and constantly shifting 'balance of terror'. The psychological climate for disarmament presupposes the acceptance of alternatives to the present situation, which equates the possession of military strength with the level of national security.

Is such a development impossible? Must we, as some people do, believe in the inevitable and resign ourselves to the immediate and long-term consequences of a balance of terror, even if we accept that this balance can indeed be maintained for any length of time? Is there not a danger that acceptance of this institutionalized violence will lead to acceptance of violations of the rights of individuals and nations? The public outcry against aggression, direct or indirect, armed conflict, executions, torture and the ill-treatment of prisoners is already becoming fainter. In many quarters there is a sense of resignation before the inevitable, while in others there are expressions of formal indignation, without any real conviction of the possibility of finding a solution or any real determination to find a new way forward.

A new way forward is possible. Experts in a great many

countries consider the halting of the arms race and a gradual, balanced and supervised disarmament as technically feasible. Peace would thus be more effectively ensured and the first human right, the right to life itself, more effectively guaranteed. The resources thereby released could make possible a general improvement of living conditions, the implementation of large-scale programmes of aid to the developing countries, better protection of the environment, the creation of amenities of every kind and widespread access to culture. New conditions would thus be created for the full development of the individual. The international organizations would be better equipped, in the words of the Constitution of Unesco,

to contribute to peace and security by promoting collaboration among the nations through education, science and culture in order to further universal respect for justice, for the rule of law and for the human rights and fundamental freedoms which are affirmed for the peoples of the world, without distinction of race, sex, language or religion, by the Charter of the United Nations.[1]

While many statesmen and an increasingly important section of world opinion have become aware of these problems, bold and persistent initiatives are seldom taken. Ingrained attitudes of mistrust and fear that a reduction in armaments would endanger individual and national security create psychological obstacles which are even more difficult to overcome than those of a purely technical kind. The attitude of serious reservations about disarmament is re-inforced by arguments about the difficulties involved. The psychological obstacles reflect attitudes that are not always governed by rational considerations. The boundaries between mental attitudes and perception of the difficulties cannot be clearly defined, since they reinforce each other. The same is true of the boundaries between education and information. Before attempting to dispel some of the commonly shared reservations about disarmament, it is useful to recognize the role of public opinion in creating a climate favourable to a disarmament psychology.

The role of public opinion

Public opinion has been variously defined as 'the collective opinion of a social group on political, moral, philosophical and religious questions', as 'the predominant attitude of mind in a society (in regard to general collective and current problems)' and also as 'all those who share these attitudes'. It follows from these definitions that public opinion may assume different forms in space and time according to the structure of the society in question, its evolution at a given moment and the issue under discussion. When speaking of influencing public opinion it is thus prudent to examine the problems in their specific context and avoid generalizations. In assessing the role of public opinion at the national level, for example, it should be studied in the context of the governmental decision-making process, which varies considerably from country to country and from one social structure and another.

As regards international public opinion, the moot point is whether to view it as the mere sum total of various national public opinions or to bestow upon it a specific character of its own. In this respect, a distinction has to be made between 'official' opinion representing the viewpoint of states given at international forums and the opinions of different social groups—for example, the international non-governmental organizations. It is hardly necessary to stress the increasingly important role that international public opinion plays, particularly as regards armed conflicts and their solution. Very few governments can sustain indefinite involvement in military conflicts without popular support, unless their political systems are wholly immune from the constraints of public opinion. The possibilities of reaching out for the minds of people widely separated by physical, political and cultural boundaries have been greatly strengthened by the impact of audio-visual mass media. The United Nations, its Specialized Agencies and other intergovernmental organizations provide wide facilities for the expression of public opinion, as understood by Member States.

In general terms, the alerting of public opinion to the problem of disarmament would seem to involve three essential aspects: the need for disarmament; its urgency, particularly in view of the serious dangers stemming from the arms race; and the practical possibilities of moving towards disarmament.

On the first two aspects, a certain awareness, which should, however, be strengthened, has been aroused. On the other hand, there seems to be widespread scepticism concerning the practical possibility of achieving disarmament, and this is one of the major psychological obstacles. Because of the diversity of factors, this scepticism is expressed in different ways in different countries or circumstances. It is partly a result of mental attitudes that reflect reservations the validity of which has not been challenged vigorously. These reservations need to be analysed and measured against actual facts and developments if convincing counter-arguments are to be found.

Major reservations about the feasibility of disarmament

One of the major reservations stems from fear of the other side. This is partly due to the mistrust that exists among states, and its immediate effect is suspicion by the different parties about each other's real intentions even when negotiations are under way. It may produce a defensive attitude that often leads to an acceptance of the arms race by a public which is averse to it, on the grounds that it is imposed by a threat inherent in the arms build-up of other countries. The general feeling of mistrust is reflected in the terminology in current use, with its frequent references to the 'balance of terror', 'deterrence', 'flexible response', 'early warning systems' and so on.

An obsessive preoccupation with strategic concepts produces several unreal reservations and negative results. It relegates to the lower levels of public consciousness concepts like peaceful co-existence, which seem to mean no more than an idealistic formulation forbidding attack on one another and a recognition of the existence of differing economic, social and political systems. In the same way, détente has been regarded by many as being of a contingent and passive nature. The persistence of actual trouble spots, the ever-growing number of conflicts, particularly in the Third World, and doubts about the effectiveness of available international institutions to resolve them generate further scepticism about the possibilities of disarmament. Preservation of national security and possession of weapons have become so inseparable in the public mind that most people are reconciled to the idea that the arms race is inevitable, even though they are aware of all the dangers involved. Even declarations that states are ready to carry out disarmament generally include the condition that the others must start first. A most distasteful consequence of a security-related approach to disarmament is the insensitivity it reveals to the global reality of the waste of resources.

An attempt to rectify the present situation must start by emphasizing that, during the last few years, ideas concerning détente and co-operation have progressed, that these words are being increasingly used and are increasingly becoming part of the language. Co-existence is tending to assume an active aspect through co-operation in every field between countries with differing economic, social and political systems and through affirmation of the right of each state, people and individual to exist. In the case of Europe, these various concepts are explicitly set forth in the Final Act of the Helsinki Conference. It is also being increasingly recognized that real détente should imply a positive effort to settle present conflicts and find a solution for problems that are likely to lead to further clashes. The states participating in the Helsinki Conference declared themselves, in the Final Act of that conference, to be

motivated by the political will in the interests of peoples to improve and intensify their relations . . . and expressed their conviction of the need to exert efforts to make détente both a continuing and an increasingly viable and comprehensive process, universal in scope.[2]

Past and present negotiations in Europe and the results already achieved reflect this evolution and highlight the need and the possibility of settling international differences without recourse to force. The new way forward that has been shown can also be followed in other regions of the world.

The dangers stemming from the growing inequality in the distribution of world resources dramatize the absurdity of the arms race and the vicious circle that it helps to estab-lish. Armaments absorb sums that could be allocated as aid to the developing countries, particularly in regard to food supplies. The continuation of the present situation aggravates the very tension and dangers of conflict which are invoked to justify the buildup of arms. Thus, while arms expenditure, which amounted to $207,000 million in 1974, exceeded $300,000 million in 1976, aid to development amounted to only $25,000 million, or twenty times less. Meanwhile, 70 per cent of the world's population has no access to drinking water, over 700 million people are living in an alarming state of poverty, and 450 million of them are likely to die of starvation. The number of unemployed is close to 300 million in the developing countries, and it is forecast that it will rise to 1,000 million by the year 2000. In 1976, a total of 800 million adult illiterates was recorded, a figure that continues to increase.

The International Labour Office has established that basic needs in food, health and education in the least developed countries could be entirely met by a 10 per cent reduction in annual arms expenditure. There are many more examples of the 'colossal wastage' involved in the arms race, and these have been continuously cited by the Stockholm International Peace Research Institute. Real security does not lie in an accumulation of arms which, by accentuating disparities between countries, aggravates tension and constitute a constant threat of conflagration, but in seeking a more equitable distribution of world resources. The various discussions and negotiations now under way and the working out of a new international economic order are steps forward along this path and should be strongly encouraged.

The effectiveness of existing international institutions reflects the attitude of member states. The validity of the principles of the United Nations Charter, as defined at San Francisco, has rarely been challenged, although they have occasionally been expanded and developed to meet the changing world situation. In implementing these principles, the United Nations and its Specialized Agencies are experiencing the difficulties inherent in the process of growth and adaptation necessitated by changes that have occurred since their foundation. The problems of adaptation notwithstanding, the role of the United Nations is irreplaceable. As pointed out by the United Nations Secretary-General, Kurt Waldheim: 'In our present world there is no rational alternative in international relations to the principles and procedures of the United Nations.'[3] At all events, if the discussions and action of the United Nations are to be really effective, its recommendations should enjoy the broadest possible measure of agreement and should be directed towards the easing of tension and the solution of conflicts.

It should be noted in this respect that continuous contacts within the United Nations and its Specialized Agencies at the level of government representatives and experts have afforded the opportunity for improving relationships and created a climate of fellow-feeling and understanding which should not be underestimated, even if it does not always find expression in official documents. Although the United Nations has not been able everywhere, and at all times, to cope with its task of maintaining peace, there is a long list of conflicts that have been settled either directly or indirectly through the intermediary of the United Nations. In several other cases the United Nations has either prevented the occurrence of a conflict through 'preventive diplomacy' or contained its duration and intensity through 'peace-keeping operations'. At the same time, undeniable progress has been achieved in the field of international co-operation by the Specialized Agencies.

As for those who consider disarmament a drag on national security efforts and want the initiative to come from the other side, it should be remembered that, if everyone persists in the same attitude, the arms race with all its dangers and absurdities will go on. A continued arms race entails new types of increasingly sophisticated weapons complicating the problems of verification and control and making subsequent agreements harder to achieve. To break this vicious circle, unilateral initiatives need to be encouraged. For those impatient with the slow progress of disarmament, it needs to be stressed that the process can be accelerated by adequate international vigilance and supervision on the part of public opinion. A study of the present situation shows that a number of countries have begun to concert their efforts for a balanced limitation of arms. Europe has already demonstrated that it is possible for the various parties to proceed together along this path.

The link established between arms and the maintenance of security stems essentially from the fact that the problem of disarmament is often viewed on a short-term basis and within the context of the present-day world. Progress towards disarmament requires a change in the nature of international relations so that co-operation and recourse to arbitration for the solution of international differences may replace mistrust and the use or the threat of force. It is this change that would seem to lie at the heart of the problem. An improvement in the international climate would facilitate the curtailment of the arms race and this, in turn, would help to establish confidence. The possibilities of opening up this new path have been demonstrated in Europe by the adoption of the Final Act of the Helsinki Conference.

Some popular misconceptions about disarmament

All the reservations about disarmament are intensified by ignorance or poor information. Because of the complexity of the strategic, technical and economic aspects, discussions on disarmament are usually confined to a small circle of experts speaking a language which is difficult for the general public to understand. The result is that the mass media fail to provide information concerning disarmament and the man in the street has the impression that such discussions, and hence the problems of disarmament itself, are beyond his comprehension and influence. The translation of technical problems into a language that can be understood by the public is important. The difficulty is particularly great when one is considering the technical and strategic factors. While the well-informed common man cannot be expected to resolve the seemingly complex issues involved, this does not entitle the 'experts' to become the sole judges in the case. There is an urgent need for divesting disarmament of the complexity of incomprehensible jargon and explaining it in a language that allows the 'man in the street' to participate in the process which can bring an end to the arms race without jeopardizing the interests of national security.

In describing the inadequacy which the 'man in the street' may feel about his contribution to disarmament, attention should be drawn to the extraordinarily rapid development of public awareness concerning environmental and pollution problems and the results that public opinion has succeeded in obtaining from governments. Ministerial departments with special responsibility for protection of the environment and for controlling pollution have been set up in a number of countries. Elsewhere, legislation has been enacted and regulations adopted in response to persistent demands by the public.

The force of public opinion and the measure of its influence can be attributed to several factors. The mass media have given wide coverage to these questions. They have dealt with highly technical problems and brought them within the grasp of all. By developing public awareness they have helped to create the political will to find a solution to these problems. The initial results have encouraged the public to continue and intensify its action. Government responses have reinforced public awareness of its influence and strengthened the belief that difficulties may be solved within the present context and without any fundamental change in the international structures.

These developments provide interesting pointers as to the possibility of action by public opinion in support of disarmament and stress the key role of the press and the information and education media as a whole. One must not, however, lose sight of the fact that 'information today means power—technological power and political power—both within countries and at the international level. But this power is unevenly distributed'.[4]

It is worth giving a random survey of some popularly held misconceptions about disarmament and the correctives which merit wider dissemination.

The arms race has always existed, and disarmament has been talked about for decades without being achieved. The same could be said of the plague, but the plague has virtually ceased to exist in an epidemic or endemic form, and there are means available for treating it. Going to the moon was also talked about for a long time. Now it has happened. Why should there not be a similar progress as regards disarmament, since such achievements are due not to chance but to human will? Space flights, aviation, even railways were long considered unfeasible. Slavery was abolished and child labour prohibited eventually. The atomic bomb itself was only a flight of fancy not so long ago. If destructive flights of fancy can become a reality why cannot visions that seek the good of humanity come to pass?

The balance of terror ensures peace by making war impossible. This is a dangerously unstable balance, always liable to be upset, and actually becomes the driving force in the headlong arms race. In fact, the creation and development of increasingly destructive new types of weapons and weapon systems constantly nourish the arms race. The deterrent value of nuclear weapons is, at present, considered to be based on two assumptions: (a) the absolute reliability of those whose responsibility it is to 'press the button', excluding any error or failure of human judgement; (b) the absolute reliability of technology that excludes any possibility of an 'accident'. This double assumption, questionable even when the number of countries with nuclear arms was limited, is now even more doubtful in the light of the proliferation of nuclear weapons in areas of growing political uncertainty. According to experts' forecasts, the present state of technological progress in a majority of non-nuclear industrialized countries enables them to manufacture nuclear weapons at fairly short notice. The threat represented by the possession of miniaturized nuclear arms by groups conducting terrorist operations should not be underestimated. The miniaturization of nuclear weapons, particularly tactical weapons, also increases the risk of their possible use. Possession of atomic weapons may avoid a nuclear conflict at the global level, but the likelihood of miniaturized nuclear arms being employed in localized conflicts leading to the destruction of entire regions is constantly increasing.

Arms, particularly nuclear weapons, provide essential support for diplomatic action. There are plenty of examples of countries which do not possess nuclear weapons and the diplomatic influence of which is in no way reduced by the level of their armaments—conventional or nuclear.

The armaments industry, particularly in the nuclear sector, is in the forefront of progress and accordingly plays an essential role in technological and economic development. Some of the industrially and economically most advanced non-nuclear countries demonstrate the fact that this progress can be just as great without the arms industry. Scientific and technological breakthroughs, both in research and development and in applied research, depend to a large extent on the financial resources available. The arms industry is probably the only one in which the notion of costs is entirely subordinated to technological requirements. If the resources now being devoted to the development of weapons were available for other ends, scientists and research workers would have probably already achieved decisive successes in the fight against cancer and epidemics and in the protection of the environment, not to mention solutions to the problems of hunger and under-development.

The arms industry is a vital driving force of the economy. It provides employment and as a source of exports contributes to the balance of payments. While the recession affecting certain countries and the resultant fear of unemployment lend special weight to this argument, it should be stressed that unproductive manufacture which, as such, does not enter the economic circuit produces stagnation, engenders inflation and tends to aggravate the economic situation. The problem is distorted when considered on a short-term basis. In the long run, the resources released through a reduction in armaments would allow the opening up of much larger markets for the export of capital goods, which would help to create more employment. Many studies, particularly under the auspices of the United Nations, have shown that the reconversion of arms industries to non-military production would not involve any major problems.* In 1945 there was an immense problem of reconverting armaments industries into non-military production, and this task was successfully carried out in a few years.

The current global military expenditure weakens the world economic potential and creates serious imbalances in trade, which themselves generate tensions and conflicts. Through the secrecy which surrounds it and the non-productive nature of its output, the armaments industry is a major contributory factor in the wastage of human, economic and energy resources that the world cannot afford. It is a wastage that directly affects the standard of living of every individual, whether in the industrialized or in the developing countries. The maintenance of powerful armaments industries deprives countries of development programmes.

If we do not export arms, others will export them in our place, to the detriment of our economy. Such apprehensions are valid only if disarmament is a restrictive goal confined to a few, leaving the field free for other competitors. In a drive towards general disarmament both the importers and exporters of weapons will be expected to limit the market.

Guidelines and ways and means of action

In the light of the above, it is possible to trace the lines along which action in support of disarmament should proceed and the way in which such action would be carried out. The following guidelines may be suggested, with a view to overcoming the psychological obstacles in particular.

* This applies especially to the reconversion projects established by the Committee for the General Assembly's Special Session on disarmament in August 1975.

If public opinion is to be strengthened in favour of disarmament, account should be taken of the complexity and diversity of the factors which determine the national decision-making process. It would be useful if a collection of studies undertaken in this field were to be made available to organizations working for disarmament. Here it should be stressed that the factors influencing public opinion and the influence that public opinion can expect to have are often difficult to assess but are a continuous and cumulative process. Apparent lack of impact does not necessarily mean failure of the action undertaken. An example is provided by the Rome Appeal issued by the Meeting of War Veterans in November 1971. During the days and weeks immediately following the meeting, the appeal seemed to have had less effect than it deserved. The subsequent months and years have shown that the interest it created has been profound and enduring and that it has not been without effect on the outcome of the Conference on Security and Co-operation in Europe.

To combat the deeply ingrained feelings of mistrust, ignorance and fear, a deeper analysis is needed of their motivations and manifestations as expressed at the level of states in their external relations and at the level of national and international public opinion. A collection of studies made along these lines would be extremely useful. A continuous international effort at defusing the global trouble spots by ensuring the establishment of social justice could be made through a reaffirmation of the principles set forth in the Final Act of the Helsinki Conference.

Wider publicity should be given to the new developments which have occurred concerning the possibility of disarmament and the institutional requirements that it implies. In this the mass media have a valuable role to play in influencing journalists and those who disseminate information to persuade the public to take a greater interest in disarmament problems. Wider coverage of appropriate information needs to be pooled.

As pointed out by the Director-General of Unesco, the balance of terror and the aggravation of inequalities could lead to an ultimate confrontation that would leave nothing but ruin and desolation in their wake and cause the destruction of everything that human genius has helped to create over so many thousands of years. Mankind is condemned to solidarity. People must not only accept their differences, but, transcending them, must build a new economic, social and cultural order. At the same time, '. . . the introduction of a "new international economic order" obviously concerns not only economics but is also a matter of social, scientific, technological and cultural relevance . . .'. Lastly,

it is not to be taken for granted that men will escape the course of events which has led them to the present dangers: the survival of the planet is at stake . . . not merely the survival of the human race, but the survival of all living things.[5]

Action, according to the guidelines set out above, demands special efforts in the field of cultural exchanges, education and information. A very special effort in the field of education appears essential and has already been initiated by Unesco, which has included disarmament as a part of its concern for human rights and peace. An important place should be set aside in educational curricula for the study of international relations, stressing the problems which the international community has to face and the new prospects for world-wide co-operation. Pluri-national institutions of education and technical training and systematic study of foreign languages in order to overcome language barriers are excellent means of fostering international co-operation and understanding. Every initiative of this kind should be encouraged and developed. The aim should be to initiate a movement where it does not exist. More frequent references to the problem of disarmament would lead the public to take a greater interest in it, and this, in turn, would arouse increased interest in those professionally involved with information.

The following practical measures may be suggested in this connection.

Disarmament education should emphasize the global nature of a problem that transcends geographical location, economic and social structure and development level, and affects every aspect of national and international life. It is not a matter that concerns only the experts but a question that is bound up with day-to-day life.

Occasional international meetings should be planned of those in charge of and professionally involved with information, in order to exchange experiences on the nature, difficulties and results of their efforts to sensitize public opinion to disarmament. Encounters of this kind would lead to a clearer identification of the difficulties and the means of overcoming them.

It would be useful to prepare specific documentation on a regular basis. Prepared in a simple way and easy to understand, it should be designed to sensitize the widest possible sectors of public opinion to the interdependent issues involved (security, disarmament, the new international economic order, survival of humanity). This documentation should be adaptable to the particular preoccupations of different countries and regions. It should be widely circulated, particularly to parliamentary documentation services, university and school libraries, teachers' associations, trade unions and employer's federations, the many non-governmental organizations, especially youth organizations and the mass media (news agencies, audio-visual organizations, journalists' associations).

The curtailment of the arms race and progress towards disarmament are not simply morally desirable goals. They represent a vital necessity in a world which technological development has rendered increasingly interdependent and increasingly vulnerable. They represent the only way to prevent the world from being sooner or later engulfed in ruin and destruction.

The obstacles hampering the advance towards disarmament are indeed considerable but not disproportionately so, in comparison with others that mankind has experienced in its history and has overcome. And mankind is certainly better equipped for this purpose today than ever before, thanks to the resources that the development of science and technology has placed at its disposal. This means, more especially, that the psychological obstacles which prevent this political determination from making progress have to be overcome. This implies an effort in the field of education and information, and also a change in the very structure of international relations, replacing mistrust by a concerted action, conflict by arbitration, and the use or threat of force by conciliation. The Final Act of the Conference on Security and Co-operation in Europe has provided a lead for such an approach.

War veterans and members of resistance movements, former deportees and prisoners of war all intend to work unflaggingly for a new way forward, particularly within their international organizations, which represent tens of millions

of members in all parts of the world and of every philosophical persuasion. Profoundly dedicated to the preservation of their respective countries' security, anxious to
contribute the wealth of their experience, determined that
young people shall be spared the destruction and suffering
that they have known, they intend to pursue and extend the
efforts that have already been initiated in Europe. In this
connection, they have held several international meetings of
war veterans on disarmament. Conscious of the fact that
'since wars begin in the minds of men, it is in the minds of
men that defences of peace must be constructed',[6] they
entertain the hope that, as has been the case in Europe,
their words and their deeds will help to overcome the
difficulties that exist, particularly those of a psychological
nature.

Notes

1. Unesco, Constitution of Unesco, Article I, Purposes and functions.
2. Final Act of the Conference on Security and Co-operation in Europe,
   Helsinki, 1 August 1975.
3. United Nations, *Report of the Secretary-General on the Activities of the
   Organization*, New York, 1975.
4. Unesco, the Assistant Director-General for Culture and Communication,
   'Unesco and World Problems of Communication', *Unesco Courier*,
   April 1977.
5. *Unesco Courier*, March 1976. For a collective text by an international
   advisory panel to survey major world problems, see 'Unesco and the
   World Outlook for Tomorrow'.
6. Preamble to the Constitution of Unesco.

The role
of the United Nations*

Professor of international
law at the Institute of State
and Law of the Soviet
Union, Moscow

O. V. Bogdanov

The United Nations: an important centre for talks on disarmament

It is current international practice to refer to disarmament as the number-one problem, the solution of which promises to benefit mankind. The numerous studies carried out both within the United Nations and outside it have conclusively proved that the achievement of disarmament would have manifold salutary effects not only in the field of international politics but also in the economic, social and cultural spheres.[1] It would, indeed, be difficult to name any other international problem that so strongly influences the international situation and has such widespread results. Disarmament is the key to a significant improvement of the international climate and to the realization of man's age-old dream of a world without war.

Such a development would have a particularly great —indeed, revolutionary—effect on people's awareness and on the world's present system of education and schooling. It is now fully recognized that the elimination or substantial reduction of expenditure on the production of armaments will make it possible to increase many times current national appropriations for social and cultural needs—education, health, science and the arts.[2] This, in turn, will create more favourable conditions for general cultural development.

The socio-economic consequences of disarmament visibly demonstrate the close connection between disarmament and Unesco's sphere of activity. A point to be firmly established is that the importance of disarmament extends in one way or another to every link of the United Nations system, including its work in culture and education. Therefore, the work on disarmament carried out within the United Nations is of direct relevance to Unesco.

* This chapter was written prior to the Tenth Special Session of the General Assembly (1978) and has been up-dated by the Secretariat as regards certain developments.

Unesco is being called upon to play an increasingly significant role in diffusing the philosophy of disarmament. One of the practical ways of fulfilling this role might be to study the activity of the United Nations organs in the field of disarmament and to provide information about their aims to a wider audience. The work currently being undertaken in connection with the long-term survey, approved by the General Conference of Unesco at its eighteenth session, of the role of international organizations in the modern world should make a positive contribution to this task.

Support for disarmament has become a clearly defined part of the activities of the United Nations, particularly during the past decade. The responsibility of the United Nations in this regard has grown steadily and in direct proportion to the growing importance of disarmament in the modern world. This development is entirely as it should be, because the United Nations, as the Organization primarily concerned with international security, must focus attention on essential contemporary international problems. One of the central purposes of the Organization now is to make an effective practical contribution to disarmament.

In the United Nations Charter, effective work towards disarmament is considered to be an inseparable part of the overall duty of the Organization to strengthen peace throughout the world. The Charter, in general, gives a fairly large place to disarmament even though it has no article that deals specifically with the issue; this has been dealt with in the context of the functions and powers of the principal organs of the United Nations for the maintenance of international peace. With respect to co-operation between states for the maintenance of peace, the Charter refers to disarmament as one of the most important means of achieving that aim. Disarmament is also referred to as one of the principal matters for the attention of the General Assembly and the Security Council, and is explicitly mentioned in the statement of the powers of each of these two organs of the United Nations. By Article II, paragraph 1 of the United Nations Charter, the General Assembly is charged with considering the general principles relating to disarmament and with making recommendations with regard to them to the Member States of the United Nations and to the Security Council. Article 26 specifically entrusts the Security Council with responsibility for formulating disarmament plans to be submitted to the United Nations. Naturally, the latter retains the right of final decision as to the acceptance or rejection of such plans. In this respect, the Charter rightly proceeds from the principle that conventions concerning disarmament can be based only on the agreement of the sovereign Member States of the United Nations.

This point deserves special attention, since certain authors commenting on the Charter have questioned this procedure as a 'weakness' in the Charter because it does not entitle the United Nations to formulate disarmament plans that are binding on the Member States of the Organization. Such a stand is taken, for examples, by the English jurists N. Bentwich and A. Martin, who write: 'The Charter confers no authority upon the United Nations to impose upon its members a system for disarmament or even for the regulation of armaments.'[3]

This view is based essentially on the rather unrealistic premise which favours the 'imposition' of the United Nations decisions on sovereign states and, therefore, restricts the possibilities of their free acceptance of their corresponding responsibilities. Any procedure other than the one adopted by the Charter might have actually hindered the inclusion of disarmament among the aims of the United Nations.

A few words should be said concerning the disarmament terminology used in the United Nations Charter, which makes use of two terms—'disarmament' and 'regulation of armaments' (Articles 11, 26, 47). The former is more comprehensive and covers practically all measures, including the abolition of armaments. The regulation of armaments is generally taken to mean their limitation and reduction; in other words, this concept may be equated with partial disarmament measures. It follows from this that the Charter covers the disarmament question fairly broadly in terms which provide for both partial and total disarmament. Many contemporary writings tend to adopt the same approach when dealing with disarmament and arms regulation. In reference works the term 'disarmament' is more often than not interpreted as embracing all kinds of measures—from the reduction of armaments to their total abolition.[4]

Some authoritative commentators on the Charter tend to attribute a disproportionately larger role to the 'regulation of armaments' by trying to show that the Charter makes the practical achievement of disarmament dependent on certain conditions. The American expert on the United Nations Charter, L. Goodrich, writes, for example: 'Furthermore, it was clearly intended that the regulation of national armaments should come after and not before the full implementation of the system of collective security.'[5]

This viewpoint is not supported by the text of the Charter, which nowhere states that disarmament measures should be implemented only after the establishment of a system of collective security. Indeed, the Charter proceeds essentially from an entirely different viewpoint, i.e. the desire to achieve both disarmament and collective security, neither being in any way conditional upon the other. In the final analysis both have the same goal—the strengthening of peace—but there should be no question of presenting one as a pre-condition for the other.

On the question of the content of the expression 'regulation of armaments' used in the Charter, it should be said that other Western scholars give a more reasonable interpretation of it. The eminent English jurist H. Lauterpacht, writing as the editor of the seventh edition of L. Oppenheim's widely-used textbook on international law, wrote that in practice there was a prevailing tendency to give a broad interpretation to the United Nations Charter wording on disarmament, interpreting it to include the reduction as well as the regulation of armaments.[6] This approach is considerably more realistic, since it emphasizes the main provisions of the Charter and their orientation towards practical disarmament, setting aside any ambitious notions of intermediate 'preliminary conditions'.

The Charter itself provides for specific machinery to achieve disarmament, and in the thirty years of the existence of the United Nations system this machinery has grown considerably, reflecting the increasing importance of the problem of disarmament in international affairs. That period saw, for the first time in the history of international relations, the establishment of several organs for examining disarmament questions. A distinctive feature of the system is its constant development and improvement, reflecting both the increasing urgency and the ever-growing dimensions of the problem.

This process of growth must certainly be considered one of the characteristic traits of post-war developments. A comparison of the state of affairs at the time when the United

Nations was set up with the present-day situation reveals clearly that the importance of disarmament increased geometrically. Whereas earlier the United Nations machinery for examining disarmament questions was fairly modest, the scale of the work in this field has multiplied. That, of course, is one of the outstanding features of the general direction of development of the United Nations during the past three decades.[7]

There were originally two special organs—the Atomic Energy Commission, set up in 1946, and the Commission for Conventional Armaments, set up in 1947. In 1952 they were replaced by the Disarmament Commission, composed of all the members of the Security Council plus Canada. The Commission had a subcommittee consisting of representatives of Canada, France, the Soviet Union, the United Kingdom and the United States. Important practical work in the field of disarmament was carried out in these working organs and particularly in the subcommittee. The fact that it did not achieve success was to a certain extent due to the inadequate membership of the Commission and of its subcommittee, which did not reflect the true balance of forces in the United Nations and did not provide genuine representation of the Organization's membership.

This state of affairs highlighted the necessity of giving adequately representative character to the actual organizational structure of the United Nations organs for examining disarmament matters. Proposals in this direction were considered at the twelfth and thirteenth sessions of the General Assembly of the United Nations. As a result, the composition of the Disarmament Commission was substantially broadened to take in all members of the Organization. However, the Commission had not met since 1965. It was replaced at the Special Session in 1978 by a new Disarmament Commission, which provides a forum for the discussion of disarmament proposals when the General Assembly is not in session.

It should be borne in mind, however, that the Commission does not play an essentially practical role in the formulation of disarmament plans. At the end of the 1950s the centre of operations in disarmament work shifted to another sector. During that period the system of working organs concerned with examining disarmament questions underwent a certain degree of reorganization aimed at improving the system and making it more effective. A step in that direction was the establishment in 1959 of a special working organ: the Ten-Nation Disarmament Committee, composed of representatives from five eastern European states (Bulgaria, Czechoslovakia, Poland, Romania and the Soviet Union) and five Western states (France, Italy, Canada, the United Kingdom and the United States). This composition represented a certain improvement on the previous position but was still rather a poor reflection of the actual alignment of forces in the world. This, no doubt, had its effect on the productivity of the Ten-Nation Committee; it did little more than initiate a debate on the examination of certain proposals for general disarmament.

The next step was taken at the end of 1961: the composition of the Disarmament Committee was enlarged to eighteen states; in addition to the ten states named above it included eight non-aligned countries (Brazil, Burma, Egypt, Ethiopia, India, Mexico, Nigeria and Sweden). The Committee continued to work with this composition until the end of the 1960s, and, for the first time in its existence, its work achieved tangible results: drafts of several important international documents were prepared, including a treaty on the non-proliferation of nuclear weapons. This achievement attested to the value of this kind of working organ to examine disarmament questions.

The composition of the Committee was extended in the following years. In 1969, two additional states were included (Japan and the Mongolian People's Republic), and then a further six countries (Argentina, Hungary, Morocco, the Netherlands, Pakistan and Yugoslavia) were made members. This brought the overall number of members of the Committee to twenty-six states; its title was also slightly modified and it became known as the Conference of the Committee on Disarmament, popularly referred to as the CCD. Thereafter, the composition of the Committee continued to grow; from 1975 it took in another five states; the German Democratic Republic, the Federal Republic of Germany, Iran, Peru and Zaire. The Committee comprised thirty-one states — France, although a Committee member, took no practical part in its work.[8]

Certain features concerning the legal position of the CCD should be noted. It was not an organ of the United Nations, although it worked in close contact with the Organization and was financed by it. Each year the General Assembly considered the Committee's reports on the work it had accomplished and adopted resolutions concerning its future activity. This arrangement involved the Committee in the United Nations' overall pattern of activity in the field of disarmament. The General Assembly also examined draft agreements on disarmament prepared by the Committee. This it did, for example, with the Treaty on the Non-Proliferation of Nuclear Weapons, the Treaty on the Prohibition of the Emplacement of Nuclear Weapons and Other Weapons of Mass Destruction on the Sea-Bed and the Ocean Floor and the Subsoil Thereof, and the Convention on the Prohibition of the Development, Production and Stockpiling of Bacteriological (Biological) and Toxin Weapons and on their Destruction. All these documents were discussed and sometimes amplified and approved by the General Assembly. Thus, in practice the CCD had assumed the role of the main organ of the United Nations for examining questions of disarmament. In 1978, the CCD was replaced by the Committee on Disarmament (CD), which has closer relations with the United Nations. It is made up of the nuclear-weapon states and thirty-five other states.*

World disarmament conference

* The Committee on Disarmament is open to the nuclear-weapon states and the following thirty-five others including twenty-one non-aligned countries and fourteen others divided between socialist and Western groups: Algeria, Argentina, Australia, Belgium, Brazil, Bulgaria, Burma, Canada, Cuba, Czechoslovakia, Egypt, Ethiopia, German Democratic Republic, Germany, Federal Republic of, Hungary, India, Indonesia, Iran, Italy, Japan, Kenya, Mexico, Mongolia, Morocco, Netherlands, Nigeria, Pakistan, Peru, Poland, Romania, Sri Lanka, Sweden, Venezuela, Yugoslavia and Zaire.

In addition, for a number of years now, plans have been under consideration within the United Nations for adopting other possible organizational means for the study and settlement of disarmament problems. The first of these is a world disarmament conference, offering the widest and most representative forum of states possible. The idea of convening such a conference has been gaining currency for many years now, since one of the main advantages of a forum of that kind would be the opportunity to involve practically every country in the world in the examination of disarmament questions. Such an approach was not used in the past apart from the well-known conferences that took place in the 1930s under the auspices of the League of Nations and were by no means noted for their representative composition. In the opinion of many states, a world conference could open up new possibilities for progress in disarmament and act as a spur to more dynamic work in that field.

The campaign for the convening of a world conference

on disarmament gained strength in the 1960s. Calls for holding it were heard within the United Nations and at a number of international conferences: for example, at the conferences of non-aligned countries in Belgrade in 1961 and in Cairo in 1964. Moves in the same direction were also made inside the United Nations in 1965, although at that time they did not have the support of the majority of the members of the United Nations.

Concrete proposals on the subject were made in the United Nations by the Soviet Union and met with wide approval. In a unanimously adopted resolution, the twenty-sixth session of the General Assembly expressed its conviction that 'it is most desirable to take immediate steps in order that careful consideration be given to the convening, following adequate preparation, of a world disarmament conference open to all states'.[9] The resolution clearly indicated the desirability of embarking on a process of practical preparation for the convening of the conference. A survey carried out on the question showed that the overwhelming majority of members of the United Nations supported the idea of holding a conference following adequate preparation. It is true that there were also opponents of the idea, who wanted to make the possibility of convening a conference dependent on a host of preliminary conditions.

Preparations for the conference nevertheless went ahead. In 1973, according to its resolution 3183 (XXVIII), the General Assembly decided to establish an *Ad Hoc* Committee to examine all the views and suggestions expressed by governments on the convening of a world disarmament conference, including conditions for the holding of such a conference. While this organizational machinery made a real contribution to the promotion of favourable conditions for convening a world conference, considerable difficulties remain which stem from the stand taken on the question by certain states. If the conference is to be truly a world conference, it is essential that the widest possible number of states should participate in it, including, of course, all the nuclear powers.

In 1976, an important step was taken when the General Assembly's resolution 31/189 B on the convening of a special session of the General Assembly devoted to disarmament, proposed by the Soviet Union, was unanimously adopted. This session, referred to as the SSD (Special Session on Disarmament) and held in 1978 in New York, called for the convening of a world disarmament conference with universal participation at the earliest appropriate date. An Ad Hoc Committee has been established on this question, which has suggested that the conference be held after the 1982 Second Special Dession (SSD (2)) 'as soon as the necessary consensus on its convening has been reached'.

One of the notable results of a growing United Nations interest is the inclusion of disarmament questions in the sphere of activity of the associated agencies of the United Nations. A well-known example is the work done by the International Atomic Energy Agency (IAEA) in supervising the implementation of arrangements aimed at ensuring non-proliferation of nuclear weapons. The IAEA has an important role in sealing off channels for the transfer of nuclear weapons to non-nuclear weapon states that have subscribed to the Non-Proliferation Treaty. This represents a valuable contribution to the overall task of limiting the spread of nuclear weapons throughout the world.

Unesco, too, within its fields of competence, has played a valuable role in support of disarmament. Propagation of the concept of disarmament is bound up in the closest possible way with realization of the clause in Unesco's Constitution that speaks of constructing the defences of peace in the minds of men—words that in recent years have increasingly influenced Unesco's activities. The latest and most important examples were the adoption, in 1976 and 1978 by the General Conference at its eighteenth and nineteenth sessions, of the resolution entitled Role of Unesco in Generating a Climate of Public Opinion Conducive to the Halting of the Arms Race and the Transition to Disarmament and the holding of a World Congress on Disarmament Education, which took place at Unesco Headquarters on 9–13 June 1980.

The resolutions of the General Conference specifically invited the Director-General of Unesco, in implementing Unesco's programme, to bear in mind the importance of taking measures that would effectively assist the cause of disarmament, to ensure wide publication in Unesco's periodicals of articles and material dealing with disarmament, to make provisions for the holding of various symposia for educators, scientists and cultural workers on the themes of disarmament and also for making wider use of other possibilities for influencing public opinion.[9]

Now more than ever it is obvious that there can be no genuine security in the world without disarmament. Peace-loving men are mobilizing the energies of all peoples for a radical shift towards refusal to accept the arms race. It would be no exaggeration to say that never before have international organizations concerned themselves on such a scale with every conceivable aspect of the question of disarmament. Further expansion of the scope of research in this area can also be foreseen for the future. This is why it is especially urgent today to analyse the effectiveness of the work already done on disarmament.

The results so far

During the first decade of the United Nations' existence, its principal organs, and in particular the General Assembly, concerned themselves only sporadically with disarmament matters. However, during the 1960s and especially during the 1970s, discussion of these matters not only became regular practice but a high priority in the work of the General Assembly. It has now become an established rule to include dozens of questions relating to disarmament in the agenda for each session of the Assembly, and the number of resolutions on the matter adopted by the Assembly has grown in proportion. This trend reflects the general and heightened importance, on a world scale, of the disarmament problem. The United Nations machinery has handled a large portion of the multilateral treaties and agreements on disarmament during the post-war period. A whole series of international treaties on disarmament are now in force. This is a new development in international relations. Formerly agreements on arms limitations were very rare and not particularly effective, although there are specific instances of attempts to examine the problems of arms limitation. The most notable example was the International Conference on Disarmament held in Geneva from 1932 to 1934. This conference did not lead to any decisions on arms limitation and did not succeed in working out any international treaties on the matter. It revealed to the whole world not only the difficulty in resolving disarmament questions but also the presence in the world of circles that were making a determined stand against disarmament. Germany, which, at the time, was preparing for military aggression and territorial annexation, took a particularly obstructive stand.

Although the current international situation is totally different, disarmament problems continue to be thorny, and their practical solution requires enormous effort. The hopeful aspect, however, is that, as compared to the 1930s, a much larger number of states are consistently giving unprecedented support to the concept of disarmament. There is also widespread recognition of the fact that continuation of the arms race can lead to disastrous results for the entire world. All these factors exert a real influence on disarmament prospects, rendering further progress possible and even inevitable. A powerful stimulus in this respect is provided by the new atmosphere that is becoming established in international relations—an atmosphere of détente based on a decisive choice against the 'cold war'.

Among the tangible results of the disarmament efforts is the 1963 Moscow Treaty, which for the first time put a partial ban on nuclear-weapon tests, and forbade experimental nuclear explosion in three areas; the atmosphere, outer space and under water.[10] The conclusion of this treaty was a most important and timely step; it came at a time when the consequences of continuing with experimental nuclear explosions in the atmosphere had become obvious and when the renunciation of such explosions had come to be seen as a matter of necessity. At the present time, the Moscow Treaty is a widely supported and authoritative international document, which has been ratified by more than 100 states and has exerted a marked influence on international affairs. The problem of eliminating atmospheric nuclear tests altogether is still not fully solved; one of the two nuclear powers which have not yet acceded to the treaty continues to carry out nuclear explosions in the atmosphere, giving understandable cause for concern.

The Moscow Treaty acted as a catalyst for the preparation of instruments on disarmament. It was followed by other significant agreements—the Treaty on the Non-Proliferation of Nuclear Weapons (which came into force in 1970), the Treaty on the Prohibition of the Emplacement of Nuclear Weapons and other Weapons of Mass Destruction on the Sea-Bed and the Ocean Floor and the Subsoil Thereof (which came into force in 1972) and the Convention on the Prohibition of the Development, Production and Stockpiling of

Bacteriological (Biological) and Toxin Weapons and on their Destruction (which came into force in 1975).

These international agreements made an important contribution to the solution of the pressing problems of disarmament. The matter of the non-proliferation of nuclear weapons may be taken as an example. The Non-Proliferation Treaty (NPT) was concluded at a time when it had become obvious to the whole world that possession of nuclear weapons could well spread across the whole globe. Such a state of affairs would naturally have entailed a multitude of grave dangers for mankind, including a manifold increase of the risk of a nuclear war breaking out. The Non-Proliferation Treaty was designed to block the avenues for the transfer of nuclear means of destruction from one state to another.

Under this treaty, each nuclear-weapon state undertook not to transfer to any recipient whatsoever nuclear weapons or other nuclear explosive devices. In addition, each non-nuclear-weapon state undertook not to manufacture and not to acquire such weapons or other nuclear explosive devices (Articles I and II). In order to comply with these requirements, the non-nuclear-weapon states undertook to conclude agreements with the International Atomic Energy Agency permitting supervision of their nuclear activities. The purpose of such control is to prevent fissionable material being diverted from peaceful uses to the manufacture of nuclear weapons. Control lies in scrutinizing the accounting documents relating to the movement of nuclear materials, by observing the activities being performed by workers at nuclear installations and by independent inspections carried out by representatives of the IAEA. While the number of states signatories to the NPT has grown to more than 100, the urgent problem of attracting more signatories still remains. Especially important is the need for all nuclear-weapon states to sign the treaty. This is also true for the 'near-nuclear' states, whose number has shown a marked increase in recent years.

Also in recent years, the problem of reconciling the non-proliferation of nuclear weapons with the development of peaceful atomic energy has acquired new dimensions. Present findings show that atomic energy possesses a number of economic advantages in relation to conventional fuels, but, at the same time, its development involves the production of plutonium, a fissionable substance. This by-product can be used for the production of nuclear weapons, a fact that lends particular urgency to the question of strengthening and improving the controls exercised by the IAEA, especially over the export of nuclear material. The strengthening of measures for the non-proliferation of nuclear weapons is now becoming a matter of paramount concern, and the successful solution of this problem could substantially increase the overall effectiveness of the Treaty on the Non-Proliferation of Nuclear Weapons. Review conferences on the operation of this treaty were held in 1975 and 1980.

Another of the treaties mentioned earlier—the Convention on the Prohibition of Bacteriological Weapons—occupies a special place, since it aims at the total prohibition of bacteriological weapons. It calls for a destruction of the existing weapons, an end to the production of such weapons or their diversion to peaceful purposes and an absolute refusal to transfer them to any other state (Articles I, II and III).

This Convention is unprecedented, inasmuch as it represents an agreement to abolish one of the means of mass destruction. Never before in the history of international relations has such a radical agreement been concluded. The Convention opens the way to the development of other similar documents applicable to the remaining means of mass destruction that exist—above all to chemical weapons. In itself the Convention provides convincing proof that practical disarmament measures are now feasible.

This point needs to be made to impress those who believe that disarmament talks are fruitless. A break-through has now been definitely achieved in these talks, opening up promising prospects for the future. The initial steps have already been taken and should be followed by even more radical achievements which could have a real effect on the international situation. Their adoption by an international security organization as extensive as the United Nations (with 153 Members) reflects mankind's growing aspiration for real and prompt disarmament measures.

Some of the recent proposals in this field are the following:
• In its resolution 3093 (XXVIII) of 1973 the General Assembly called for the reduction of the military budgets of the permanent members of the Security Council (China, France, the Soviet Union, the United Kingdom and the United States), by 10 per cent and the utilization of part of

the funds saved to provide assistance to developing countries. Such a step could make a weighty contribution to detente. After all, 10 per cent of the military appropriations of the five states mentioned represents a sum running into hundreds of millions of dollars. It is, therefore, natural that the General Assembly should attach considerable importance to the implementation of this resolution, which is justifiably regarded as a valuable and extremely opportune measure.

• In 1974 the General Assembly recommended by its resolution 3264 (XXIX) that an international convention be worked out prohibiting action to influence the environment for military and other purposes incompatible with the maintenance of international security, human well-being and health. That recommendation laid the foundation for practical work by the CCD, which two years later submitted an appropriate draft to the General Assembly at its thirty-first session in 1976. After discussion and certain amendments, this draft received majority approval, and the Convention on the Prohibition of Military or Any other Hostile Use of Environmental Modification Techniques was signed in Geneva on 18 May 1977 and entered into force on 5 October 1978. It represents one of the latest examples of the continuing development of international agreements on pressing aspects of arms race limitation.

• A similar matter which was being examined by the CCD concerns the prohibition of the development and manufacture of new types of weapons of mass destruction, the General Assembly's resolution 3479 (XXX) in 1975 having recommended that a convention be drafted. The recommendation was prompted by the fact that, given the rapid scientific and technological developments taking place today, it is probable—not to say inevitable—that new types and systems of mass-destruction weapons will be developed which may be even more dangerous and devastating than those we know now. To prevent such a development, an international agreement prohibiting states from developing and manufacturing new types and new systems of weapons of mass destruction needs to be adopted. A draft agreement on these lines was submitted to the CCD after discussions by the General Assembly indicated that the idea found support in United Nations circles. In 1979, the General Assembly, by its resolution 34/79, requested continued efforts of the CD in the preparation of a draft comprehensive agreement prohibiting the development and manufacture of new types of mass destruction weapons and, where necessary, specific agreements on particular types of such weapons.

The task ahead

A total ban on nuclear tests

Among the urgent disarmament problems that have long defied a solution is the question of the total prohibition of nuclear-weapon tests. Since the conclusion of the Moscow Treaty, fifteen years ago, there has been an urgent need to take the ban on nuclear tests to its logical conclusion by extending it to underground nuclear explosions. Such nuclear-weapon explosions are to this day being carried out in many parts of the world—yet another reminder of the pressing need to impose a broad international ban on all forms of nuclear-weapon tests. In 1975, a step was taken in this direction by General Assembly resolution 3478 (XXX), to which was annexed a draft treaty on the complete and general prohibition of nuclear-weapon tests. Agreement on the issue has been complicated by a divergence of views on the question of supervision. Some states maintain that effective supervision can be achieved by the use of national technical resources and international co-operation in the exchange of seismic data. Other countries continue to insist on the establishment of a special supervisory body with powers to carry out on-site verification. A new compromise proposal was submitted to the thirty-first session of the General Assembly (1976) with a view to overcoming the differences on supervision without further delay; this made provision for on-site verification on a voluntary basis. This proposal provides a means of overcoming the basic obstacle to the speedy achievement of a total and comprehensive ban on nuclear-weapon tests. In resolutions 3466 (XXX), 31/66, 32/78 and 33/60, the General Assembly called upon all nuclear powers to participate, together with the non-nuclear powers, in talks on the complete and general prohibition of nuclear weapon tests. A total cessation of these tests requires all the nuclear powers to adhere to the treaty in question; hence the importance of the requirement that (together with the non-nuclear states) they take part in the negotiations on the drafting of that treaty.

In 1979, the General Assembly, in its resolution 34/73, requested that the CD initiate negotiations on a treaty prohibiting 'all nuclear test explosions by all states for all time'.

Non-use of force in international relations

Closely related to the problem of disarmament is the issue of the non-use of force in international relations. This has attracted considerable attention at recent sessions of the General Assembly. At the thirty-first session (1976) a concrete proposal was submitted in the form of a draft world treaty, which, according to resolution 31/9, Member States were invited to examine. A Special Committee on Enhancing the Effectiveness of the Principle of Non-Use of Force in International Relations, composed of thirty-five Member States, was established in 1977 by resolution 32/150. In 1978 the General Assembly decided that the Special Committee should continue its work with the goal of drafting, at the earliest possible date, a world treaty on the non-use of force in international relations, as well as on the peaceful settlement of disputes and such other recommendations as the Committee deems appropriate (resolution 33/96). The purpose of these measures was to give greater strength to the famous principle proclaimed in the Charter of the United Nations that 'all members shall refrain in their international relations from the threat or use of force' (Article 2 paragraph 4). While in principle it is exceptionally important for the favourable development of contemporary international relations, in practice there are numerous instances of failure to observe it. It was precisely in order to turn this principle into an immutable norm of international relations that a proposal was made to embody it in a special treaty to be signed by every country in the world. Signing of such an instrument would substantially enhance the real effectiveness of the principle of the non-use of force. The document would explicitly stress that the principle extends to modern means of mass destruction, including nuclear weapons. The significance of such a provision would be considerable at present, when the threat of a nuclear-missile war overshadows international relations. A widely accepted treaty on non-use of force would contribute directly to alleviating the security concerns of Member States of the United Nations and make them more amenable to other disarmament measures.

Prohibition of chemical weapons

One of the existing means of mass destruction—bacteriological weapons—is already the subject of a total ban established by an international convention which came into force in 1975. Other means of mass destruction, in particular chemical and nuclear weapons, are still not covered by a ban of this sort. Attempts to ban them have been carried on for many years through the preparations for a treaty on the total banning and elimination of chemical weapons. The urgency of accomplishing this task is indisputable. The pernicious nature of chemical agents is widely known, as their use during the First World War caused dreadful human suffering and death on a large scale. Chemical-warfare technology has made immense progress since then. New types of chemical weapons have been developed that are capable of inflicting even more agonizing death on human beings. Improvements have been made upon the methods of delivering chemical weapons, so that they can now be employed not only in the battle zone (i.e. against military personnel) but also against the civilian population of a country's towns and cities.

All this is yet another reminder of the need to produce a treaty on the prohibition and destruction of chemical weapons. The solution to the problem offered by the 1925 Geneva Protocol, in force at present, is far from complete. First, although it forbids the use of chemical agents, it does not provide for their abolition. Second, the number of states parties is too small to rule out the use of these substances. The need to produce a more radical document that not only forbids the use of all chemical agents, but provides for their abolition thus remains urgent. The negotiations on the subject, however, have so far not confirmed the possibility of such a solution. Instead, it has been suggested that a start could be made by aiming at agreement on the banning and liquidation of the most dangerous and lethal types of chemical weapons.

The question of the prohibition and destruction of chemical weapons was on the agenda of the CCD. It is now assigned to the CD, which, according to General Assembly resolution 34/72 of 1979, was urged 'to undertake . . . negotiations on an agreement on the complete and effective prohibition of the development, production and stockpiling of all chemical weapons and on their destruction as a matter of high priority'. In March 1980, the CD set up an Ad Hoc Working Group on Chemical Weapons, which is to define the issues to be dealt with in negotiations on a chemical-weapons convention.

Nuclear disarmament

An effective solution to the problem of disarmament is inconceivable without decisive measures on nuclear disarmament. Nuclear weapons present a huge threat to mankind. The conclusions reached in the course of the authoritative studies carried out in the United Nations on the consequences of the possible use of nuclear weapons are well known. The overall conclusion reached by the experts is that:

Were such weapons ever to be used in numbers, hundreds of millions of people might be killed, and civilization as we know it, as well as organized community life, would inevitably come to an end in the countries involved in the conflict.[11]

The difficulties of bringing about nuclear disarmament are increasingly compounded by continuous technological innovations in nuclear weaponry. At an earlier stage in the development of nuclear weapons it would have been very much simpler: stocks of nuclear weapons were then smaller, and agreement on their abolition was more easily attainable. The nuclear arsenal has now grown into a massive array of weapon types and systems with a variety of purposes, yields and methods of delivery. Only a gradual approach holds hope for an ultimate liquidation of the existing nuclear arsenals. A beginning can be made through a cessation of the arms race. We must put an end to the production of nuclear weapons, their supply to national armed forces and the development and manufacture of new models and types. Then a start must be made on reducing stockpiles of nuclear weapons and diverting the nuclear materials thereby released to peaceful sectors of the economy. The ultimate goal of this reduction should be the complete abolition of every type of nuclear weapon—strategic and tactical, offensive and defensive. The means of delivering nuclear weapons to the target must also be cut back along with the weapons themselves.

The participation of all states possessing nuclear weapons

is indispensable for any credible proposals to achieve nuclear disarmament. Even a single exception can jeopardize the entire effort. Any deviation from this principle would create an obvious threat to the other nuclear countries. It would be absurd to have a situation in which some nuclear powers were working towards liquidating their nuclear arsenals while others were enlarging and perfecting theirs. Nuclear disarmament must, therefore, be undertaken by all the nuclear powers. This does not, of course, mean that negotiations on this subject must be limited solely to the circle of nuclear powers. On the contrary, the non-nuclear powers should also take part in these negotiations, since nuclear disarmament is in reality a global problem the solution of which concerns everyone.

The United Nations has more than once discussed the problem of nuclear disarmament, and a number of concrete proposals on the subject have been put forward. The series of treaties already in operation—among others the Moscow Treaty on the Banning of Nuclear Weapon Tests, the Treaty on the Non-Proliferation of Nuclear Weapons and the Treaty of the Prohibition of the Emplacement of Nuclear Weapons and other Weapons of Mass Destruction on the Sea-bed and the Ocean Floor, and in the Subsoil Thereof—form a kind of prelude to practical nuclear disarmament and set a course towards increasingly decisive measures for the reduction and eventual abolition of nuclear weapons.

Conventional arms reduction

The field of nuclear disarmament, for all its overriding importance, does not eliminate the need for measures to reduce conventional weapons and armed forces as well. Here too, there are many urgent problems, such as a reduction of the national armed forces and weapons stockpiles. These and similar problems were discussed throughout the 1950s and 1960s at the United Nations, but no decisions were reached. The problem has now grown more acute in proportion to the technical improvement in the destructive power of modern conventional armaments, a fact that serves as yet another reminder of the need to adopt practical measures. The beginning of conventional arms restraint talks (CART) between the Soviet Union and the United States has so far, unfortunately, made no headway.

Foreign military presences

Both inside and outside the United Nations concrete proposals were repeatedly made for reducing military forces.
An issue which remains even today is that of closing foreign
military bases on alien territory and withdrawing foreign
troops from such territories. Experience has clearly demonstrated the importance of ensuring that powers which do
not belong to a region do not implant their armed forces
there nor set up military bases. This problem is at present
relevant to the Indian Ocean area, to take but one example.
In this connection, the Declaration of the Indian Ocean as
a Zone of Peace, adopted by the General Assembly in 1971,
is particularly important. Moreover, in 1979 in Resolution 34/80 A, the General Assembly stated that 'the continued military presence of the great Powers in the Indian
Ocean, conceived in the context of great-Power rivalry with
the danger of a competitive escalation of such a military
presence, gives greater urgency to the need to take practical
steps for the early implementation of the Declaration of the
Indian Ocean as a Zone of Peace'. It urged that talks between
the Soviet Union and the United States regarding their
military presence in the Indian Ocean be resumed without
delay, and that they should refrain from any activity prejudicial to implementation of the Declaration.

The same principle applies to the Mediterranean, where
there is an evident need for active steps towards a military
détente. Even though these goals remain unattained so far,
attempts to pursue them have increased significantly in recent
years, with negotiations on disarmament extending over a
broader range of topics. New ventures and organizational
centres working on diverse aspects of these problem have
made their appearance. Although not all of these ventures are
formally included in the United Nations system, they are
certainly very closely associated with the objectives of the
Organization. It is, therefore, necessary to touch on them,
even if only briefly.

Mutual Force Reductions (MFR)

Important in this context are the ongoing negotiations in
Vienna, since October 1973, on the reduction of armed
forces and armaments in Central Europe.[12] Eleven states are

participating directly in these negotiations: Belgium, Canada, Czechoslovakia, the German Democratic Republic, the Federal Republic of Germany, Luxembourg, the Netherlands, Poland, the Soviet Union, the United Kingdom and the United States. In addition, eight states are attending with a special status: they contribute to the discussions and distribute documents on matters under consideration, but do not participate in the taking of decisions, since they will not be parties to any agreements that may be concluded. These eight states are Bulgaria, Denmark, Greece, Hungary, Italy, Norway, Romania and Turkey.

The Vienna talks are seen as a timely step towards the achievement of military détente in Central Europe. Even before the beginning of the talks, agreement was reached at the preliminary consultations on certain principles that should form the basis of such a détente. Strict observance of these principles was recognized as being an absolute prerequisite to successful work on the reduction of armed forces and armaments in Central Europe. These principles of mutuality of reductions, equality of obligations and exclusion of unilateral military advantages involve no impairing of the security of any of the parties. It is widely recognized that these principles form a suitable basis for the attainment of significant practical results in the consolidation of security in Central Europe.

Several rounds of the Vienna talks have already taken place, although no concrete agreements have been achieved so far. These talks, nonetheless, have constantly attracted the attention of all who are interested in the strengthening of European security. There is no doubt that the Vienna talks constitute one of the key factors in the drive towards military détente in Europe and that a real diminution of the threat of war in that part of the world depends directly on their successful conclusion. The continent of Europe has suffered more than any other part of the world from the dire results of the arms race. Twice in history Europe has been turned into a 'powder keg', an experience which cost tens of millions of lives. It is now important to exclude any possibility of the renewed development of such a state of affairs. This is what makes genuine measures to strengthen European security so vital.

Implementation of the Final Act adopted at Helsinki

A major contribution to the formulation of such measures was provided by the Conference on Security and Co-operation in Europe that took place in 1975 in Helsinki. The Final Act adopted by the Conference points unequivocally to the necessity of achieving military détente on the continent of Europe. A section of the act dealing specifically with this point is headed 'Questions relating to disarmament' and reflects the interest of the participating states in 'efforts aimed at lessening military confrontation and promoting disarmament, which are designed to complement political détente in Europe'.[13]

An outstanding feature of the Final Act is the inclusion of a section containing detailed provisions regarding prior notification of major military manoeuvres. The participating states expressed their conviction of 'the political importance of prior notification of major military manoeuvres for the promotion of mutual understanding and the strengthening of confidence, stability and security'.[14] Provision is made in particular for notification, through diplomatic channels, of major military manoeuvres by land forces where the total number of men involved exceeds 25,000. It is important to point out that this clause of the Final Act has already been put into practice. During 1976, for example, the Soviet press published information on three occasions about the holding of troop manoeuvres.[15] In accordance with the provision of the Final Act, this information was sent within the prescribed time to the states that had participated in the Helsinki Conference and observers—notably from the NATO countries—attended the manoeuvres. Continuation of such practices will certainly help to create an atmosphere of greater trust in Europe and contribute towards the achievement of disarmament measures.

Elsewhere, too, efforts are being made towards furthering the Helsinki Principles. Practical proposals for implementing the Helsinki decisions have already been put forward. With a view towards easing military confrontation in Europe, for example, the Warsaw Pact countries proposed that at the end of 1976 all thirty-six states party to the Final Act should pledge themselves not to be the first to use nuclear weapons against one another; a draft treaty to this effect was worked out and made available for closer study.[16] Article I of this draft requires the signatories 'not to be the first to use nuclear weapons, one against the other, either on land, on the sea, in the air or in outer space'. It is intended that the parties should accept a common obligation to refrain from being the first to use nuclear weapons against one another in all the four environments. This obligation would be binding on four of the five existing nuclear powers—France, the Soviet Union, the United Kingdom and the United States. This would inevitably make a substantial contribution to security in Europe—and beyond.

Essentially, the draft subjects nuclear weapons to a specific kind of international prohibition, namely a ban on their first use. Its acceptance would considerably broaden the scope of existing international law, which as of now contains no provisions directly prohibiting the use of nuclear weapons. These weapons made their appearance relatively recently—some three decades ago—and no specific international agreements on their prohibition have been reached during that period. None of the existing international treaties lays down rules prohibiting the use of nuclear weapons.

There are, however, certain bilateral instruments, like the Soviet-American and Soviet-French agreements on averting nuclear war. While these make an appreciable contribution to the containment of the nuclear threat, they do not constitute universal agreements on prohibition of the use of nuclear weapons. The Agreement between the Soviet Union and the United States on the Prevention of Nuclear War was signed in 1973. In Article I of the agreement the parties declare 'that they will act in such a manner as to prevent the development of situations capable of causing a dangerous exacerbation of the relations, as to avoid military confrontations, and as to exclude the outbreak of nuclear war between them and between either of the parties and other countries'.[17] In general, the agreement enjoins the two parties to do everything possible to prevent a nuclear war. The concrete obligations deriving from it are spelt out in Article 4 of the agreement, which states that if at any time the risk of a nuclear conflict arises the parties 'shall immediately enter into urgent consultations with each other and make every effort to avert the risk',

The agreement concluded in July 1976 between France and the Soviet Union aims at preventing the accidental or unauthorized use of nuclear weapons. Under the terms of this document the parties agree to continue to carry out and improve measures to prevent accidental or unauthorized use of nuclear weapons and to notify one another of any incident that might lead to the explosion of one of their combat nuclear devices and be interpreted as potentially detrimental to the other party.[18] It is provided that all available channels of communication should be used for such a notification, including the direct line between the Kremlin and the Elysée Palace.

The General Assembly has also given considerable attention to forbidding the use of nuclear weapons. The Assembly's resolutions, however, do not have the same legal weight as international treaties, since under the Charter of the United Nations, they constitute no more than recommendations. The most significant of these, resolution 1653, was adopted by a simple majority at the sixteenth session in 1961. Called the Declaration on the Prohibition of the Use of Nuclear and Thermo-Nuclear Weapons, it declares the use of nuclear weapons to be a violation of the Charter of the United Nations and 'contrary to the rules of international law and to the laws of humanity'.[19] The Declaration also calls for a convention on the prohibition of the use of nuclear weapons, but does not in itself constitute a substitute for such a convention.

This explains the tremendous importance of the proposal made by the Warsaw Pact countries. The idea of the proposal is that all the states which signed the Final Act of the Helsinki Conference should assume a treaty obligation not to be the first to use nuclear weapons against one another. The result of such a step would be the creation of a local rule of international law prohibiting the first use of nuclear weapons. This proposal embodies the 'spirit of Helsinki' and has been proposed by Warsaw Pact countries for discussion at meetings devoted to carrying further the process begun at the European Conference.

Limiting strategic armaments

In the field of nuclear weaponry a new term has appeared in recent years covering the most dangerous and destructive forms of armaments, that is the strategic armaments. The task of finding ways of limiting these armaments now constitutes a new and extremely important aspect of the work on disarmament. It is intimately linked to the Soviet-American top-level talks that have become a regular occurrence over the past few years and that constitute a striking illustration of the way in which an atmosphere of détente is gradually developing. Discussion at the bilateral Soviet-American Strategic Arms Limitation Talks (SALT) is determined by the fact that the Soviet Union and the United States, as states possessing the greatest military potential, are in duty bound to make a special contribution to the work of limiting the arms race. These talks can exert a direct influence on the accomplishment of a vital mission—that of sparing the world the possibility of a nuclear-missile war. The process of limiting strategic armaments was begun in 1972. As a result of the Soviet-American top-level talks, two agreements were worked out, opening the way to limitation of the production and development of the most dangerous and expensive forms of modern weapons.[20] The first of these is a treaty of unlimited duration between the Soviet Union and the United States on the limitation by the contracting parties of their anti-ballistic missile systems on the principle of equal security (SALT-ABM Treaty). Under this treaty the two parties undertook to restrict their anti-ballistic-missile systems to two areas. The second, signed in 1972, is an Interim Agreement between the Soviet Union and the United States on specific measures concerning the limitation of strategic offensive arms and provides that during the period of its operation (the agreement having been concluded for a period of five years), the parties shall not augment the number of their land-based missiles (SALT I). Limitations are also placed on the number of submarines equipped with ballistic missiles and on the total number of ballistic missile launchers installed on nuclear-powered submarines.

Subsequent work on the limitation of strategic armaments has produced a number of new and worthwhile results. During the Soviet-American talks in Moscow in 1974, agreement was reached on a more substantial limitation of anti-ballistic-missile systems than that achieved by the 1972 Soviet-American talks: a protocol to the 1972 treaty was signed limiting the deployment of anti-ballistic-missile systems to one area (instead of the two areas permitted to each side under the earlier agreements).[21] In other words, the extent to which such systems could be deployed was reduced by half.

In 1974 a Soviet-American Treaty on the Limitation of Underground Nuclear-Weapon Tests[22] was signed. This treaty totally bans underground testing of nuclear weapons exceeding a specified yield (150 kilotons) and limits the number of other underground nuclear weapon tests to a minimum. Article III of the Soviet-American treaty provided that it would come into force only after the conclusion of a complementary treaty concerning underground nuclear explosions for peaceful purposes. This complementary treaty was signed in 1976[23] and opened the way for both instruments to come into force after ratification.

In recent years, Soviet-American negotiations have concentrated on the problem of limiting strategic offensive arms. As the 1972 Interim Agreement expired in October 1977, proposals were made to replace it by a long-term treaty. Basic guidelines for such a treaty were agreed during the Soviet-American meeting in Vladivostok at the end of 1974. Both parties to the Joint American-Soviet Statement of Vladivostok decided that a new agreement would be worked out incorporating the relevant provisions of the 1972 Interim Agreement and covering the period from October 1977 to 31 December 1985. The agreement will include a provision for further negotiations beginning no later than 1980–81 on the question of further limitations and possible reductions of strategic arms after 1985. The Soviet-American Treaty on the Limitation of Strategic Offensive Arms (SALT II) and Protocol, as well as several other documents, were signed in Vienna on 18 June 1979. The treaty is to remain in force until 31 December 1985. In its resolution 34/87 F, the General Assembly stated that the treaty constituted 'a vital element for the continuation and progress of the negotiations between the two states possessing the most important arsenals of nuclear weapons'. The Assembly also expressed its trust that the treaty will enter into force at an early date, and that the SALT III negotiations will begin promptly thereafter.

The Soviet-American negotiations on the strategic-arms limitation, after a relatively short time, deserve to be regarded as one of the major forums for the solution of urgent disarmament problems.

With so many forums discussing disarmament, much is being attempted and achieved. This does not mean that the problems of disarmament can be easily solved. On the contrary, they are still to be counted among those problems requiring the greatest effort and perseverance. This is to some extent understandable, because decisions on disarmament are linked to the vital security interests of states and, in fact, to their very survival. But one of the characteristic features of modern life is that difficulties in the resolving of such problems are now being overcome with increasing regularity. The series of treaties on disarmament that have made their appearance in recent years is by no means accidental. It reflects the shift that has taken place on the international scene towards refusal to continue the ruinous arms race and a growing awareness of the urgent need for practical steps to put an end to it.

In recent years the shape of international events has been increasingly moulded by the spirit of détente. The need to supplement political détente with military détente has now become axiomatic. It is very widely recognized that the time has come to halt and reverse the stockpiling of means of annihilation, which has grown to colossal proportions. National governments, international organizations and world public opinion can and must play their part in accomplishing this task. The number of unresolved problems in the field of disarmament is still very large. Widespread and co-ordinated efforts are needed to ensure increasing momentum in this sphere. This is the urgent summons of our time, which the United Nations, in its role as the international organization primarily responsible for world peace, must answer with all the influence it commands. It can do this by strengthening its own commitment to disarmament and by promoting an international climate in which agreements reached outside the United Nations framework, as in the MFR and SALT negotiations, become meaningful.

Notes

1. A report on the economic and social consequences of disarmament, prepared by eminent specialists from all over the world, asserted, for example, 'There should thus be no doubt that the diversion to peaceful purposes of the resources now in military use could be accomplished to the benefit of all countries and lead to the improvement of world economic and social conditions', *Economic and Social Consequences of Disarmament*, p. 52, New York, 1962.
2. Another study prepared by the United Nations in 1971 made the point that 'the cost of the arms race is enormous and because of it resources have been denied almost every other field of social activity'. *Economic and Social Consequences of the Arms Race and of Military Expenditures*, p. 36, New York, 1972. Pursuant to General Assembly

resolution 3462 (XXX) of 11 December 1975, this study was updated and re-issued in 1978.

3. N. Bentwich and A. Martin, *A Commentary on the Charter of the United Nations*, p. 64, London, 1951.
4. A French dictionary of international law terminology, for instance, gives the following definition for the term 'disarmament': 'A term which in its true sense signifies the abolition by one or more states of their armed forces, military materials and installations, and retention of only their police forces. In negotiations on the subject the term is frequently used to include the reduction and limitation of armaments'. *Dictionnaire de la terminologie du droit international*, p. 207, Paris, 1960.
5. L. Goodrich, *The United Nations*, p. 219, New York, 1959.
6. L. Oppenheim, *International Law*, Vol. II, p. 127, London, 1952.
7. For further details of the organization of disarmament talks, see the collection entitled *The United Nations and Disarmament, 1945–70*, New York, 1970.
8. Resolution 2833 (XXVI) adopted on 16 December 1971; see also *Disarmament: Progress towards Peace*, p. 53, New York, 1974.
9. See Unesco resolutions 19 C/13.I and 20 C/II.I. For further details see Y. Kashlev and L. Kutanov, 'Results of the Nineteenth Session of the General Conference of Unesco', *Mezdunarodnaja zizn*, No. 2, pp. 94–102, 1977, and Unesco documents 20 C/16 and 21 C/14.
10. For the text of this and other treaties, see *The United Nations and Disarmament: 1945–70*, op. cit.
11. *Effects of the Possible Use of Nuclear Weapons and the Security and Economic Implications for States of the Acquisition and Further Development of these Weapons*, New York, 1968, p. 1.
12. For fuller details of these talks, see O. Khlestov, 'The Vienna Negotiations: Problems and Prospects', *Mirovaja ekonomika i mezdunarodnye otnosenija*, No. 6, pp. 42–51, 1974.
13. *In the Name of Peace, Security and Cooperation: Results of the Conference on Security and Co-operation in Europe held at Helsinki from 30 July to 1 August 1975*, p. 31, Moscow, 1975.
14. Ibid., p. 27.
15. See *Izvestia*, 26 January, 24 May and 17 September 1976.
16. For the text of the draft treaty, see *Meeting of the Political Consultative Committee of the States participating in the Warsaw Treaty* (Bucarest, 25–26 November 1976), pp. 26–7, Moscow, 1976.
17. For the text of this agreement, see *List of Treaties, Agreements and Conventions in Force, Concluded between the USSR and Foreign States*, Part XXIX, pp. 27–8, Moscow, 1975.
18. *Soviet-French Relations, 1965–76. Documents and related papers*, pp. 244–6, Moscow, 1976.
19. *Resolutions Adopted by the General Assembly at its XVIth Session*, Vol. I, p. 5, New York, 1962.
20. The texts of the documents drawn up at the Soviet-American meeting are reproduced in *List of Treaties Agreements and Conventions in Force, Concluded between the USSR and Foreign States*, Part XXVIII, pp. 31–8, Moscow, 1974.
21. *Documents and Materials Relating to the Third Soviet-American Summit Meeting (27 June–3 July 1974)*, pp. 55–6, Moscow, 1974.
22. Ibid., pp. 57–9.
23. *Izvestia*, 29 May 1976.

Bibliography

Assistant Librarian, Institute for Defence Studies and Analysis, New Delhi

Uma Chopra

UNESCO PUBLICATIONS

ALBRECHT, U.; ERNST, D.; LOCK, P.; WULF, H. Arming the Developing Countries. *International Social Science Journal*, Vol. XXVIII, No. 2, 1976, pp. 326–40.

AWOKOYA, S. O. The Failure to Disarm: Main Obstacle to Development? *Impact of Science on Society*, Vol. XXV, No. 1, 1975, pp. 25–35.

BARNABY, F. The Dynamics of World Armaments: an Overview. *International Social Science Journal*, Vol. XXVIII, No. 2, 1976, pp. 245–65.

BÖNISCH, A. Disarmament, Peace Research and the Policy of Peaceful Coexistence. *International Social Science Journal*, Vol. XXVIII, No. 2, 1976, pp. 268–75.

DIAZ, J. Disarmament Education and Social Justice: Arms are the Symptom of a Deep-seated Ill Which must be Tackled at the Roots. *The Unesco Courier*, Vol. XXXIII, No. 8, 1980, pp. 14–15.

EIDE, A. The Transfer of Arms to Third World Countries and their Internal Use. *International Social Science Journal*, Vol. XXVIII, No. 2, 1976, pp. 307–25.

EKLUND, S. Disarmament and International Control. *Impact of Science on Society*, Vol. XXII, No. 3, 1972, pp. 263–77.

Expert Meeting for the Preparation of the World Congress on Disarmament Education, Prague, 1979. *Final Report*. 15 June 1979.

GAMBRELL, L. Teaching Disarmament at Universities: a World Survey. *The Unesco Courier*, Vol. XXXIII, No. 8, 1980, pp. 30–1.

International Scientific Symposium on Research and Teaching on Disarmament in Various Disciplines of Higher Education, Vienna, 1980. *Final Report*. 1 April 1980.

KASTLER, A. Suicide or Survival? The Challenge of the Century. *Cultures*, Vol. III, No. 4, 1976, pp. 31–5.

LEITENBERG, M. Social Responsibility II: the Classical Scientific Ethic and Strategic-Weapons Development. *Impact of Science on Society*, Vol. XXI, No. 2, 1971, pp. 123–36.

M'BOW, A.-M. Address at the Special Session of the United Nations General Assembly on Disarmament, May 1978.

MYRDAL, A. The Game of Disarmament. *Impact of Science on Society*, Vol. XXII, No. 3, 1972, pp. 217–33.

NE'EMAN, Y. Coherence, Abstraction and Personal Involvement: Albert Einstein, Physicist and Humanist. *Impact of Science on Society*, Vol. XXIX, No. 1, 1979, pp. 17–25.

NOEL-BAKER, P. Science and Disarmament. *Impact of Science on Society*, Vol. XV, No. 4, 1965, pp. 211–46.

——. The Super-nuclear Arms Monster. In: *Suicide or Survival? The Challenge of the Year 2000*, 1978, pp. 75–80.

PRICE, C. C. Weapons of Mass Destruction and Public Policy. *Impact of Science on Society*, Vol. XXVI, No. 1/2, 1976, pp. 17–24.

PRIMAKOV, E. M. The Outlook on Disarmament. *International Social Science Journal*, Vol. XXVIII, No. 2, 1976, pp. 276–87.

RANA, S. Education for Disarmament—Freedom from Fear is a Fundamental Human Right. *The Unesco Courier*, October 1978, pp. 12–13.

REARDON, B. Disarmament and Peace Education. *Prospects*, Vol. VIII, No. 4, 1978, pp. 395–405.

Review of Research Trends and an Annotated Bibliography: Social and Economic Consequences of the Arms Race and of Disarmament. 1978. 44 pp. (Reports and Papers in the Social Sciences, 39.)

ROLING, B. International Law and the Right to Possess Arms. *The Unesco Courier*, Vol. XXXIII, No. 8, 1980, pp. 20–4.

STARES, J. The Strategic Nuclear Arms Race. *Impact of Science on Society*, Vol. XXVI, No. 1/2, 1976, pp. 27–38.

SUBRAHMANYAM, K. Can Nuclear Arms Proliferation Contribute to World Security? *Impact of Science on Society*, July–September 1972, pp. 243–52.

Ten Principles for Disarmament Education. *The Unesco Courier*, Vol. XXXIII, No. 8, 1980, pp. 18–19. (Taken from the Report and Final Document of the World Congress on Disarmament Education, Paris, June 1980.)

THEE, M. (ed.). *Armaments, Arms Control and Disarmament: A Unesco Reader for Disarmament Education*. (In press.)

——. The Dynamics of the Arms Race, Military R&D and Disarmament. *International Social Science Journal*, Vol. XXX, No. 4, 1978, pp. 904–25.

——. International Arms Control and Disarmament Agreements: Promise, Fact and Vision. *International Social Science Journal*, Vol. XXVIII, No. 2, 1976, pp. 359–74.

TORNEY, J. V.; GAMBRELL, L. Education, Disarmament and Human Rights. *The Unesco Courier*, Vol. XXXIII, No. 8, 1980, pp. 5–9.

UNESCO GENERAL CONFERENCE. Nineteenth session, Nairobi, 1976. Role of Unesco in Generating a Climate of Public Opinion Conducive to the Halting of the Arms Race, the Reduction of Accumulated Weapon Stocks, the Systematic Diminution of Military Expenditure and the Transition to Disarmament. 7 pp. (Paper containing the covering letter and the draft resolution proposed by the Union of Soviet Socialist Republics; includes observations of the Director-General.)

——. Twentieth session, Paris, 1978. Role of Unesco in Generating a Climate of Public Opinion Conducive to the Halting of the Arms Race and the Transition to Disarmament. 21 pp. (Paper setting out the measures taken by the Secretariat to implement the programme of 1977–78 with the special importance of the problem of disarmament in mind.)

——. Twenty-first session, Belgrade, 1980. Role of Unesco in Generating a Climate of Public Opinion Conducive to the Halting of the Arms Race and the Transition to Disarmament. 22 pp. (Paper submitting information on the measures taken.)

WALDHEIM-NATURAL, L. World Opinion: the Weapon to End All Weapons. *The Unesco Courier*, Vol. XXXIII, No. 8, 1980, pp. 10–13.

OTHER PUBLICATIONS*

Books

ALFORD, Jonathan. *Future of Arms Control*. Pt. III: *Confidence Building Measures*. London, IISS, 1979. (Adelphi Paper No. 149.)

ALLEN, Thomas J. *Managing the Flow of Technology: Technology Transfer and the Dissemination of Technological Information with the R&D Organization*. Cambridge, Mass., MIT Press, 1978.

BARKER, Charles A. (ed.). *Problems of World Disarmament*. Boston, Mass., Houghton Mifflin, 1963.

BATSANOV, Boris; IVANOV, Vladimir. *Disarmament—Mankind's Future*. Moscow, Novosti Press Agency, 1968.

BECKER, Abraham S. *Military Expenditure Limitation for Arms Control: Problems and Prospects*, Cambridge, Mass., Ballinger Pub. Co., 1977.

BELL, M. J. V. *Military Assistance to Independent African States*. London, IISS, 1964. (Adelphi Paper No. 15.)

BENOIT, Emile (ed.). *Disarmament and World Economic Interdependence*. New York, Columbia University Press, 1967.

——. The Economic Impact of Disarmament in the United States. In: Seymour Melman (ed.), *Disarmament: Its Politics and Economics*, pp. 134–57. Boston, American Academy of Arts and Science, 1962.

BERKOWITZ, Martin. *Conversion of Military-oriented Research and Development to Civilian Uses*. New York, Praeger, 1970.

BERTRAM, Christoph. *Future of Arms Control*. Part I: *Beyond SALT II*. London, IISS, 1977. (Adelphi Paper No. 141.)

——. *Future of Arms Control*. Part II: *Arms Control and Technical Change-elements of a New Approach*. London, IISS, 1978. (Adelphi Paper No. 146.)

BHARGAVA, Mahesh Kumar. *Disarmament from Versailles to Test Ban Treaty*. New Delhi, National Publishing House, 1979. (Special Problems of the Future, pp. 165–89.)

BIDDLE, W. F. *Weapons Technology and Arms Control*. New York, Praeger, 1972.

BOSTON, J. H.; WEILBER, L. D. (eds.). *International Arms Control: Issues and Agreements*. Stanford, Calif., Stanford Arms Control Group, 1976.

BOULDING, Kenneth E. Economic Implications of Arms Control. In: Donald G. Brennan (ed.), *Arms Control, Disarmament and National Security*, New York, Braziller, 1961.

CAHN, Anne Hessiog, *Controlling Future Arms Trade*, New York, McGraw Hill Book Co., 1978.

CLARK, Grenville, et al. (eds.). *World Disarmament and World Development Organization*. Cambridge, Mass., Harvard University, 1965.

COFFEY, Joseph I. (ed.). *Arms Control and European Security: A Guide to East-West Negotiations*. New York, Praeger, 1977.

——. *New Approaches to Arms Reductions in Europe*. London, IISS, 1974. (Adelphi Paper No. 105.)

COFFEY, Joseph I.; LAULICHT, Jerome. *The Implications for Arms Control of Perceptions of Strategic Weapons Systems*. 6 Vols. Washington, D.C., ACDA, November 1971. (ACDA Report E-163.)

COX, Donald W. *America's New Policy Makers: The Scientists' Rise to Power*. Philadelphia, Chilton, 1964.

DOUGHERTY, James E. *Arms Control and Disarmament: The Critical Issues*. Washington, D.C., Centre for Strategic Studies, 1966.

——. *How to Think About Arms Control and Disarmament*. New York, Crane, Russak & Co., 1973.

* This section is necessarily selective as regards the origin of the references. For more complete bibliographical information covering numerous languages and countries of publication, the reader's attention is drawn to the offprints of the chapter on 'Disarmament, Peace and Security' of the Monthly Bibliography (Part II) prepared by the United Nations Library in Geneva in collaboration with the Research Collection of the Geneva Unit of the United Nations Centre for Disarmament. Requests for that bibliography may be addressed to the Geneva Unit, Centre for Disarmament, Palais des Nations, Geneva, Switzerland.

DOUGHERTY, James E.; LEHMAN, John F. (eds.). *Prospects for Arms Control*. New York, MacFadden-Bartell, 1965.

DRUCKMAN, D. *Human Factors in International Negotiations*. Beverly Hills, Calif., Sage Publications, 1973.

DUPRE, J. S.; LAKOFF, S. A. *Arms and the Scientists. Science and the Nation: Policy and Politics*, Englewood Cliffs, N.J., Prentice Hall, 1962.

Dynamics of the Bargaining Process in a Bureaucratic Age. (Symposium discussion.) In: William R. Kintner and Robert L. Pfaltzgraff (eds.), *SALT: Implications for Arms Control in the 1970's*, pp. 187–96. Pittsburgh, Pittsburgh University Press, 1973.

EDWARDS, David V. *Arms Control in International Politics*. New York, Holt, Rinehart and Winston, 1969.

ERICKSON, John (eds.). *The Military Technical Revolution*. New York, Praeger, 1966.

FARAMAZYAN, R. A. *Disarmament and Economy*. Moscow, Mysl Publishers, 1978.

FELD, Bernard T. et al. (eds.). *Impact of New Technologies on the Arms Race*. Cambridge, Mass., MIT Press, 1971.

FISHER, Roger D. Constructing Rules that Affect Governments. In: Donald G. Brenman (ed.), *Arms Control, Disarmament, and National Security*, pp. 56–7, New York, Braziller, 1961.

FRANK, Jerome D. Psychological Aspects of the Disarmament Problem. In: Charles A. Barker (ed.), *Problems of World Disarmament*, pp. 82–97. Boston, Mass., Houghton Mifflin, 1963.

——. *Sanity and Survival: Psychiatric Aspects of War and Peace*. New York, Random House, 1967.

FRANK, Lewis A. *Arms Trade in International Relations*. New York, Praeger, 1969.

GARRIS, Jerome; WISEBERG, Laurie. *Security Studies Project*. Vol. 7: *Trends in International Polarity: Implications for Arms Control*. Los Angeles, University of California, Arms Control Special Studies Program, 1968. (ACDA Report WEC-126.)

GHATATE, Narayan M. *Disarmament in India's Foreign Policy, 1947–65*. Ph.D. thesis at the American University, Washington, D.C., 1966.

HALLE, Louis J. *Question of Commitments*. Santa Monica, Calif., Arms Control and Foreign Policy Seminar, 1973.

HARNAM, Singh (ed.). *Studies in World Order*. Delhi, Kitab Mahal, 1972.

HOAGLAND, John H. *World Combat Aircraft Inventories and Production 1970–75. Implications for Arms Transfer Policies*. Cambridge, Mass., MIT Press, 1970.

HOOVER INSTITUTION ON WAR, REVOLUTION AND PEACE. *Arms Control Arrangements for the Far East*. Stanford, Calif., Stanford University Press, 1967.

IKLE, Doris M. *How Arms Controls Would Affect the National Security Budget*. Santa Monica, Calif., Rand, 1961.

INDIAN COUNCIL OF WORLD AFFAIRS et al. *Seminar on American Arms to Pakistan and the Implications for India's Security*. New Delhi, Sapru House, 1970.

INTERNATIONAL WORKSHOP ON DISARMAMENT. *Disarmament Development and a Just World Order*. Delhi, Centre for the Study of Developing Societies, 1978.

JAIN, J. P. *India and Disarmament*. Vol. 1: *Nehru Era—an Analytical Study*. New Delhi, Radiant Publishers, 1974.

——. *Nuclear India*, 2 Vols. New Delhi, Radiant Publishers, 1974.

JOLLY, Richard (ed.). *Disarmament and World Development*. Oxford, Pergamon Press, 1978.

KALYADIN, Alexander; KADE, Gerhard (eds.). *Détente and Disarmament: Problems and Prospectives*, Vienna, Gazzetta Pub. House, 1976. (International Institute for Peace.)

KAPUR, R. K. *Post-War Disarmament Negotiations: A Study of the Narrowing of Differences Between the East and the West*. Ph.D. thesis at New York University, 1966.

KAUSHIK, Devendra; KHAN, M. A. S. *U.S. Arms for Pakistan: an Exercise in Tension Building*. Moscow, Novosti Press Agency, 1970.

KEMP, Geoffrey. *Classification of Weapons Systems and Force Designs in Less Developed Country Environments: Implications for Arms Transfer Policies*. Cambridge, Mass., MIT Press, 1970.

——. *Some Relationships Between U.S. Military Training in Latin America and Weapons Acquisition Patterns: 1959-69*. Cambridge, Mass., MIT Press, 1970.

KLEIN, Peter; ENGELHARDT, Klous. *Disarmament—World Problem No. 1*. Berlin, GDR National Institute for International Politics and Economy, 1979.

KNORR, Klaus E.; MORGENSTERN, Oskar. *Science and Defense: Some Critical Thoughts on Military Research and Development*. Princeton, N.J., Princeton University Press, 1965.

LAPP, Ralph E. *Arms Beyond Doubt: The Tyranny of Weapons Technology*. New York, Cowles, 1970.

LEISS, Amelia C. *Changing Patterns of Arms Transfers: Implications for Arms Transfer Policies*, Cambridge, Mass., MIT Press, 1970.

LEISS, Amelia C. et al. *Arms Control and Local Conflict*. Vol. 3: *Arms Transfers to Less Developed Countries*. Cambridge, Mass., MIT Press, 1970.

LEVINE, Robert A. General Disarmament as a Policy Goal: Economic Aspects. In: Dougherty and Lehman, op. cit., pp. 163–70.

MACQUEEN, James B. *Security Studies Project*. Vol. 8: *A Statistical Analysis of Some International Confrontations: Implications for Arms Control*. Los Angeles, University of California, Arms Control Special Studies Program, 1968. (ACDA Report WEC-12.)

MAHMOUD, Abdel-Aziz. *Nuclear Proliferation and National Security*. New Delhi, Lancers Publishers, 1978.

MARTIN, Anthony D. *Negotiation Strategies for Arms Control: Some Alternatives for the Next Decade and Beyond*. Santa Monica, Calif., Arms Control and Foreign Policy Seminar, 1972.

MEERLO, Joost. A. M. *That Difficult Peace*. New York, Channel Press, 1961.

MELMAN, Seymour (ed.). *The Defense Economy: Conversion of Industries and Occupations to Civilian Needs*. New York, Praeger, 1970.

MYRDAL, Alva. *Game of Disarmament: How the United States and Russia Run the Arms Race*. New York, Pantheon Books, 1976.

NEAL, Fred Warner. *Disarmament and the Communist Threat*. Philadelphia, American Friends Service Committee, 1962.

NIEZING, Johan. *Sociology, War and Disarmament: Studies in Peace Research*. Rotterdam, Rotterdam University Press, 1970.

PEAR, T. H. (ed.). *Psychological Factors of Peace and War*. New York, Philosophical Library, 1950.

RAYMOND, Richard C. Problems of Industrial Conversion. In: Seymour Melman (ed.), *Disarmament: Its Politics and Economics*, pp. 158–76, Boston, American Academy of Arts and Sciences, 1962.

REFSON, Jacob S. *U.S. Military Training and Advice: Implications for arms Transfer Policies*, Cambridge, Mass., MIT Press, 1970.

RESEARCH BOARD (ed.). *United Nations and Disarmament*, Delhi, Research, 1972.

RIVKIN, Steven R. *Technology Unbound: Transfering Scientific and Engineering Resources from Defence to Civilian Purposes*. Elmsford, N.Y., Pergamon, 1969.

RUSSETT, Bruce M. *What Price Vigilance? The Burdens of National Defense*. New Haven, Conn., Yale University Press, 1970.

SAMPSON, Anthony. *Arms Bazaar*. London, Hodder & Stoughton, 1977.

SARIN, H. C. *Defence and Development*. New Delhi, United Service Institution of India, 1979. (USI National Security Lectures.)

SAWYER, Jack; GUETZKOW, Harold. Bargaining and Negotiating in International Relations. In: Herbert C. Kelman (ed.), *International Behaviour: A Social-Psychological Analysis*. New York, Holt, Rinehart & Winston, 1965.

SCHELLING, Thomas C. Reciprocal Measures for Arms Stabilization. In: Donald G. Brenman (ed.), *Arms Control, Disarmament, and National Security*, pp. 167–86. New York, Braziller, 1961.

SEED, Philip. *The Psychological Problem of Disarmament*. London, Hovsmans, 1966.

SIPRI. *Arms Trade Register: The Arms Trade with the Third World*. London, MIT Press, 1975.

——. *Arms Trade with the Third World*. Stockholm, SIPRI, 1971.

SIVARD, Ruth Leger. *World Military and Social Expenditures, 1974*. New York, Institute for World Order, 1974.

STANLEY, John; PEARTON, Maurice. *International Trade in Arms*. London, Chatto & Windus, 1972.

STONE, Jeremy J. *Strategic Presuasion: Arms Limitations Through Dialogue*. New York, Columbia University Press, 1967.

SUBRAHMANYAM, K. *Defence and Development*. Calcutta, Minerva Associates, 1973.

SUTTON, John; KEMP, Geoffrey. *Arms to Developing Countries, 1945– 1965*. London, IISS, 1966. (Adelphi Paper No. 28.)

Technological Change and the Strategic Arms Race. (Symposium discussion.) In: William R. Kintner and Robert L. Pfaltzgraff (eds.), *SALT: Implications for Arms Control in the 1970's*, pp. 107–24, Pittsburgh, Pittsburgh University Press, 1973.

THAYER, George. *War Business: The International Trade in Armaments*. London, Weidenfeld & Nicolson, 1969.

ULLMANN, John E. (ed.). *Political Civilian Markets for the Military-Electronics Industry: Strategies for Conversion*. New York, Praeger, 1970.

UNITED NATIONS, *Basic Problems of Disarmament: Reports of the Secretary-General*. New York, United Nations, 1970.

——. *United Nations and Disarmament 1945–65*. New York, United Nations, 1967.

——. *United Nations and Disarmament 1970–75*. New York, United Nations, 1976.

UNITED STATES. *Analysis of Export Control of U.S. Technology—A DOD Perspective: A Report of the Defense Science Board Task Force on Export of U.S. Technology*. Washington, D.C., Director of Defense, Research and Engineering, 1976.

U.S. ARMS CONTROL AND DISARMAMENT AGENCY. *Implications of Future Weapons Technology on Arms Control and Disarmament*. New York, Hudson Institute, 1965. (ACDA Report ST-51.)

—— *The Potential Transfer of Industrial Skills from Defense to non-defense Industries*, 2 Vols. State of California, Department of Labor, June 1968. (ACDA Report E-102.)

——. *World Military Expenditures and Arms Transfers, 1966–1975.* Washington, D.C., U.S. Arms Control and Disarmament Agency, 1976.

U.S. SENATE. Committee on Foreign Relations. *Developments in Military Technology and their Impact on United States Strategy and Foreign Policy.* Staff Study No. 8. Washington, D.C., G.P.O., 1959.

——. Committee on International Relations. *Hearings: Psychological Aspects of International Relations.* 89th Cong., 2nd Sess., 1966.

VON BREDOW, Wilfried (ed.). *Disarmament Forum: Economic and Social Aspects of Disarmament—Contributions from East and West Europe.* Oslo, Norway, BPP Pubs., 1973.

WAELDER, Robert. *Psychological Aspects of War and Peace.* Geneva Research Centre, 1939.

WEIDENBAUM, Murray L. The Transferability of Defense Industry Resources to Civilian Use. In: Roger E. Bolton (ed.), *Defense and Disarmament*, pp. 101–13. Englewood Cliffs, N.J., Prentice-Hall, 1966.

ZUCKERMAN, Solly. *Scientists and War: The Impact of Science on Military and Civil Affairs.* New York, Harper & Row, 1967.

Articles

ABARENKOV, V. Disarmament Towards Lasting Peace—Opponents of Disarmament and Detente. *International Affairs* (Moscow), Vol. 4, 1979, pp. 80–8.

AGNEW, Harold M. Technological Innovation: A Necessary Deterrent of Provocation? *Air Force and Space Digest*, Vol. 50, No. 5, May 1967, pp. 66–70.

ALCOCK, Norman. U.N. Special Session on Disarmament. *Peace Research*, Vol. 10, No. 4, October 1978, pp. 135–40.

ALLISON, Graham T.; MORRIS, Frederic A. Armaments and Arms Control: Exploring the Determinants of Military Weapons. *Daedalus*, Vol. 104, No. 3, Summer 1975, pp. 99–129.

ANDERSON, Richard M. Anguish in the Defense Industry. *Harvard Business Review*, Vol. 47, November-December 1969, pp. 162 et seq.

Arms Control and Human Rights. Report of a Seminar. *RUSI Journal*, Vol. 123, No. 2, June 1978, pp. 3–10.

ART, Robert J. Restructuring the Military-industrial Complex: Arms Control in International Perspective. *Public Policy*, Vol. 22, Fall 1974, pp. 423–59.

BANDYOPADHYAYA Jayantanuja. Disarmament and Development: Structural Linkages. *Alternatives*, Vol. 4, No. 1, July 1978, pp. 11–34.

BASOV, Nikolai. The Scientists' Social Responsibility. *New Times* (Moscow), Vol. 42, October 1976, pp. 26–7.

BERI, H. M. L. Arms Control: Prospects and Problems. *Democratic World*, Vol. 8, No. 29, 22 July 1979, pp. 7–8.

BLOOMFIELD, Lincoln P.; LEISS, Amelia C. Arms Control and the Developing Countries. *World Politics*, Vol. 17, No. 1, October 1965, pp. 1–20.

BLUESTONE, Irving. Problems of the Worker in Industrial Conversion. *Journal of Arms Control*, Vol. 1, No. 3, 1963, pp. 589–96.

BONHAM, G. Mathew. Simulating International Disarmament Negotiations. *Journal of Conflict Resolution*, Vol. 15, No. 3, 1977, pp. 299–315.

BORAWSKI, John. Mutual Force Reduction in Europe from a Soviet Perspective. *Orbis*, Vol. 22, No. 4, Winter 1979, pp. 845–73.

BORISOV, K. Disarmament—Towards Lasting Peace: Today's Key Problem. *International Affairs* (Moscow), November 1979, pp. 83–91.

BRODIE, Bernard. Military Demonstration and Disclosure of New Weapons. *World Politics*, Vol. 5, No. 9, January 1953, pp. 281–301.

BROWN, Harold. Arms Control: A Balanced and Effective Defense. *U.S. Department of State Bulletin*, Vol. 78 (2020), November 1978, pp. 14–17.

BULL, Hedley. Disarmament and the International System. *Australian Journal of Politics and History*, Vol. 5, No. 2, 1959, pp. 41–50.

BURHOP, E. H. S. Scientists and Soliders. *Bulletin of the Atomic Scientists*, Vol. 30, No. 11, November 1974, pp. 4–8.

BURHOP, E. H. S. The Social Responsibility of the Scientists, *Scientific World*, Vol. 18, Spring 1974, pp. 20–3.

CAMBERN, John R. Skill Transfers: Can Defense Workers adapt to Civilian Occupations? *Monthly Labour Review*, Vol. 92, No. 6, June 1969, pp. 21–5.

CANBY, Steven L. Mutual Force Reductions: A Military Perspective. *International Security*, Vol. 2, No. 3, Winter 1978, pp. 122–35.

CHARI, P. R. Disarmament and Conventional Arms. *Peace and Solidarity*, Vol. 9, No. 9, September 1978, pp. 31–5.

——. International Trade in Arms. *Foreign News and Features*, Vol. 9, No. 24, 17 June 1978, pp. 5–6.

——. U.N. Special Session on Disarmament. *Strategic Analysis*, Vol. 2, No. 5, August 1978, pp. 187–91.

CHENEY, John, et al. The Effects of Communicating Threats and Promises upon the Bargaining Process. *Journal of Conflict Resolution*, Vol. 19, No. 2, 1972, pp. 99–107.

CHITIKOV, Alexei. Problems of Disarmament—World on Threshold of 1980's: Deploying U.S. Missiles on Western Europe would Endanger and Threaten Peace. *New Perspectives*, Vol. 10, No. 1, 1980, pp. 5–7.

CHOPRA, Maharaj K. Arms and Stability in the Indian Subcontinent. *Military Review*, Vol. 55 (ii), November 1975, pp. 66–76.

CIVIC, Milutin. International Security and Nuclear Weapons, UN Study on Nuclear Weapons. Pt I, *Review of International Affairs*, Vol. 30, No. 707, 20 September 1979, pp. 83–6; Pt II, op. cit., No. 708, 5 October 1979, pp. 9–12.

CLARK, Joseph S. Congress and Disarmament. *Bulletin of the Atomic Scientists*, Vol. 19, No. 7, September 1963, pp. 3–7.

CORY, Robert H. Images of the United States Disarmament Policy in the International Disarmament Negotiating System. *Journal of Conflict Resolution*, Vol. 7, No. 3, 1963, pp. 560–8.

CRITCHLEY, Julian. Community Policy for Armaments. *NATO Review*, Vol. 27, No. 1, February 1979, pp. 10–14.

DAVID, Robert N. The International Influence Process: How Relevant is the Contribution of Psychologists? *American Psychologist*, Vol. 21, No. 3, March 1966, pp. 236–43.

DEUTSCH, Karl W. The Impact of Science and Technology on International Politics, *Daedalus*, Vol. 88, No. 4, February 1959, pp. 669–85.

DOBROSIELSKI, M. Problems of Disarmament. Stopping the Arms Race: Prerequisite to Preventing Nuclear Holocaust. *Soviet Review*, Vol. 15, No. 26, 5 June 1978, pp. 42–6.

DORONINA, N.; NIKOLAYEV, D. Disarmament: A Solution in Sight? *International Affairs*, November 1978, pp. 50–8.

DOTY, Paul. The Community of Science and the Search for Peace. *Science*, Vol. 173, 10 September 1971, pp. 998–1002.

DUBOFF, Richard B. Converting Military Spending to Social Welfare: The Real Obstacles. *Quarterly Review of Economics and Business*, Vol. 12, Spring 1972, pp. 7–22.

DUNN, Frederick S. Peace Strategies in an Unstable World. *Yale Review*, Vol. 37, Winter 1948, pp. 226–40.

ECKHARDT, William. Psychology of War and Peace. *Journal of Human Relations*, Vol. 16, No. 2, 1968, pp. 239–49.

EPSTEIN, William. Banning the Use of Nuclear Weapons. *Bulletin of the Atomic Scientists*, Vol. 35, No. 4, April 1979, pp. 7–9.

——. U.N. Special Session on Disarmament: How Much Progress? *Survival*, Vol. 20, No. 6, November-December 1978, pp. 248–54.

Europe after the Conference for Security and Cooperation in Europe. Regional and Global Problems of Security and Disarmament. *Peace and the Sciences*, October 1976, pp. 1–114.

FAIRBAIRNS, Zoe. War Research at British Universities. *New Scientist*, Vol. 63, No. 909, August 1974, pp. 312–15.

FALK, Richard A. Arms Control, Foreign Policy and Global Reform, *Daedalus*, Vol. 104, No. 3, Summer 1975, pp. 35–52.

——. Nuclear Policy and World Order: Why Denuclearization? *Alternatives*, Vol. 3, No. 3, March 1978, pp. 321–50.

FEINGLASS, Abe. Problems of Disarmament—Increased Military Spending in U.S.A. Must Stop. *New Perspectives*, Vol. 9, No. 5, 1979, p. 5.

FELD, Bernard T. Scientists' Role in Arms Control. *Bulletin of the Atomic Scientists*, Vol. 26, No. 1, January 1970, pp. 7–8, 47–8.

FRANK, Jerome D. Emotional and Motivational Aspects of the Disarmament Problem. *Journal of Social Issues*, Vol. 17, No. 3, 1961, pp. 20–7.

FREEMAN, Harrop A.; YARKER, Stanley. Disarmament and Atomic Control: Legal and Non-legal Problems. *Cornell Law Quarterly*, Vol. 43, Winter 1958, pp. 132–5.

FULTON, Joseph F. Employment Impact of Changing Defense Programs. *Monthly Labor Review*, Vol. 87, No. 5, May 1964, pp. 508–17

GELBER, Harry G. Technical Innovation and Arms Control. *World Politics*, Vol. 26, No. 4, July 1974, pp. 509–41.

GILL, Ken. Alternative to Arms Production is Feasible and Necessary. *New Perspectives*, Vol. 9, No. 2, 1979, pp. 5–8.

GIEBER, Harry G. Technical Innovation and Arms Control. *World Politics*, Vol. 26, No. 4, July 1974, pp. 509–41.

GLEDITSCH, Nils P. Six Arguments Against Research for the Military. *Bulletin of Peace Proposals*, Vol. 6, No. 2, 1975, pp. 172–5.

GORDON, King. Development and Security and the UN Special Session. *International Perspectives*, November-December 1978, pp. 14–19.

GRAMPP, William D. False Fears of Disarmament. *Harvard Business Review*, Vol. 42, No. 1, January-February 1964, pp. 28–30.

GREEN, Harold P. The New Technological Era: A View from the Law. *Bulletin of the Atomic Scientists*, Vol. 23, No. 11, November 1967, pp. 12–18.

GURNEY, R. Arms and Men. *Bulletin of the Atomic Scientists*, Vol. 31, No. 10, December 1975, pp. 23–33.

GUSTAVSON, M. R. Evolving Strategic Arms and the Technologist. *Science*, Vol. 190, 5 December 1975, pp. 955–8.

HART, Thomas G. Cognitive Paradigms in the Arms Race: Deterrence, Détente and the Fundamental Error of Attribution. *Co-operation and Conflict*, Vol. 13, No. 3, 1978, pp. 147–61.

HOLST, John Jorgen. Is There a Strategic Arms Race? What is Really Going On? *Foreign Policy*, No. 19, Summer 1975, pp. 155–63.

HONKASALO, Antero. Problems of Disarmament—Arms Race Depletes Resources and Pollutes Environment. *New Perspectives*, Vol. 10, No. 1, 1980, pp. 10–11.

HVEEM, Helge. Arms Control Through Resource Control. The Link Between Military Consumption of Raw Materials and Energy and the Disarmament Question. *Bulletin of Peace Proposals*, Vol. 9, No. 1, 1978, pp. 15–23.

IGNATIEFF, George. Negotiating Arms Control. *International Journal*, Vol. 30, No. 1, Winter 1975, pp. 91–101.

ISRAELYAN, V. Constructive Approach. *International Affairs* (Moscow), No. 1, 1980, pp. 20-8.

JACK, Homer A. An International Disarmament Movement? *Bulletin of Peace Proposals*, Vol. 9, No. 3, 1978, pp. 234–8.

JAIPAL, Rikhi. Development and Disarmament. *Man and Development*, Vol. 1, No. 1, May 1979, pp. 75–80.

JOHANSEN, Robert C. Global Humanist Critique of National Policies for Arms Control. *Journal of International Affairs*, Vol. 3, No. 2, Fall/Winter 1977, pp. 215–41.

KALIADIN, A. Global Aspects of Disarmament Problems—Mobilising World Scientific Community to End Arms Race. *New Perspectives*, Vol. 9, No. 6, 1979, pp. 5–7.

KAPUR, Ashok. Evaluating the Progress of Test Ban Negotiations. *International Perspectives*, January–February 1979, pp. 29–33.

KAUSHIK, B. M. Arms Control Policy for India. *Strategic Analysis*, Vol. 1, No. 2, March 1978, pp. 1–4.

KAZAKOV, Y. Problems of Disarmament—Arms Race and the Struggle for Peace. *Soviet Review*, Vol. 15, No. 51, 6 November 1978, pp. 34–6.

KINCADE, William. Strategy for All Seasons: Targeting Doctrine and Strategic Arms Control. *Bulletin of the Atomic Scientists*, Vol. 34, No. 5, May 1978, pp. 14–20.

KINTNER, William R.; SICHERMAN, Harvey. Technology and International Politics: The Crisis of Wishing. *Orbis*, Vol. 15, No. 1, Spring 1971, pp. 13–27.

KISTIAKOWSKY, G. B. Good and the Bad of Nuclear Arms Control Negotiations—Commentary. *Bulletin of the Atomic Scientists*, Vol. 35, No. 5, May 1979, pp. 7–9.

KOTHARI, Rajni. Disarmament, Development, and a Just World Order. *Alternatives*, Vol. 4, No. 1, July 1978, pp. 1–10.

KUCZYNSKI, Jurgen. International Scientific Co-operation and the Limitation of Armaments. *Scientific World*, Vol. 12, No. 4/5, 1968, pp. 29–31.

KUTSENKOV A. Developing Countries and the Arms Race. *Soviet Military Review*, No. 1, 1979, pp. 47–9.

LALL, Betty Goetz. Arms Reduction Impact. *Bulletin of the Atomic Scientists*, Vol. 22, No. 7, September 1966, pp. 41–4.

——. Conversion of Defense Resources. *Bulletin of the Atomic Scientists*, Vol. 22, No. 1, January 1966, pp. 46–8.

LEITENBERG, Milton. Disarmament and Arms Control Since 1945—A Brief Survey. *Review of International Affairs*, Vol. 30, No. 694, 5 March 1979, pp. 18–21.

LEONTIEF, Wassily W. Alternatives to Armament Expenditures. *Bulletin of the Atomic Scientists*, Vol. 20, No. 6, June 1964, pp. 19–21.

LONG, F. A. Arms Control from the Perspectives of the Nineteen-seventies. *Daedalus*, Vol. 104, No. 3, Summer 1975, pp. 1–13.

LUTTWAK, Edward N. Why Arms Control Has Failed. *Commentary*, Vol. 65, No. 1, January 1978, pp. 19–28.

MADAN PAL SINGH. Problems of Implementation of Disarmament. *Vikrant*, Vol. 9, No. 11, August 1979, pp. 15–18.

MERLE, Marcel. Can the World Bring Itself to Say Farewell to Arms? A Footnote to the Special Session. *International Perspectives*, November–December 1978, pp. 10–14.

MESSING, Aubrey R. University Campus: Why Military-sponsored Research? *Military Review*, Vol. 52, No. 12, December 1972, pp. 54–62.

MIHAJLOVIC, Miodrag. Disarmament—Non-nuclear Weapon States and Security Guarantees. *Review of International Affairs*, Vol. 30, No. 692, 5 February 1979, pp. 26–30.

MISHRA, Indu Shekhar. NTP is not Enough for India. *Bulletin of the Atomic Scientists*, Vol. 24, No. 6, June 1968, pp. 4–5.

MOJSOV, Lazar. Road to Disarmament—New Obstacles in the Way. *Review of International Affairs*, Vol. 30, No. 712, 5 December 1979, pp. 1–3.

MORSE, John H. New Weapons Technologies: Implications for NATO. *Orbis*, Vol. 19, No. 2, Summer 1975, pp. 497–513.

MRAZEK, Josef. Some Notes on the Prohibition of Use of Nuclear Weapons and the Possibilities of Liquidating Them. *Peace and the Sciences*, Vol. 2, 1978, pp. 51–7.

NACHT, Michael L. Is There a Strategic Arms Race? The Delicate Balance of Error. *Foreign Policy*, No. 19, Summer 1975, pp. 163–77.

NELSON, Bryce. M.I.T.'s March 4: Scientists Discuss Research. *Science*, Vol. 163, March 1969, pp. 1175–8.

NELSON, Richard R. Adjusting Research and Development. *Bulletin of the Atomic Scientists*, Vol. 20, No. 4, April 1964, pp. 15–19.

——. Impact of Arms Reduction on Research and Development. *American Economic Review*, Vol. 53, No. 5, May 1963, pp. 435–46.

NOGEE, Joseph L. Propaganda and Negotiation: The Case of the Ten-nation Disarmament Committee. *Journal of Conflict Resolution*, Vol. 7, No. 3, 1963, pp. 510–21.

OBERG, Jan. Report of Commission I: Armament Dynamics and Repressive Violence. *International Peace Research Newsletter*, Vol. 13, No. 6, 1975, pp. 10–21.

OLIVER, Richard P. The Employment Effect of Defense Expenditures. *Monthly Labor Review*, Vol. 90, No. 9, September 1967, pp. 10–11.

——. Employment Effects of Reduced Defense Spending. *Monthly Labor Review*, Vol. 94, No. 12, December 1971, pp. 3–11.

On Practical Ways to End the Arms Race: Proposals of the Soviet Union at the Special Session of the UN General Assembly on Disarmament. *Soviet Review*, Vol. 15, No. 28, 19 June 1978, pp. 5–18.

ORWANT, Jack E. Effects of Derogatory Attacks in Soviet Arms Control Propaganda. *Journalism Quarterly*, No. 49, Spring 1972, pp. 107–15.

PALME, Olaf J. Disarmament and Development. *Review of International Affairs*, Vol. 29, No. 683, 20 September 1978, pp. 13–21.

PETKOVIC, Ranko. Non-alignment and Disarmament. *Review of International Affairs*, Vol. 29, No. 677, 20 June 1978, pp. 7–9.

PETKOVSKI, Dane. Disarmament: Condition for Peace and Progress. *Review of International Affairs*, Vol. 29, No. 676, 5 June 1978, pp. 9–10.

PETRUS, Behnam. Development and Disarmament are Interlinked. *New Perspectives*, Vol. 9, No. 5, 1979, pp. 15–16.

PIEL, Gerard. Science, Disarmament and Peace. *Bulletin of the Atomic Scientists*, Vol. 14, No. 6, June 1958, pp. 217–19.

PIERRE, Andrew J.; MOYNE, Claudia W. Nuclear Proliferation: A Strategy for Control. *Headline Series*, No. 232, October 1976.

PILISUK, Marc; RAPOPORT, Anatol, Stepwise Disarmament and Sudden Destruction in a Two-person Game: A Research Tool. *Journal of Conflict Resolution*, Vol. 7, No. 1, 1964, pp. 36–49.

PLISCHAKE, Elmer. Summit Diplomacy: Its Uses and Limitations. *Virginia Quarterly Review*, Vol. 48, Summer 1972, pp. 321–44.

PRICE, Charles C. A Look at Disarmament. *Bulletin of the Atomic Scientists*, Vol. 14, No. 6, 1958, pp. 229–31.

Problems of Disarmament Under Conditions of International Détente. *Peace and the Sciences*, March 1976, pp. 1–147. (Papers presented at a Symposium of the International Institute for Peace, Vienna, July 1975.)

PULU, Alexandru. Problems of Disarmament. Arms Race Distorts Scientific Research and Development. *New Perspectives*, Vol. 10, No. 1, 1980, pp. 12–14.

RAJASHEKARA, H. M. Disarmament Problems and Prospects. *Indian Journal of Political Science*, Vol. 39, No. 1, January-March 1978, pp. 121–9.

RAJHJENS, G. W. Changing Perspectives on Arms Control. *Daedalus*, Vol. 104, No. 3, Summer 1975, pp. 201–15.

RAM, Prasad. Scientists and Disarmament. *Mainstream*, Vol. 14, No. 8, 25 October 1975, pp. 21–3.

RAMA RAO, R. Arms Transfer. *Seminar*, June 1976, pp. 26–36.

RANA, Swadesh. Approaches to Disarmament. *Strategic Analysis*, Vol. 1, No. 11, February 1978, pp. 31–4.

——. Disarmament and Development. A Third World Perspective. *Strategic Analysis*, Vol. 3, No. 9, December 1979, pp. 338–41.

RAPACKL, Adam. Socialist Diplomacy of Peace in the World Arena. *World Marxist Review*, Vol. 5, No. 6, June 1962, pp. 12–18.

RIEFLER, Roger F.; DOWNING, Paul B. Regional Effects of Defense Effort on Employment. *Monthly Labor Review*, Vol. 91, No. 7, July 1968, pp. 1–8.

ROACH, E. Hugh. Transfer of Technology: The Need for Pragmatism. *Behind the Headlines*, Vol. 37, No. 5, 1979.

RUDZINSKI, Alexander W. Soviet Peace Offensives. *International Conciliation*, April 1953, pp. 175–225.

SCHMIDT, Max. Problems of Disarmament: Menace of Military-Industrial Complex, Profit Motive of Transnationals Intensifies Arms Race. *New Perspectives*, Vol. 9, No. 6, 1979, pp. 5–7.

Scientific Symposium: Disarmament Problems from Different Ideological Standpoints, USSR, 24–26 April 1978. *Peace Research and the Sciences*, Vol. 3, 1978, pp. 1–12. (Series of articles.)

SCOVILLE, Herbert. Strategic Weapons and their Control. *India International Centre Quarterly*, Vol. 5, No. 3, July 1978, pp. 147–54.

SENGHAAS, D. Armament Dynamics and Disarmament. *Instant Research on Peace and Violence*, Vol. 6, No. 1/2, 1976, pp. 3–17.

SHERWIN, C. W. Securing Peace through Military Technology. *Bulletin of the Atomic Scientists*, Vol. 12, No. 5, May 1956, pp. 159–64.

SHULMAN, Marshall D. Arms Control in an International Context. *Daedalus*, Vol. 104, No. 3, Summer 1975, pp. 53–61.

SIMAI, Mihaly. What Can Science Do for Disarmament? *New Perspectives*, Vol. 9, No. 2, 1979, pp. 9–10.

SIMONYAN, R. Disarmament Towards Lasting Peace: Curbing the Arms Race—A Key Problem of our Time. *International Affairs*, January 1979, pp. 70–7.

SLOCOMBE, Walter. Controlling Strategic Nuclear Weapons. *Headline Series*, No. 226, June 1975.

SOHN, Louis B. Disarmament at the Crossroads. *International Security*, Vol. 2, No. 4, Spring 1978, pp. 4–31.

SOLOMON, Mark. Problems of Disarmament—Movement Against Increased Military Spending in U.S.A. *New Perspectives*, Vol. 10, No. 1, 1980, pp. 8–9.

STEIN, Eric. Legal Restraints in Modern Arms Control Agreements. *American Journal of International Law*, Vol. 66, No. 4, April 1972, pp. 255–89.

STEINBRUNER, John; CARTER, Barry. Organizational and Political Dimensions of the Strategic Posture: The Problems of Reform. *Daedalus*, Vol. 104, No. 1, Summer 1975, pp. 131–54.

STEINER, Barry H. On Controlling the Soviet-American Nuclear Arms Competition. *Armed Forces and Society*, Vol. 5, No. 1, Fall 1978, pp. 53–71.

SUINN, Richard W. The Disarmament Fantasy: Psychological Factors that May Produce Warfare. *Journal of Human Relations*, Vol. 15, No. 1, 1967, pp. 36–42.

SULLIVAN, I.; MICHAEL, J. Indian Attitudes on International Atomic Energy Controls. *Pacific Affairs*, Vol. 44, No. 3, Fall 1970, pp. 353–69.

THEE, Marek. Armaments Dynamic and Military Research and Development. *Alternatives*, Vol. 4, No. 1, July 1978, p. 35.

——. Disarmament through Unilateral Initiatives. *Bulletin of Peace Proposals*, No. 4, 1974, pp. 381–4.

——. Nuclear Arms Race: Trends, Dynamics, Control. *Instant Research on Peace and Violence*, Vol. 6, No. 1–2, 1976, pp. 18–28.

U.S. Arms and Foreign Aid. *Current History*, Vol. 77, No. 448, July-August 1979. (Special issue: series of articles and arms-trade charts.)

USTINOV, V. New Weapons Threaten Peace. *International Affairs* (Moscow), October 1979, pp. 33–8.

VAYRYNEN, R. Cutting Down Military Budgets: Some Perspectives. *Instant Research on Peace and Violence*, Vol. 6, No. 1/2, 1976, pp. 72–80.

VAYRYEN, Raimo. Curbing International Transfers of Arms and Military Technology. *Alternatives*, Vol. 4, No. 1, July 1978, pp. 87–113.

VELLODI, M. A. Problems of Disarmament. *India International Centre Quarterly*, Vol. 6, No. 3, July 1979, pp. 205–16.

VERMA, Shreekant. Arms Race in a Hungry World. *Vikrant*, Vol. 9, No. 8, May 1979, pp. 29–31.

VERONA, Sergiu. Structural Negotiating Blockages to Disarmament. *Bulletin of Peace Proposals*, Vol. 9, No. 3, 1978, pp. 200–9.

VESA, Unto. Special Session on Disarmament: A Turning Point? *Current Research on Peace and Violence*, Vol. 1, No. 1, 1978, pp. 1–12.

WALLENSTEEN, Peter. Disarmament and Development: A School for Action. *Bulletin of Peace Proposals*, Vol. 9, No. 1, 1978, pp. 11–13.

WARIAVWALLA, B. K. Problems of Disarmament. *Sainik Samachar*, Vol. 25, No. 25, 18 June 1978, pp. 4–5.

WARNKE, Paul C. Arms Control: A Global Imperative. *Strategic Digest*, Vol. 9, No. 2, February 1979, pp. 145–7.

WEDGE, Bryant; MUROMCEW, Cyril. Psychological Factors in Soviet Disarmament Negotiations. *Journal of Conflict Resolution*, Vol. 9, No. 2, 1965, pp. 18–36.

WEIDENBAUM, Murray L. Economic Adjustments to Disarmament. *University of Washington Business Review*, Vol. 22, February 1963, pp. 3–11.

——. Reductions in Defense Spending: The Problem and the Government Response. *University of Washington Business Review*, Vol. 24,
April-June 1965, pp. 5–12.

WEILER, Lawrence D. Reflections on the Disarmament Session. *Bulletin
of the Atomic Scientists*, Vol. 34, No. 10, December 1978, pp. 7–9.

WEINBERG, Alvin M. The Many Dimensions of Scientific Responsibility.
Bulletin of the Atomic Scientists, Vol. 32, No. 11, November 1976,
pp. 21–5.

WESTING, Arthur H. Military Expenditures and their Reduction.
Bulletin of Peace Proposals, Vol. 9, No. 1, 1978, pp. 24–9.

WILKES, Owen. Military Research and Development Program: Problems
of Control. *Bulletin of Peace Proposals*, Vol. 9, No. 1, 1978, pp. 3–10.

WOOLSEY, R. James. Chipping Away at the Bargains. *Daedalus*,
Vol. 104, No. 3, Summer 1975, pp. 175–85.

YUTER, S. C. The Role of World Law in Arms Control. *Bulletin of
the Atomic Scientists*, Vol. 25, No. 8, Ocober 1969, pp. 23–5.

Appendices

1. Report of the expert meeting on the obstacles to disarmament and the ways of overcoming them, Paris, 3–7 April 1978

I. Introduction

General background

1. Pursuant to resolution 3.171 concerning the programme of Unesco on human rights and peace and taking into account resolution 12.1 on Unesco's contribution to peace, and resolution 13.1 on the role of Unesco in generating a climate of public opinion conducive to the halting of the arms race and the transition to disarmament, adopted by the General Conference at its nineteenth session (Nairobi, 1976), an expert meeting on 'Obstacles to disarmament and the ways of overcoming them' took place at Unesco Headquarters, Paris, from 3 to 7 April 1978.

2. The purpose of the meeting was to draw from an analysis of obstacles which may be identified as preventing or slowing down the process of disarmament, a series of conclusions regarding the steps which may be taken in the fields of education, science, culture and information in order to overcome the obstacles thus identified.

3. The meeting carried out its work bearing in mind that the ideas and conclusions would be brought to the attention, in an appropriate way, of the special session of the General Assembly of the United Nations devoted to disarmament.

4. Twelve experts from research institutions in various countries participated in their personal capacities. Several international non-governmental organizations sent observers. The list of participants appears at the end of this report.

Opening of the meeting

5. The meeting was opened by Mrs Martha Hildebrandt, Assistant Director-General for Social Sciences and their Applications. She welcomed the participants on behalf of the Director-General and explained the mandate the General Conference had given to the Secretariat to promote studies and research on 'the contribution that can be made by Unesco, in its fields of competence, to knowledge of the problems of disarmament and to their solution, by employing all possible ways of making world opinion alive to these problems' (19 C/Resolution 12.1, Part I, paragraph 2(b)). She also described the place activities relating to disarmament have in Unesco's current programme and in particular in the Medium-Term Plan. In this regard she drew the attention of the meeting to Objective 2.1 of the Medium-Term Plan entitled 'Promotion of peace research, in particular on manifestations of violation of peace, causes preventing its realization, ways and means to eliminate them and proper measures to be taken in order to maintain and reinforce a just, lasting and constructive peace at the level of groups, societies and the world' and in particular to the principle of action (c) of that objective which reads as follows: '(c) Increased emphasis should also be placed on studies which can be used to explain the origin of the tensions in the world and the factors determining the arms race, and which can be used to promote disarmament and eliminate the obstacles to it.' In conclusion she stated that the present meeting would provide important guidance for future activities in the field of disarmament and expressed the hope that the special session of the United Nations General Assembly would take account of the meeting's recommendations.

Organization of work

6. In accordance with Rule 4 of the Rules of Procedure, the meeting elected the following officers: Chairman: Mrs Swadesh Rana; Vice-Chairmen: Mr Sean MacBride, Mr V. V. Zhurkin; Rapporteur: Mr Sergiu Verona.

7. Thirteen working papers dealing with the various obstacles to disarmament and the ways of overcoming them were presented to the meeting. After general statements, these

papers were introduced and discussed in the following order, as agreed by the meeting:

Obstacles to disarmament

Obstacles relating to the world economic and political structures: International Political Structures—paper by J. Owona; International Economic Structures—papers by P. Lock and A. Bönisch; International Legal and Diplomatic Aspects—paper by S. Verona.

Obstacles relating to internal and cultural factors: Psychological Factors—paper by the World Veterans Federation in conjunction with the European Confederation of War Veterans, the International Confederation of Former Prisoners-of-War and the International Federation of Resistance Movements; Determination of Strategic Interests —paper by S. Rana; Militarism in Developing and Developed Countries—paper by War Resisters International.

Ways of overcoming the obstacles to disarmament

The Role of Education and Proposals for Disarmament Education—papers by B. Reardon and J. Diaz.

The Role of Scientists and Proposals Concerning Research on Military Research and Development—paper by M. Thee.

The Role of Culture and Communication and Proposals for Influencing Public Opinion—paper by M. Lumsden.

The Role of the United Nations, its Organs and Programmes in Furthering Disarmament and Putting an End to the Arms Race—paper by O. V. Bogdanov.

The Role of Non-governmental Organizations and Proposals for Future Action—paper by the World Federation of United Nations Associations.

8. In addition to the above-mentioned background papers, several information documents were distributed. The first of these was the report of the International Expert Seminar on 'Research, education and information on questions related to disarmament and international co-operation in this field', organized on 1–2 December 1978 by the Finnish National Commission for Unesco at Siikaranta, near Helsinki. The complete proceedings of the seminar were published as No. 12 in the series of publications of the Finnish National

Commission. The other information documents distributed were:

Report on Research Trends and an Annotated Bibliography on the Economic and Social Aspects of the Arms Race and Disarmament, Unesco, 1978 (Reports and Papers in the Social Sciences, No. 39).

The Role of the Military in the World Economic Order, by Malvern Lumsden.

Final Report of the Non-Governmental Organization Symposium on 'Disarmament, Development and Education for Peace and How they Interact' (Unesco doc. ONG/78/19/DES/Final Report, 30 March 1978).

Final Declaration of the Non-Governmental Organization Committee on Disarmament, International Conference on Disarmament, Geneva, 27 February–2 March 1978.

9. Following the presentation and discussion of the working papers, the meeting concentrated on specific proposals relating to the contribution Unesco could make within the framework of the special session of the General Assembly devoted to disarmament and, more generally, through the programmes and activities in all the Organization's spheres of competence.

Adoption of report and closure of the meeting

10. The Rapporteur and another expert designated by the Committee (M. Lumsden) prepared a draft report which was considered at the final session. The general orientation and recommendations of this draft report were approved on the understanding that a final version would be prepared on the basis of the modifications and suggestions made by the participants during the final session. It was also understood that the conclusions of the meeting would be brought to the attention of the special session of the General Assembly in an appropriate way.

11. At the closing of the meeting the Chairman presented her conclusions and noted that, although such a meeting could not resolve any of the issues and controversies relating to disarmament, it had clarified some of them and hopefully had been useful for Unesco.

12. The representative of the Director-General expressed the gratitude of Unesco to the participants in the meeting which had, in his view, accomplished four tasks: (i) it had

elucidated a number of obstacles to the process of disarmament in a way which could form the basis of a publication by Unesco on this theme; (ii) it had provided very pertinent suggestions regarding the matters which Unesco could stress at the special session of the General Assembly devoted to disarmament; (iii) it had formulated recommendations which could guide Unesco's future activities in this field; and (iv) it had established the beginning of a network of specialists representing scholarly opinion in various parts of the world on which Unesco could call for additional advice and for contributions to research projects on disarmament questions.

II. Identification
of the obstacles to disarmament

Definition of disarmament

13. While holding different and sometimes opposing views on various aspects of the analysis of the obstacles to disarmament (some examples of which appear in the following paragraphs), all the experts agreed to emphasize that the goal of international action in the field of disarmament must be general and complete disarmament, and that this goal, while it does not rule out intermediate measures of arms limitations and reductions, is the only one which is compatible with development and human rights.

14. On the question of *defining general and complete disarmament*, some experts felt that the most comprehensive definition was contained in the Joint Statement of Agreed Principles for Disarmament Negotiations by the USSR and the United States, which were endorsed by the General Assembly in resolution 1722 (XVI) adopted on 20 December 1961.[1] Several experts stressed the importance of subsequent resolutions by the General Assembly on the subject.

15. Several of the participants from Third World countries noted that most of the talk and scientific work on disarmament was coming from 'overarmed' countries and that too little account was being taken of the *'non-armament'* of many Third World countries, particularly in Africa. It was thus necessary to take a *regional approach* to the study of the obstacles to disarmament and to consider that it was

mainly the countries which favour the status quo who call for disarmament, whereas for other countries, such as those in Africa contending with the military might of the apartheid regime in South Africa, disarmament could mean suicide.

The present international climate

16. The meeting expressed satisfaction that the United Nations General Assembly had decided to convene a special session devoted to disarmament which should be a new stage in achieving substantial progress toward disarmament.

17. Disarmament was considered a vital element in the efforts to achieve a New International Economic Order as it would release human and material resources which could be used for development, abolishing illiteracy and for cultural progress. But more important, disarmament was necessary to remove the military obstacles, at the global and the national level, to a New International Economic Order permitting greatly increased investment in useful production in the developing countries and an equitable distribution of income within and between countries.

18. Several participants regarded the development of *political détente in Europe* as an essential feature of the international climate in that the failure to achieve collateral progress in arms limitation constituted a serious challenge to the value of the relaxation of political tensions achieved by the Conference on Security and Co-operation in Europe. In this regard one participant saw the lack of concrete results at the Belgrade Conference as a sign of the loss of élan of the CSCE. One expert mentioned that a conference of the type of the CSCE would not be suitable for other regions composed of developing countries.

Typologies relating to the obstacles to disarmament

19. While considering the points under discussion (see above paragraph 7) as a good starting point for the identification of obstacles to disarmament, some participants suggested different typologies of these obstacles, while others offered subclassifications within the overall classification of obstacles proposed by the Secretariat.

20. One participant, for example, stressed the following as

the essential obstacles to achieving substantial progress toward disarmament:

Historically, going to war is a habit of the human race whereas the concept of not having wars is new.

The glorification of war, for example in history books and monuments, is common to practically every country.

The military industrial complex constitutes the most powerful financial and political lobby in the world reaching even non-military matters.

Military establishments in every country prepare for war, even though their work is often referred to as 'defence', and determine, through advice based on a vested interest and often distorted information, the position of diplomats in disarmament negotiations.

The control of the press is passing from independent owners to multinational corporations who often have an interest in the military establishment and thus in generating a climate of mutual distrust on military matters.

Updated planning for reconversion of industry from military to civilian purposes is required to meet the challenge of unemployment which disarmament would create,

21. Another participant referred to the *conservatism of military forces* as such and the resulting influence of military policy on foreign policy. He also stressed the importance that planning by the military establishment had on the continuation of the arms race, resulting sometimes in the decision to continue production of a weapon simply because it is in the plan. In the view of this expert, the existence of military pacts is itself an obstacle to disarmament as the organizations based on them tend to justify their own existence. The conditions of the labour market constitute another factor that can contribute to the arms race since the jobless may be attracted to the army.

22. Referring to the agenda of the meeting, one participant found useful the distinction between '*structural*' *obstacles*, on the one hand, and '*cultural*' or '*super-structural obstacles*' on the other, the latter being more relevant for proposals to Unesco while necessarily based on an understanding of the former. He suggested that another concept which helps better to understand the structural obstacles to disarmament is that of *symmetry and asymmetry*. While states have equal status, they have unequal military power which determines the relations between major arms producers and smaller countries.

23. Another participant drew attention to two parallel trends: international society is *receptive to conflicts*, on the one hand, and *reticent to any international control* of armaments, on the other. Evidence of the receptiveness to conflicts may be found in the fact that the armed states stay armed and exercise exclusive jurisdiction over armed forces, that the poles of power are multiplying (nuclear polycentrism and proliferation of medium-sized powers), that ideological sensitivity results in difficulty to achieve consensus, and that charismatic militaristic figures continue to appeal to masses. As evidence of the reticence to arms control, he noted that no international arms control administration had been created but partial results had been achieved by treaty on specific points (SALT, denuclearization).

Economic obstacles

24. In addition to the general approaches to the identification of the obstacles to disarmament mentioned above, many participants focused on various economic determinants in the arms race, particularly as regards the relations between *disarmament and development*. It was pointed out, for example, that certain states or groups of states which are major arms producers compete to maintain access to sources of raw materials and markets, using for this purpose direct or indirect military means. Some experts saw a particular danger in the increase in arms sales, particularly through multinational corporations.

25. Some participants saw the present economic obstacles to disarmament as resulting from the historical process which led to the present world economic order. It was noted in this regard that military force was commonly used to acquire access to raw materials and to markets during the colonial period and that certain possessions acquired then continue to have strategic importance for the former colonialist powers.

26. The *transfer of military technology* was, in the view of some experts, a crucial factor for economic development. Once a developing country decides to prepare its defences against a feared threat to its security it accepts the military technology of the arms-supplying developed country and it is this technology which affects the development process in the country, forces its economy into a certain role in the world market and, consequently, hinders the application of alterna-

tive development strategies. In this way the arms race has an absolutely detrimental effect on developing countries.

The negotiation process

27. Numerous observations were made concerning the system of negotiation that has developed since the Second World War. It was pointed out that this system had evolved qualitatively following the entry into the international scene of many newly-independent countries and that the negotiation process could no longer be a concern for only a few countries. One expert felt in this regard that participation of all countries on an equal footing should be assured and that the special session of the General Assembly provided an opportunity to advance proposals based on these principles.

28. It was generally agreed that *existing negotiating machinery*, including the Conference of the Committee on Disarmament in Geneva, in spite of the efforts and proposals made, has failed to produce tangible results commensurate with the objective of general and complete disarmament.

29. Several participants expressed the view that the process of political decision-making was of paramount importance and that the principal factor in the negotiation was the *political will* of governments to disarm and to allow control of arms reduction.

30. While *treaties* concluded in recent years have contributed to creating a climate of understanding, they have not proved capable of curbing the arms race or ensuring the implementation of effective disarmament measures. Moreover, they do not deal with the root causes of the arms race nor with the major weapons, particularly nuclear weapons.

31. One expert did express the view that existing negotiating machinery was quite adequate and opposed destructive approaches to this machinery as dangerous for disarmament. He also considered it was wrong to underestimate the positive role of international agreements in this field.[2] However, this expert expressed grave concern at the continuation of the arms race which called for new and effective measures.

Security doctrines

32. The meeting repeatedly referred to the effect of doctrines of national security on the potential for disarmament. For

many participants, the underlying justification for armaments in practically every country is the conviction that the only means of protecting the security of the state is military preparedness. While practically all countries consider disarmament desirable, very few find it feasible. *Parity*, which has come to be regarded as a major precondition for arms control in the SALT and MFR contexts, is a doctrine which contributes to an unavoidable spiral in the arms race. *Deterrence* and the worst-case assumption in the strategic relations between the major military powers were also cited as doctrines based on national security which hampered the process of disarmament. One participant felt that it is not these doctrines which are to blame but the activities of those forces which are opposing disarmament. He stressed that disarmament should be carried out without prejudice to the security of any party and that in every conflict situation the concrete responsibilities of the aggressors, militarists, etc., should be identified. Some experts referred in this connection to the negative role of the development of new types of weapons of mass destruction lowering the nuclear threshold, citing as an example the neutron bomb. Other experts believed that any use of any nuclear weapon was a crime against humanity.

33. Several participants considered that it was urgent to find *alternatives* to the national security doctrine. One approach that was suggested consisted in reinforcing the means of pacific settlement of disputes in accordance with the provisions of the United Nations Charter. Some participants felt that bold new action was required, including unilateral measures which could contribute to a climate of hope and change. One expert emphasized that for certain countries no amount of talk about alternative approaches will convince the leaders or the people to renounce the use of armaments in the interests of national security, whatever the price.

34. It was generally agreed that more study was needed on the impact of strategic doctrines in shaping a climate of war and peace and on alternatives to these doctrines.

Cultural and psychological factors

35. Many participants recognized the essential role *public opinion* can have in determining policy over matters of vital concern to the population at large. Public opinion was under-

stood as the publicly expressed values and beliefs of a given social group capable of influencing the decisions of the policy-makers of that group. One participant pointed out that the difficulty of mobilizing public opinion in favour of disarmament stemmed from the complexity of the issues at stake and the feeling of impotence people often have regarding their capacity to do anything about them. However, some participants cited the case of environmental protection which popular opinion at local and international levels was able to influence in order to bring about change.

36. One participant explained that the arms race gained support from the public through the manipulation by the mass media of fear and anxiety and of group identification. Another participant referred to the self-centred, inner-directed psychosis which creates popular support for armaments.

37. The existence of *fear and distrust* between peoples and nations was seen by most participants as the major psychological obstacle to disarmament. The lack of public information on military and disarmament issues, often due to official policies of secrecy or controlled leaks of selected information, contributes to these factors. The meeting recognized the need for the media to present reality as it is and for governments to revise policies of secrecy which lead to miscalculation and misperception rather than protect national security. It was pointed out that international organizations had no rule concerning the period of time after which secret information could be released nor did they apply the principle which exists in certain countries of freedom of access to administrative records. The participants agreed that more information should be provided to the public on alternatives to the war system, such as non-violent defence and conflict resolution, so that secrecy or controlled leaks would be less of an inducement to the arms race. Some experts felt that while the role of information at disarmament negotiations was important, it was necessary to pay special attention to developing a climate of confidence among states through détente and improvement of the international atmosphere. They considered that inflating the so-called 'secrecy issue' led to diverting attention from actual disarmament issues and problems of confidence-building which were of paramount importance.

38. The role of *non-governmental organizations* was gener-

ally regarded as essential to ensure that public opinion is fully informed and also to enable ordinary people to influence their respective governments. The responsibility of journalists not to distort the facts and of research institutes to disseminate all pertinent information on armaments as widely as possible was stressed by several participants.

39. One participant mentioned the *ideologization of violence and of war* as an obstacle to disarmament. The ideology of violence and war is transmitted through literature and films and reinforced by military service, which, in the view of this expert, was based on an outmoded and faulty hypothesis and wasted the forces of youth. Some experts argued that conscription was a form of forced labour and furthered militarism by building up the armed forces and subjugating young people to military discipline and ideology. As a step toward the abolition of conscription they expressed the view that the right of conscientious objection should be universally recognized.[3] Some others did not share this view.

40. The broader *cultural dimensions* of the problem of disarmament were also discussed. The role of mythology as an ecological factor maintaining the social system was one such dimension. The propensity of a culture to promote a militaristic ideology was another. Variations were noted between the cultural manifestations of military ideology in 'educated' or 'high' culture and in 'popular' or 'low' culture, i.e. in official forms of literary and artistic expression and in mass forms of cultural expression. The contribution of culture to the cause of disarmament should be at both these levels and efforts should be made to mobilize all the forces at work in the creation of culture (artists, writers, scientists, etc.) toward this end.

The role of educators and scientists

41. The meeting agreed that *disarmament education* should be encouraged at all levels. The purpose of such education is to promote the goal of general and complete disarmament and of a peace system; it thus involves the socialization of youth in favour of this goal ('education for disarmament') and training and instruction regarding the various historical, political, economic and other aspects of the problem of disarmament in international relations and domestic policy ('education about disarmament'). One of the tasks of disarmament

education was thus to demystify the question of armaments and the arms race and to provide the intellectual preparation for finding alternatives.

42. The development of disarmament education was seen as a way of implementing the Recommendation on Education for International Understanding, Co-operation and Peace and Education Relating to Human Rights and Fundamental Freedoms, adopted by the General Conference of Unesco on 19 November 1974. It was felt that much more should be done to implement this recommendation by all member states and that the approach contained in it was suitable for disarmament education.

43. Among the purposes of disarmament education, one participant mentioned the promotion of a spirit of tolerance, the development of intellectual capacities, training in skills of non-violent social change and establishment of a commitment to a value system based on human rights. She argued that peace studies deserved special attention and that peace educators should attain wider recognition and be invited to participate in all symposia relating to disarmament.

44. Another expert stressed the effect of the transmission of belligerent ideologies through the school, which he considered as the 'mother and daughter' of such ideologies. No progress could be made to prepare youth to contribute to the elimination of the ideology of war until schools ceased to play this role and disarmament education was, in his view, a step in the right direction.

45. Another expert drew the attention of the meeting to the fact that formal education was not very widespread in certain regions and that the realities of developing countries in this regard should be kept in mind.

46. The role of scientists was also considered a major factor in the search for disarmament since they occupy the key position in the technology race which, in fact, is what the arms race is all about. *Military research and development* affects many aspects of life and creates a technological momentum and a technological imperative which, in the view of some of the experts, was stronger than governments, although others saw the will of governments as paramount.

47. The *rights and duties of scientists* as set out in the Recommendation on the Status of Scientific Researchers adopted by the General Conference of Unesco on 20 November 1974, should be scrupulously respected. Some experts drew par-

ticular attention to their right to speak out on disarmament questions and one suggested an oath for scientists which could reinforce their commitment to contribute to disarmament.

III. Recommendations

A. Recommendations for the United Nations General Assembly Special Session on Disarmament (SSD)

48. Fully conscious of the importance of the special session's work, the experts strongly felt that the declaration which the General Assembly will adopt would be incomplete without reference to the need for measures to create the psychological, social and cultural conditions and a climate of public opinion conducive to disarmament.

49. Further, the experts considered that the Plan of Action to be adopted by the General Assembly should contain specific recommendations with regard to programmes which can be undertaken by Unesco, within its spheres of competence, in order to promote the psychological, social and cultural conditions and a climate of public opinion conducive to disarmament. Amongst the specific recommendations which could be included in the Plan of Action are the following:

(a) The SSD could request Unesco to increase its efforts, in the fields of education, science, culture and information, to identify further the obstacles to disarmament and the ways of overcoming them.

(b) The SSD could invite Unesco to pursue its work in the field of education to promote peace and human rights and endorse the proposal to organize a world congress on disarmament education.

(c) Noting the General Assembly's endorsement of the proposal for a study of disarmament and development, and emphasizing the negative impact of the arms race on efforts to achieve a new international economic order, on the human environment, on natural resources, on social change, on cultural progress and on human rights, the SSD could invite Unesco to contribute to this project within its spheres of competence.

(d) Aware that many obstacles to disarmament are of a regional nature, and noting the proposal to establish a world institute for disarmament with regional branches, but aware of the very limited number of qualified researchers in the field of disarmament, Unesco could be urged to accelerate its efforts to promote relevant research, training and information centres in Africa, Asia and Latin America taking into account the specific needs and conditions of these regions.

(e) Having regard to the important role of public opinion in the promotion of world disarmament, it was deemed desirable to extend special facilities to non-governmental organizations and institutes involved in the promotion of disarmament.

B. Recommendations relating to Unesco's programmes and activities

1. Major projects in the field of disarmament

50. While proposing the general development of activities in the field of disarmament throughout Unesco's programmes, the meeting considered that three projects should be highlighted because of their potential impact on promoting the cause of disarmament and because they exemplify the specific contribution Unesco can make in this area.

51. The first of these projects is the holding of a *world congress on disarmament education*, preferably in 1979 or 1980. Such a congress should bring together several hundred specialists from appropriate government ministries, peace research institutes, groups of educators, etc., who can both recommend measures aimed at the establishment of specialized education in favour of disarmament and implement such measures.

52. The second major project recommended to Unesco relates to the extent to which armament is itself *a challenge to international law*. Bearing in mind the work Unesco is doing concerning the challenges of such concepts as human rights and the establishment of a new international economic order to international law, the experts urged Unesco to take up the study of the relationship between armament, disarmament and international law. This study should deal with the concept of the 'law of disarmament' as a new branch of international law in response to the challenge the maintenance of the arms race poses to the efforts of the United Nations and to the provisions of the United Nations Charter.

53. The third major project is the application, in a truly creative way, of *audio-visual means of communication to disseminating ideas and information about disarmament.* This project would take the form of organizing every year a 'disarmament day' or 'disarmament week' during which essential information about the negative aspects of the arms race and the positive aspects of disarmament would be disseminated through films, including a film festival, art exhibits, concerts and other forms of expression aimed at reaching all segments of the population. Those in charge of and professionally involved with information should be brought together to exchange experiences and find ways to improve their efforts to sensitize public opinion to disarmament.

2. Development of other specific activities
in Unesco's fields of competence

(a) Education
54. In addition to the congress mentioned above, the meeting agreed that other activities should be carried out or encouraged by Unesco with a view to creating a genuine field of disarmament education. It was felt that the full implementation of the Recommendation concerning Education for International Understanding, Co-operation and Peace and Education relating to Human Rights and Fundamental Freedoms, adopted by the General Conference at its eighteenth session on 19 November 1974, should contribute to this end. Efforts should therefore be reinforced relating to implementing this recommendation with particular reference to disarmament.

55. A set of guidelines and criteria should be worked out by a group of educators competent in this field. A handbook on teaching and learning practices on disarmament would also be useful. Developments of this type should be disseminated through periodical publications of educators and a programme of teacher education should be established taking into account the specific conditions prevailing in the various regions.

56. Unesco should also promote the creation in universities and other academic institutions of special courses and seminars on the arms race, military expenditure and disarmament. Its goal in this regard should be the es-

tablishment of at least one such course in every country.

57. Unesco should continue to encourage efforts by member states, particularly through their National Commissions, to revise school textbooks, especially on history and geography, in the spirit of the above-mentioned Recommendation.

(b) Science

58. The meeting considered proposals relating both to natural sciences and social sciences. International co-operation relating to research in both these fields was considered as an essential task for Unesco in overcoming the obstacles to disarmament in its spheres of competence.

59. Unesco is urged to expand its efforts to involve scientists in the study of disarmament problems. In this regard it was suggested that Unesco convene a conference of scientific and other workers engaged partly or entirely in military industries to consider the problems of conversion and of ways of bringing pressure on their governments to begin such conversion.

60. Research programmes co-ordinated by Unesco should be implemented in close co-operation with relevant international scientific organizations, universities and research institutions. It was suggested that the institutions represented at the meeting could constitute a starting point for such co-operation.

61. The responsibility of scientists was considered one of the key factors in overcoming the obstacles to disarmament. It was suggested that an oath for scientists could be drafted according to which they would commit themselves to working toward disarmament. In this regard, the meeting urged Unesco to step up efforts to implement the Recommendation on the Status of Scientific Researchers, adopted by the General Conference at its eighteenth session on 20 November 1974.

62. Among the numerous themes for research projects and/or symposia which Unesco could carry out or encourage were the following:

Military research and development and its impact on the arms race.

Role of various scientific disciplines in developing new military technology.

Impact of contemporary strategic doctrines on the international climate.

Costs and consequences of war in general and of nuclear
   war in particular.
Non-military alternatives and strategies for assuring security
   of states, including non-violent ones.
The semantics of disarmament and its impact on the various
   negotiations.
Human rights aspects of the arms question including the
   relationship between militarization and repression.
New developments in the problem of reconversion of military industries to civilian uses.
The decision-making process as applied to disarmament
   negotiations.
63. Unesco could do more to bring the role of scientific
research in fuelling the arms race to the attention of scientists
and science teachers through scientific organizations, conferences and journals. One or more semi-popular publications
on the impact of science, technology and medicine on war,
both in historical and in modern times, could be a useful
way of stimulating the interest of scientists and science
teachers and in promoting public opinion in favour of
disarmament.

(c) Culture
64. The meeting considered proposals relating both to
culture in the broad sense, and to various fields of cultural
activity, which are of major importance in determining the
climate of public opinion. It was felt that there was a need
for international co-operation in the study of cultural influences on the formation of values and beliefs, fears and
prejudices, with particular reference to issues of war, peace
and disarmament. To this end a number of recommendations
for research were made, including:
(a) A study of the influence of traditional values and beliefs
    (as reflected in various religions, mythology, classical
    literature, philosophy, and so on) and of contemporary
    philosophical and political theories on current thought
    on peace and war in different cultures.
(b) A study of the ways in which war and peace are portrayed
    in literature, art, music, theatre, dance and films, as a
    basis for promoting disarmament as a means to the
    cultural progress of mankind.
(c) A synthesis of studies of the motivations and manifes-
    tations of fear and distrust which affect the possibilities

of disarmament in interstate relations and in national and international public opinion.

65. It was suggested that Unesco could stimulate international organizations in the cultural sphere to contribute to promoting a climate of opinion conducive to disarmament. In addition, Unesco could produce books and films relating disarmament to the cultural progress of mankind. One or more semi-popular publications on the impact of war and peace on culture (the arts, literature, music, dance, films, philosophy, mythology, etc.)—and the impact of culture on war and peace—could be a useful way of stimulating the interest of cultural workers and of promoting public opinion conducive to disarmament.

(d) Information

66. The meeting suggested that the recommendations relating to the press and the mass media be brought to the attention of the International Commission for the Study of Communication Problems in the hope that it may be in a position to conduct studies and give advice in these matters.

67. The expert meeting urged that the press and mass media should take the utmost care not to allow themselves to be used in the propagation of false or misleading information on strategic armament or other military matters.

68. Likewise it is hoped that the press and media will focus more public attention on the escalating danger of the arms race and the need for general and complete disarmament.

69. Considering that freedom of information is an inalienable human right, all Member States of the United Nations should be urged to promote greater freedom of information with respect to military and disarmament affairs.

70. In order to improve international standards of information in the armament/disarmament field, Unesco itself should organize seminars and training programmes in order to increase professional competence in utilizing documentary sources and information systems, and in accounting military expenditures and other military-related statistical operations.

71. A special study to analyse the sources, content and impact of military-related information in the international mass media should be carried out by or through Unesco in order to promote subsequently adequate steps to minimize the dangerous effects of false or misleading information as an obstacle to disarmament.

72. The expanding influence of advertisements promoting the sale of implements of war upon the mass media in general, as well as the proliferation of specialized magazines relying upon such advertisements, should be investigated by Unesco. Special reference should be made to the legal and constitutional implications of this problem.

73. Unesco is encouraged to continue and develop its own information activities in the field of disarmament, in the first instance by publishing the reader on disarmament which has been prepared during the 1977–78 biennium. It is recommended that this could be followed by several other publications in the same series thereby building up a basic library, such as:

A collection of articles on the obstacles to disarmament and the ways of overcoming them.

A reader on the conversion of military industries and labour forces to civilian production, the use of military forces in public works, etc.

A disarmament and peace education handbook.

A reader on strategic doctrines and critiques of them and related issues.

A reader on the impact of war and military activities on human environment, social development and cultural progress.

74. In addition, the Division of Human Rights and Peace is encouraged to continue its efforts to provide bibliographies and other information services; to collaborate further with the Unesco periodicals in the production of relevant materials; and to promote the use of other media such as television and films which can reach a wide public.

List of participants

Experts

Alfred Bönisch (German Democratic Republic), Professor, Academy of Sciences of the German Democratic Republic.

Jaime Diaz (Colombia), Director, Corporación integral para el desarrollo cultural y social (CODECAL), Bogotá.

Peter Lock (Federal Republic of Germany), Working Group on Armaments and Underdevelopment, Hamburg.

Malvern Lumsden (United Kingdom), Stockholm International Peace Research Institute, Oslo (SIPRI).

Sean MacBride (Ireland), Nobel and Lenin Peace Prize
Winner; President, International Peace Bureau.

Wojciech Multan (Poland), Polish Institute of International
Affairs, Warsaw.

Joseph Owona (United Republic of Cameroon), Director,
International Relations Institute of Cameroon (IRIC),
Yaoundé.

Swadesh Rana (India), Institute for Defence Studies
and Analysis, New Delhi.

Betty Reardon (United States of America) Chairperson,
Consortium on Peace Research, Education and
Development; Executive Secretary, World Council for
Curriculum and Instruction.

Marek Thee (Norway), Editor-in-Chief, *Bulletin of Peace
Proposals*, International Peace Research Institute,
Oslo (PRIO).

Sergiu Verona (Romania), Institute of Political Science,
Bucharest.

V. V. Zhurkin (Union of Soviet Socialist Republics),
Vice-Director, Institute of the United States
and Canada of the Academy of Sciences of the USSR,
Moscow.

*Specialists representing non-governmental organizations
which contributed working papers*

Michael Randle, War Resisters International.

Louis Beaudoin, International Confederation of Former
Prisoners-of-War.

Max Girou, European Confederation of War Veterans.

Robert Vollet, International Federation of Resistance
Movements.

Serge Wourgaft, World Veterans Federation.

Representative of the United Nations

Aminoto Djireokoye, United Nations Information Centre,
Paris.

*List of non-governmental organizations
represented by observers or experts*

Consortium on Peace Research, Education and Development
(COPRED), United States of America.

International Institute for Peace (IIP), Vienna.

International Peace Bureau (IPB), Geneva.

International Peace Research Association (IPRA).

International Peace Research Institute (PRIO), Oslo.

Stockholm International Peace Research Institute (SIPRI).

Members of the Unesco Secretariat

Martha Hildebrandt, Assistant Director-General for Social
  Sciences and their Applications.
Karel Vasak, Director, Division of Human Rights and
  Peace.
Stephen Marks (Secretary of the Meeting), Division of
  Human Rights and Peace.
Vitali Shelopoutov, Division of Human Rights and Peace.
Rosemary Castelino, Division of Human Rights and Peace.
Peter Lengyel, Editor-in-Chief, *International Social
  Science Journal.*
Wolfgang Schwendler, Division of Philosophy.
Antony Brock, Office of Public Information.

Notes

1. According to this text the programme for general and complete disarmament should provide with respect to the military establishment of every
   nation: '(a) disbanding of armed forces, dismantling of military establishments, including bases, cessation of the production of armaments as
   well as their liquidation or conversion to peaceful uses; (b) elimination of
   all stockpiles of nuclear, chemical, bacteriological, and other weapons of
   mass destruction and cessation of the production of such weapons;
   (c) elimination of all means of delivery of weapons of mass destruction;
   (d) abolishment of the organizations and institutions designed to organize
   the military effort of states, cessation of military training, and closing
   of all military training institutions; (e) discontinuance of military
   expenditure'.
2. In this regard this participant referred to the following instruments: the
   Test Ban Treaty, the Non-Proliferation Treaty; the Treaty Prohibiting
   Bacteriological (biological) Weapons, Environmental Modifications for
   Military Purposes; Treaty Prohibiting the Use of Weapons of Mass
   Destruction in Space and Sea-bed and bilateral agreements such as SALT.
3. These experts drew special attention to the comprehensive definition of
   the Right to Refuse to Kill (Conscientious Objection), which has now
   been generally accepted by the churches and recalled that the Baden
   Consultation, 3–9 April 1970, and the Kyoto Conference on Religion and
   Peace, 16–21 October 1970 defined the rights of Conscientious Objectors
   in the following terms: 'the exercise of conscientious judgement is inherent
   in the dignity of human beings and, accordingly, each person should be
   assured the right, on the grounds of conscience or profound conviction,
   to refuse military service, or any other direct or indirect participation in
   wars or armed conflicts. The right of conscientious objection also extends
   to those who are unwilling to serve in a particular war because they
   refuse to participate in a war or conflict in which weapons of mass
   destruction are likely to be used. This Conference also considers that
   members of armed forces have the right, and even the duty, to refuse to
   obey military orders which may involve the commission of criminal
   offences, or of war crimes, or of crimes against humanity.'

2. Final Report and Document of the World Congress on Disarmament Education, Paris, 9–13 June 1980

I. Final Report

Introduction

1. The World Congress on Disarmament Education was convened by the Director-General of Unesco in pursuance of decision 7.1.2 adopted by the Executive Board of Unesco at its 105th session and of resolutions 3/2.1/2 and 11.1 adopted by the General Conference at its twentieth session. The Congress took place at Unesco Headquarters in Paris from 9 to 13 June 1980.

    2. The organization of the Congress constituted a significant contribution by Unesco to the implementation of the provisions of the Final Document of the Tenth Special Session of the United Nations General Assembly. The Congress itself was to be seen in the context of the launching of the Second Disarmament Decade proclaimed by the General Assembly in resolution 34/75 of 11 December 1979. At the same time, it was a manifestation of Unesco's efforts 'to step up its programme aimed at the development of disarmament education as a distinct field of study', as the General Assembly urged it to do in paragraph 107 of the Final Document of the Tenth Special Session.

Participants

3. The Congress was attended by 132 specialists from 48 countries, together with 122 observers from 97 non-governmental organizations and 55 Member States and 9 representatives from organizations in the United Nations system, 2 international governmental organizations and 2 liberation movements. The participants attended in their

personal capacity, in conformity with the rules applying to this type of meeting. They included educators, mass media specialists, scientific researchers in the fields of peace and disarmament, and officials responsible for education and information from the Member States.

4. In pursuance of the recommendations of the preparatory meeting of experts for the Congress, held in Prague, Czechoslovakia, from 4 to 8 June 1979, an open discussion took place during which different points of view on disarmament were put forward. A substantial volume of documentation, comprising reports and studies prepared by experts and institutions, was made available to the Congress. A variety of teaching materials were put on exhibition, a series of films were shown to illustrate the cultural dimension of disarmament education, and mural painting was produced.

Opening of the Congress

5. The Congress was opened on behalf of the Director-General by Mr Federico Mayor, Deputy Director-General, who recalled that disarmament education came within the context of one of Unesco's priority objectives and that Unesco's fundamental task, as defined in its Constitution, was to work for peace through education, the spread of culture and the broadest possible dissemination of information. Mentioning the declaration of an international consultation of outstanding figures which had just been held at Unesco, he drew attention to the close link existing between disarmament, the effective protection of human rights and development. He said that a new outlook favouring peace and co-operation had to be created within public opinion, and he expressed the hope that the Congress would contribute to the establishment of the ethical, intellectual and psychological bases that would be instrumental in working out a solution to the problems involved in the arms race.

6. In his opening address, H.E. Mr Rodrigo Carazo, President of the Republic of Costa Rica, spoke of the example of his country, which at the end of the Second World War had decided to abolish its army and had since then lived in a state of unprecedented security. He asserted that peace and security were not the corollary of the number and quality of arms and that over-armed countries were always liable to become their own gaolers. He also emphasized that mankind

was running the risk of war if it did not soon embark on a process of disarmament. He drew the attention of the assembly to the essential role of education and information, which were the only paths which could lead to the ending of war and the abolition of hatred and violence. He concluded by urging that peace, in its positive, universal and engulfing dimension, be the axis of the most varied studies and methods. He proposed that the University for Peace, now in its formative stages in Costa Rica, should become a leading world centre for high-level cultural action in that field.

7. Mr Jan Martenson, United Nations Assistant Secretary-General for Disarmament, said that the Congress was the first occasion on which the question of relating education to the goals of disarmament and peace would be systematically explored. He recalled that the Final Document of the Special Session of the United Nations General Assembly in 1978 conferred a central role on the world organization in the sphere of disarmament. The implementation of these recommendations calls for careful co-ordination, in order to ensure that the actions taken duly meet the desiderata expressed by the General Assembly. He also mentioned that co-ordination was called for to ensure that the various activities of the institution of the United Nations system were mutually reinforcing. This was especially important in view of the fact that the available resources—both financial and human—were very limited. Commenting on the activities of the United Nations Centre for Disarmament, he pledged to do the utmost possible to ensure that the task entrusted to it was fulfilled and, in particular, to support all efforts towards that end undertaken in the United Nations system. He drew attention to the importance of mobilizing world opinion in favour of disarmament. In that connection, he said that the primary goal of a programme of disarmament education should be to explain to the largest number of people that, in the nuclear age, security was not to be found in an ever-expanding accumulation of arms, but in the development of international co-operation.

8. The last speaker at the opening meeting was Mr Rodolfo Stavenhagen, Assistant Director-General for the Social Sciences and their Applications. After speaking of the importance which the United Nations Tenth Special Session had attached to the democratization of the disarmament

negotiation process, Mr Stavenhagen emphasized that disarmament education constituted a new phase in the democratization of disarmament. He also said that a great many
obstacles still had to be overcome before the demilitarization
of the world became a reality. He mentioned, *inter alia*, the
need to redirect the flow of economic development of peoples;
the international arms trade; the abundance of different
political and strategic doctrines concerning the foreign or
domestic security of states; the conditioning of public opinion
and of children from an early age to accept a glorified vision
of military personalities, feats of arms, wars and conquests;
the spread of certain fashionable theories in the sphere of
mass psychology; the impact of the mass media, and the
sale of games and toys of a military nature. He recalled the
three approaches to disarmament education proposed by the
Director-General at the Prague preparatory meeting: edu-
cating in the spirit of disarmament, incorporating appropriate materials in existing disciplines and developing a
distinct field of study. He concluded by suggesting that there
was a need for a global multilateral effort to promote
disarmament with the active participation of peoples and
not just governments. Education had a key role in these
efforts.

Structure and functioning of the Congress

9. Pursuant to the recommendations of the preparatory meeting of experts held in Prague, Czechoslovakia
(4–8 June 1979), the Congress met in plenary and in two
Commissions, the terms of reference of which were as follows:
Commission I: Education—formal and non-formal education
   at different levels; the training of teaching personnel; the
   working out of appropriate teaching material; the revision of existing textbooks, particularly history and
   geography, etc.
Commission II: Information—the training of professional
   workers in the field of information, information ethics
   relating to questions of armament and disarmament,
   methods of informing the general public, scientific
   circles, military personnel, etc.
The two Commissions each held three meetings; the plenary
met six times.

10. In pursuance of Rule 4 of the Rules of Procedure, the Congress elected its Bureau, as follows:

President:	Mr Jaime Diaz (Colombia)
Vice-Presidents:	Mrs Swadesh Rana (India)
	Mrs Mabel Segun (Nigeria)
	Mr Louis Sohn (United States of America)
	Mr Vladimir Tropine (Union of Soviet Socialist Republics)
General Rapporteur:	Mr Franco Casadio (Italy)

Commission I (Education):

Chairman:	Mr Zdenek Ceska (Czechoslovakia)
Rapporteur:	Mr Nasser-Eddine Ghozali (Algeria)

Commission II (Information):

Chairman:	Mrs Birgit Brock-Utne (Norway)
Rapporteur:	Mr Ibrahima Fall (Senegal)

11. The programme of the Congress was as follows:
1. Opening of the Congress (plenary)
2. The situation of disarmament education at all levels of formal and non-formal education (plenary)
   (a) The present status of disarmament education at primary and secondary levels
   (b) The present status of disarmament education at university level
   (c) The present status of disarmament education in teacher training
   (d) The present status of disarmament education in adult education and non-formal education
   (e) The present situation concerning disarmament education through the mass media
3. Problems of and prospects for the development of disarmament education within the school system (Commission I)
   (a) Curriculum and materials
   (b) Teaching methods
   (c) Teacher training
   (d) Teaching of military personnel
4. Problems of and prospects for the development of

disarmament education outside the school system (Commission I)
  (a) Informal educational approaches
  (b) Non-formal education
  (c) Education within the family
  (d) Education within trade unions
5. Problems and prospects for the development of disarmament education through the mass media (Commission II)
  (a) Formation of public opinion on disarmament questions through the media
  (b) Approches to problems of professional ethics in relation to disarmament education through the media
  (c) Improvement of media coverage of disarmament problems
  (d) Development of audio-visual materials
6. Promotion and development of research on disarmament (both Commissions as indicated)
  (a) Research as part of education (Commission I)
  (b) Research as part of information (Commission II)
  (c) Co-operation among research bodies (both Commissions)
  (d) Problems of documentation (both Commissions)
7. Structural questions (plenary)
  (a) Co-ordination of efforts among educators, education officials and the scientific community to develop disarmament education
  (b) The role of Unesco and its National Commissions
  (c) Co-operation and co-ordination with other United Nations bodies
  (d) The role of non-governmental organizations
8. Adoption of the Final Document (plenary)
9. Closing of the Congress (plenary)

Adoption of the Final Document

12. The last plenary meeting adopted the following Final Document by consensus, it being understood that certain stylistic improvements and modifications based on observations and proposals made during the final session would be incorporated into the final version by the Secretariat in consultation with the President and the General Rapporteur of the Congress. The Final Document contains: (A) Guiding principles and considerations for disarmament education,

and (B) Recommendations addressed to the Director-General. The recommendations of the two Commissions as formulated by the rapporteurs on the basis of the proposals from participants and observers appears in Annex I. Annex II contains the list of participants and Annex III the list of documents.

II. Final Document of the Congress

The World Congress on Disarmament Education, convened by the Director-General of Unesco and meeting at Unesco Headquarters in Paris from 9 to 13 June 1980, in accordance with resolution 3/2.1/1 adopted by the General Conference at its twentieth session,

1. *Deeply concerned* by the lack of real progress towards disarmament and by the worsening of international tensions which threaten to unleash a war so devastating as to imperil the survival of mankind,
2. *Convinced* that education and information may make a significant contribution to reducing tensions and to promoting disarmament, and that it is urgent to undertake vigorous action in these areas,
3. *Taking into account* the Final Document of the Tenth Special Session of the General Assembly and in particular paragraph 106, according to which the General Assembly urged governments and governmental and non-governmental organizations to take steps to develop programmes of education for disarmament and peace studies at all levels, and paragraph 107, according to which the General Assembly welcomed the holding of this Congress and urged Unesco to step up its programme aimed at the development of disarmament education as a distinct field of study,
4. *Bearing in mind* other pertinent resolutions of the General Assembly, such as resolution 34/75 according to which the General Assembly declared the decade beginning in 1980 the Second Disarmament Decade, and resolution 33/73 by which the General Assembly adopted the Declaration on the Preparation of Societies to live in Peace,
5. *Considering* resolution 11.1 adopted by the General Conference at its twentieth session concerning the role of Unesco in generating a climate of public opinion

conducive to the halting of the arms race and transition to disarmament,

6. *Considering* further the Declaration on fundamental principles concerning the contribution of the mass media to strengthening peace and international understanding, to the promotion of human rights and to countering racism, apartheid and incitement to war, adopted by the General Conference at its twentieth session (1978),

7. *Desiring* to promote the implementation of the Recommendation concerning Education for International Understanding, Co-operation and Peace and Education relating to Human Rights and Fundamental Freedoms, adopted by the General Conference at its eighteenth session (1974),

8. *Recalling* the Expert Meeting for the preparation of the World Congress on Disarmament Education held in Prague, Czechoslovakia, on 4–8 June 1979 at the invitation of the Czechoslovak Socialist Republic,

A

Believes that disarmament education should be guided by the following *principles and considerations:*

1. *Relation of education to disarmament.* Disarmament education, an essential component of peace education, implies both education about disarmament and education for disarmament. All who engage in education or communication may contribute to disarmament education by being aware and creating an awareness of the factors underlying the production and acquisition of arms, of the social, political, economic and cultural repercussions of the arms race and of the grave danger for the survival of humanity of the existence and potential use of nuclear weapons.

2. *Definition of disarmament.* For the purpose of disarmament education, disarmament may be understood as any form of action aimed at limiting, controlling or reducing arms, including unilateral disarmament initiatives, and, ultimately, general and complete disarmament under effective international control. It may also be understood as a process aimed at transforming the current system of armed nation States into a new world order of planned unarmed peace in which war is no

longer an instrument of national policy and peoples determine their own future and live in security based on justice and solidarity.

3. *Role of information*. Disarmament education requires the collection and dissemination of reliable information from sources offering the highest degree of objectivity in accordance with a free and more balanced international flow of information. It should prepare learners, in the strictest respect for freedom of opinion, expression and information, to resist incitement to war, military propaganda and militarism in general.

4. *Relation to economic and political realities*. Disarmament education cannot, however, confine itself to the dissemination of data and information on disarmament projects and prospects nor even to commenting on the hopes and ideals which inspired them. It should recognize fully the relationship disarmament has with achieving international security and realizing development. To be effective in this regard, disarmament education should be related to the lives and concerns of the learners and to the political realities within which disarmament is sought and should provide insights into the political, economic and social factors on which the security of peoples could be based.

5. *Research and decision-making*. In addition to reaching the general public, disarmament education has a more specific and equally crucial task of providing rational arguments for disarmament based on independent scientific research which can guide decision-makers and, to the extent possible, rectify perceptions of a potential adversary based on incomplete or inaccurate information.

6. *Substantive approaches*. As a approach to international peace and security, disarmament education should take due account of the principles of international law based on the Charter of the United Nations, in particular, the refraining from the threat or use of force against the territorial integrity or political independence of States, the peaceful settlement of disputes, non-intervention in domestic affairs and self-determination of peoples. It should also draw upon the international law of human rights and international humanitarian law applicable in time of armed conflict and consider alternative approaches to security, including such non-military defence systems

as non-violent civilian action. The study of United
Nations efforts, of confidence-building measures, of
peace-keeping, of non-violent conflict resolution and of
other means of controlling international violence take
on special importance in this regard. Due attention
should be accorded in programmes of disarmament
education to the right of conscientious objection and
the right to refuse to kill. Disarmament education should
provide an occasion to explore, without prejudging the
issue, the implications for disarmament of the root
causes of individual and collective violence and the
objective and subjective causes of tensions, crises, disputes and conflicts which characterize the current
national and international structures reflecting factors
of inequality and injustice.

7. *Links with human rights and development*. As an integral
   part of peace education, disarmament education has
   essential links with human rights education and development education, in so far as each of the three terms
   peace, human rights and development must be defined
   in relation to the other two. Moreover, disarmament
   education offers an occasion to elucidate emerging concepts such as the individual and collective rights to peace
   and to development, based on the satisfaction of material
   and non-material human needs.

8. *Pedagogical objectives*. Whether conceived as education
   in the spirit of disarmament, as the incorporation of
   relevant materials in existing disciplines or as the
   development of a distinct field of study, disarmament
   education should apply the most imaginative educational
   methods, particularly those of participatory learning,
   geared to each specific cultural and social situation and
   level of education. It aims at teaching *how* to think
   about disarmament rather than *what* to think about it.
   It should therefore be problem-centred so as to develop
   the analytical and critical capacity to examine and
   evaluate practical steps towards the reduction of arms
   and the elimination of war as an acceptable international
   practice.

9. *Values*. Disarmament education should be based upon
   the values of international understanding, tolerance of
   ideological and cultural diversity and commitment to
   social justice and human solidarity.

10. *Sectors of society concerned.* Disarmament education should be the concern of all sectors of society and public opinion. Indeed, schools, non-formal and informal education circles such as the family, community organizations and the world of work, universities and other research centres and information media, all have a part to play in this task. Educators and communicators should strive to develop the most appropriate and effective language and teaching methods for each situation. The challenge is all the greater as the stakes are so high.

B

The World Congress on Disarmament Education,

Considering that in this initial year of the Second Disarmament Decade special impetus should be given to the development of disarmament education,

Accordingly *requests* the Director-General to:

(a) set out, on the basis of the aforementioned principles and considerations, elements to be included in the Declaration of the 1980s as the Second Disarmament Decade aimed at making disarmament education one of the vital means of achieving the objectives of the Decade, and transmit them to the United Nations Secretary-General for submission to the General Assembly at its thirty-fifth session;

(b) encourage initiatives designed to make adequate funds available for the significant development of disarmament education, by supporting, *inter alia*, the suggestion of the United Nations Secretary-General that one-tenth of one per cent of military spending should be devoted to national and international efforts in favour of disarmament, including disarmament education and information;

(c) strengthen social science research activities on disarmament, peace and international relations with a view, *inter alia*, to improving education and information programmes in these fields, in collaboration with the United Nations, in particular with the Centre for Disarmament and the Institute for Disarmament Research, with national and international research bodies, and with appropriate non-governmental organizations;

(d) investigate the possibility of drawing up standard clauses whereby States parties to arms control or limitation agreements would undertake, on the one hand, to foster the dissemination of the instrument in question and, on the other, to promote, to the greatest possible extent, and by appropriate means, disarmament education in general;

(e) examine, in collaboration with the Secretary-General of the United Nations, the possibility of setting up a United Nations–Unesco Radio Station, to provide information and to promote the objectives of the United Nations relating, *inter alia* to disarmament, human rights and development;

(f) draw up, on the basis of the work of the Congress, a detailed, phased action plan, on the understanding that this plan will coincide with Unesco's next Medium-Term Plan.

For the purpose of implementing this final recommendation, the Congress took note of the recommandations contained on the working papers and of the points proposed by the rapporteurs of the commissions on the basis of suggestions submitted by the participants and observers.

3. Resolution 21 C/11.1 adopted by the General Conference of Unesco at its twenty-first session on 24 October 1980

Creation of a climate of public opinion conducive to the halting of the arms race and the transition to disarmament[1]

The General Conference,

Mindful that the purpose of Unesco, in accordance with Article I of its Constitution, is 'to contribute to peace and security by promoting collaboration among the nations through education, science and culture in order to further universal respect for justice, for the rule of law and for the human rights and fundamental freedoms which are affirmed for the peoples of the world, without distinction of race, sex, language or religion, by the Charter of the United Nations',

Convinced that Unesco's activity, based on the purposes and functions set out in its Constitution, will continue to influence world public opinion in favour of promoting the ideals of peace, mutual respect and understanding between peoples,

Emphasizing in this connection that the arms race, the dimensions of which are growing and which is imperilling the future of all mankind, remains one of the chief obstacles to the strengthening of peace,

Recognizing the terrible dangers to which a nuclear war would expose mankind,

Noting the obligation of all States to refrain in their international relations from the threat or use of force against the sovereignty, territorial integrity or political independence of any State, and from any other action inconsistent with the purposes and principles of the Charter of the United Nations, and convinced that the imple-

mentation of those principles is indispensable for generating a climate conducive to the halting of the arms race,

Drawing attention to the fact that the development process
and the establishment of a new international economic
order are seriously inhibited by the growing expenditure
of human and material resources on the arms race,

Recalling that the problem of disarmament constitutes one
of the major preoccupations of our century, and *further
recalling* the decisions adopted in this field by the United
Nations General Assembly,

Realizing that the dangers threatening mankind call for
redoubled efforts to solve the problems of halting the
arms race and of the transition to disarmament,

Noting with satisfaction that the United Nations has proclaimed the 1980s a Second Disarmament Decade,

Welcoming the decision to hold a special session of the
United Nations General Assembly devoted to disarmament in 1982,

Recognizing further that disarmament could afford possibilities of improving the lives of the peoples of the world
and of promoting the solution of a multitude of urgent
socio-economic problems,

Noting that the Final Document of the Tenth Special Session
of the General Assembly urged governments and governmental and non-governmental international organizations
to take steps to develop programmes of education for
disarmament and peace studies at all levels, with a view
to contributing to a greater understanding and awareness
of the problems created by the armaments race and of
the need for disarmament, and that it specifically urged
Unesco to step up its programme aimed at the development of disarmament education as a distinct field of
study through the preparation, *inter alia*, of teachers'
guides, textbooks, readers and audio-visual materials,

Noting with satisfaction the substantial and constructive
efforts that Unesco has made within its fields of competence to promote understanding of the problem of
disarmament, as reflected in the Director-General's
report on the implementation of resolution 11.1 adopted
by the General Conference at its twentieth session,

Considering that, in the present international situation,
Unesco should continue and make more effective its
efforts to generate a climate of public opinion conducive

to the halting of the arms race and the transition to disarmament,

Noting in particular that Unesco's action to promote public education, research and information activities, in consultation with the competent United Nations bodies and the non-governmental organizations concerned, with a view to contributing, within its spheres of competence, to international peace, disarmament and security and to respect for human rights, can constitute a substantial contribution to international efforts in this field,

Taking note with interest of the Final Document of the World Congress on Disarmament Education (Paris, 9–13 June 1980),

Recalling in this connection that the United Nations General Assembly, at its Tenth Special Session devoted to disarmament, drew particular attention to the potential influence of world public opinion for halting the arms race and achieving disarmament, and welcomed Unesco's contribution to understanding of these problems whose urgency brooks no delay,

I

1. *Calls upon* all those active in Unesco's spheres of competence to participate in the Organization's efforts to generate a climate of public opinion conducive to the halting of the arms race and the transition to disarmament;

II

2. *Invites* Member States:
   (a) to continue to encourage the development of the activities in Unesco's fields of competence set out in the relevant paragraphs of the Final Document adopted by the United Nations General Assembly at its Tenth Special Session, and to publicize the results of such efforts;
   (b) to take note of the Final Document of the World Congress on Disarmament Education;
   (c) to encourage public and private scientific research institutions which could usefully contribute to a better understanding of the problems relating to disarmament;

(d) to take the necessary steps to make adequate information available on matters concerning disarmament, in order to make meaningful and informed disarmament education possible;

(e) to respond actively to the call of the General Assembly at its special session to observe the week beginning 24 October as a week devoted to fostering the objectives of disarmament;

III

3. *Invites* the Director-General:

(a) to continue efforts to implement those recommendations of the Tenth Special Session of the United Nations General Assembly which fall within Unesco's spheres of competence;

(b) to concentrate and streamline present activities in this field and elaborate suitable projects within the present framework of Unesco's Programme and Budget for 1981–1983, and in the Second Medium-Term Plan for 1984–1989, taking account *inter alia* of the results of the World Congress on Disarmament Education;

(c) to take appropriate measures, within Unesco's fields of competence, to assist the achievement of the goals of the Second Disarmament Decade proclaimed by the United Nations;

(d) to make an appropriate contribution, within Unesco's spheres of competence, to the preparation of the special session of the General Assembly of the United Nations to be devoted to disarmament in 1982;

(e) to focus research on multidimensional themes, including differing perceptions of security and the linkage between disarmament education and the social and educational context in which it takes place, and to encourage intersectoral and multi-disciplinary research where appropriate;

(f) to make the most effective use of Unesco's information channels to improve international understanding of the issues raised by the arms race and of the need in all countries for education about disarmament as an essential component of education for peace, through the publication of books and appropriate articles in the Organization's periodicals, particularly in connection with the Disarmament Week (24–30 October) proclaimed by the United Nations;

(g) to encourage and promote various activities to mark Disarmament Week in Unesco's Member States, and to assist National Commissions therein by sending them useful information and audio-visual material prepared by Unesco for that purpose;

(h) to maintain co-operation with the institutions of the United Nations system, and in particular with the United Nations Centre for Disarmament and the United Nations Institute for Disarmament Research attached to the United Nations Institute for Training and Research;

(i) to continue to stimulate and support activities of the international non-governmental organizations which are directed to achieving disarmament objectives within Unesco's fields of competence;

(j) to report to the General Conference at its twenty-second session on the progress made in implementing this resolution.

Note

1. Resolution adopted on the proposal of the Drafting and Negotiation Group at the thirty-sixth plenary meeting, on 24 October 1980.